LIVES OF THE PHILOSOPHERS

Diogenes Laertius

3ᵈ C. A.D.

translated and edited by A. Robert Caponigri

A Gateway Edition
HENRY REGNERY COMPANY
CHICAGO

Henry Regnery Company, Chicago
Translation copyright 1969 © A. Robert Caponigri.
All rights reserved.
Manufactured in the United States of America.
Library of Congress Catalog Card Number: 70-88855

table of *CONTENTS*

Introduction

PRO CAPTU *lectoris habent sua fata libelli,*
Terentianus Maurus wrote, and though the *Lives of the Philoso-*
phers by Diogenes Laertius lay in the distant future when this
line was written, it might almost have been composed with his
work in mind. Certainly, the fortune of this work is a tale to be
told; indeed, it possesses something of the picaresque. From a
nameless pen (its very authorship a matter of doubt and schol-
arly debate), the *Lives of the Philosophers* has itself become a
pedagogic tool, known, as Macauley would say, to every school-
boy. A modest work, Diogenes Laertius's book has endured
when works of greater worth, such as the *Hortensius* of Cicero
that so enthralled the mind of Augustine, have come to us only
as memories or, worse still, have perished utterly. No paradigm
of scholarship, the *Lives of the Philosophers* has influenced the
weightiest of scholars: a Zeller employs it with confidence, the
ponderous Grote defers to it, the self-assured Brehier leans
upon it. Inevitably, therefore, the question must arise: Whence
springs this fortune?

Sheer historical chance, some might reply.[1] But the more
sagacious will demur. Chance as principle suggested itself to
the most ancient metaphysicians, and no one even today would
care to deny its sway. But history is not the field of its activity,
as Machiavelli warned us long ago. Rather, as Vico with
brilliant intuition discerned and, by laborious effort, estab-

---

[1]*For example, R.D. Hicks (ed.),* Diogenes Laertius *(Loeb Classical Library), Harvard,*
1959, Vol. I, p. 1, speaks of the "lucky accident."

lished, history is the work of man, and its principles must therefore be sought in the modifications of the human mind itself. But the ruling principle of the human mind, through all its historical transformations of modifications, is never chance, but truth. In short, the reason for the great fortune and the amazing authority and influence of this book must be sought elsewhere than in chance.

A more solid clue may be found, it would seem, in Vico's doctrine of the *borie* of the human mind. Chief among these *borie*, illusory attitudes, as they may be called, is that which he calls the *boria* of the learned. This illusion leads the learned men of every age to think that the wisdom or the knowledge that they possess has existed as long as man and thus induces a kind of illusory picture of the past as a golden age. This illusion, in turn, leads man to misapprehend history and man in history; specifically to misapprehend the rude beginnings of all the values that man has generated in history and the great labor by which, against the blackness of ignorance, the harshness of nature, and the detrition of time, man has raised the structures of ideas, the arts, and institutions in which his culture consists and which keep him from falling back into tenebrous barbarism. For this reason, the real function of history, as Vico saw, is to make man aware of these rude beginnings, and of the millennial labor of the spirit by which culture is generated, in order that he may know and possess himself in reality, that he may know and value the past, cherish his cultural heritage, and see it as the ground from which he can strive for new creations of the spirit: truer sciences, firmer institutions, more subtle arts, a life more consonant with his nature.

The *Lives of the Philosophers* of Diogenes has, over the centuries, contributed to the dissipation of the *boria* of the learned in one specific and very important area, that of philosophy. One can appreciate its impact if one picks up any standard history of philosophy, such as come into the hands of any student routinely, and compares it with these *Lives*.

The usual history of philosophy inevitably generates a vision of the unbroken march of ideas over the centuries, of the early magnificence and the uninterrupted progress of this discipline. The history is conducted in transcendent terms, as though the realm of philosophical ideas were an empyrean, untouched and unsullied by any contact with the meaner and earthier concerns of man. Inevitably, in all but the professional reader, such accounts create a sense of alienation, which makes philosophy appear as an activity that does not touch the mass of human kind.

By contrast, the *Lives of the Philosophers,* in its awkward and pedestrian way, contributes much to the creation of a truer image of philosophy and of its history (which are, after all — at least from the point of view of the history of culture — identical). In the first place, by the simple and obvious device of writing this history in the form of biography, Diogenes Laertius makes an important truth clear; namely, that philosophy is the work of men, individual concrete men, living in definite times and places. He creates, by his procedure, at once a vision of philosophy as the personal striving of concrete men for clarity and wisdom in what pertains most to man, a wisdom that through the strenuous pursuit of few, at any point in time, is by its nature meant for the many and indeed, in one degree or another, for all. Diogenes, with a certain naïveté and a passionate concern for detail, coupled with a not too subtle discernment of the relative value of competing details and a childlike repetitiousness that draws close to the edge of tedium, succeeds in making these men, so remote in time, so enshrouded in myth, strangely immediate and plainly present. Most effectively of all, he makes their speculations upon nature and their pursuit of values, virtues, and moral maxims in life, however lofty they may become, appear as the direct outcome of this concrete presence.

In the second place, Diogenes's narratives generate a truer picture of philosophy itself, as the basic and most sustaining ingredient of Western culture. His narratives make philosophy appear as it truly is, the result and the achievement of the labor of the spirit toward some sort of comprehension of itself and of the world of existence, natural and human, into which it finds itself plunged. Fingering these pages, there comes over one a certain sense of awe, the sense of awe which is inseparable from the presence of the birth of things. There is communicated to the reader, not a sense of distance and alienation, but a sense of direct sympathy and participation with this utterly human and, at the same time, manifestly divine attempt to reach the *ratio* of things. The undertaking would have to be considered presumptuous of man in the extreme, did it not clearly constitute the very essence of humanness, that which makes him man and rational in the fullest sense of those terms; for the rational man is not the calculating intellect of the logicians but the seeker after true reasons, of the sources of what is, of what can be, of what must be. And Diogenes holds this image constantly before us.

Finally, the narratives of Diogenes launch one, as it were, into the moving stream of philosophy as it advances through time and history to the present. They do so by the artless art of communicating the sense of the presence of the beginnings. They possess inestimable antiquarian value, as will presently be noted, but they are utterly futuristic in outlook. Being so manifestly a record of the beginnings of philosophy, they are oriented toward what philosophy *has been* only as the point of departure for what it *must become*. That world of the ancients to which he turns our eyes is heavy with the future. Nothing there is an end. Everything is a beginning. Diogenes speaks at the close of his work of its completion, but it is clear from the spirit of the work that it is anything but completed, that it is manifestly only the opening chapter of a narrative that time itself will take up. Something like the prophetic shades of Dante's nether world, Diogenes seems to foretell and to foreshadow the great who, as yet unnamed, are yet to come, dim in outline but inevitable.

When all these reasons are regarded, the fate of this little work, a fate reserved for few at best and refused to greater works, becomes somewhat less strange, somewhat more comprehensible. The *Lives of the Philosophers* is not a mere history of philosophy. It is a very human document, and it attracts with the irresistible attraction that everything human has for every man.

It is therefore inevitable that, when one turns to a more detailed consideration of this book, one's first concern should be with its author, the man of the book, Diogenes called Laertius. It would be strange, indeed, if the historical reality, the concrete humanity of the creator of a work so teeming with living concrete figures, should not himself become the object of our interest.

The irony appears at once. This man who devoted so much of his energy to the investigation and the recording of the lives and thoughts of others is practically unknown in his personal identity and career. His very name is a subject of dispute. In some authoritative sources he is referred to as Laertius Diogenes. Eustathius records the name simply as Laertes. There is even evidence for interpreting the name simply as a pen name, taken deliberately by the actual author or perhaps assigned to him through convention by a long succession of editors, emendators, and borrowers. A similar obscurity shrouds important items such as the date and place of his birth, items to which, in the case of all those whose intellectual biographies he composed, he devoted the greatest care. But all resources are not lacking. It is possible to turn to the internal evidence of the text itself and thence to glean by inference some bits of information that no other witness has taken the trouble to record.

First, it is possible to decide fairly accurately, that he lived during the first three decades of the third century A.D. This conclusion is reached by a process of "blocking off" the possibilities, by reference to ascertained dates and events prior and subsequent to this period. With regard to the points of reference prior to this date, it is universally noted by editors that the sole notice of record of a certain philosopher Saturninus is contained in the pages of Diogenes Laertius. Saturninus is referred to as a pupil and follower of the more famous Sextus Empircus, whose period of activity is securely fixed as the end of the second century A.D. Obviously, this sets a line of demarcation in time prior to which these biographies could not have been written. More accurately, it may reasonably be said that Diogenes was, at most, a contemporary of Saturninus. A subsequent point of reference, which would exclude placing him at any later date, is found by scholars in the fact that Diogenes apparently knew nothing of the very important philosophical movement called Neo-Platonism. He makes no allusion to it in his work, despite the fact that he displays a considerable interest in and knowledge of Plato, and it is only reasonable to expect that, had the Neo-Platonic movement begun to emerge, he would have taken either of two courses with regard to it. He might, in his relatively extensive treatment of Plato, have mentioned this new development; or he might have devoted a specific study to its outstanding proponent, Plotinus. Indeed, given the range of Diogenes's interests, it is safe to assume that he would have done both. The fact that he did not makes it impossible to place the date of his own activity as late as that of this movement, that is, the fourth century.

To place Diogenes within these parentheses, the second and fourth centuries, is to assign him to a period of great literary, scientific, and philosophical productivity—the names that fall within this period are names to be reckoned with in every field of culture: Lucian, Galen, Clement of Alexandria, Athenaeus—though to do so is to assign him to an age that is not accorded the highest esteem for the quality of its work.

The same type of evidence makes it clear that the *Lives* is not the first book written by Diogenes. Frequently, if not consistently, throughout the work he appends compositions of his own, regarding, in each case, the subject of the preceding life. These compositions are all in verse and seem to be extracted from an earlier work that he had composed, the *Pammetros.* The *Pammetros* seems to have been composed of epigraphs to famous men, celebrating, in each case, some aspect of the subject's life or death or, less frequently, his doctrine. Their original composition, as well as their being attached to the end of the account of the *Lives,* makes it clear that Diogene's interest in the philosophers had antedated the composition of this work, for on no occasion does he say that his contribution to the subject's memory had been composed for the occasion. Some critics have noted that a certain error of taste may be attached to the fact that many of these epigraphs touch on the manner of the subject's demise, but this does not seem unequivocally so, since many of these philosophers placed great emphasis on death and on the importance of a man's manner of meeting it. Not all of the epigraphs or words of commemoration placed at the end of the *Lives* come from Diogenes's own pen. A number come from much more celebrated authors and poets and indicate not only the range but also the high quality of Diogenes's own taste. In a number of instances, especially to be noted in the case of the lines from Callimachus, Diogenes has performed a valuable service by this custom of quoting, for these lines would otherwise be irretrievably lost to us.

Another discovery that rests on this kind of internal evidence has caused no little bewilderment among students of his work: the ambivalence of his attitude toward philosophy itself. On the one hand, Diogenes must have possessed an avid interest in the subject, otherwise it is difficult to conceive of his expending the time and energy that obviously have gone into the present collection. On the other hand, he exhibits scant comprehension of philosophy, as such comprehension would be measured by a critical handling of the doctrinal aspects of his subject. On the contrary, he exhibits little or no critical acumen or intention. His chief concern seems to be to repeat as accurately as he can the substance of the teaching of his subjects, without entering into the refinements that distinguish them or the basic sympathies and insights that unite them. He distinguishes the schools but identifies himself with none. Moreover, the distinctions that he establishes are more conventional than judicative and penetrating. The impression that is thus created is that of a singular detachment, or perhaps aesthetic distance, between the author and his subject, that is, between philosopher and philosophy. At least two possible reasons may be suggested for this detachment: the extreme deference in which the matter was held, and a cautious treatment of the unknown. In either case, the question that remains is the same: Why would the author elect for treatment a subject matter toward which he could find himself only in this ambivalent and, on the whole, negative position? No definite answer can ever be given, of course, but the whole matter is richly compensated for by the fact that, whatever the spring of this rather incomprehensible selection, it has resulted in the preservation for us of documents, data, and ideas that might otherwise have been lost to us.

Finally, the picture emerges of a busy and energetic man of letters rather than of a philosopher or historian of philosophy working from within the discipline. But Diogenes was also a writer of serious intent, with considerable personal dedication to the mechanics (searching out the sources) of his com-

mitment, endless industry, and inexhaustible but not always
critical curiosity (in an age that has been identified as being
uncritical, this latter characteristic was, perhaps, more of an
advantage than a drawback). Diogenes reflects the tastes of his
age, too, in his passion for personal anecdote, personal documents (wills, for example, of which he presents, in detail, no
fewer than six, including that of Aristotle), and personal correspondence, of which he preserves several priceless examples.
In short, Diogenes seems to have been an agreeable character,
with modest literary aims, who chose a topic in many aspects
larger than himself, and by this won a fame far beyond his
strictly personal merits.

The preceding paragraphs had intended to concentrate
upon Diogenes the writer; imperceptibly and inevitably, however, they have come to speak of the works or, more precisely,
of the man as seen in his works. This is, however, not at all
surprising, for what, eventually, is a writer, to all who come
after him, but his works? Croce was certainly right. Shakespeare without the plays, or outside the plays, is an object of
curiosity, but the plays, in themselves, are forever Shakespeare
and all of Shakespeare that is, in the last analysis, significant for
history. We may, therefore, pass on to note more specifically
some outstanding characteristics of the work that may be of
some help to the reader in his perusal of these few selections
from the *Lives*.

There is, first of all, an interesting point concerning the
structure of the work. Upon the surface, its form is that of a
series of individual biographies arranged in a sequence the
principle of which, at first glance, may seem puzzling. The
sequence is not chronological, in a strict sense, nor does it seem
to follow an order of importance in the strictly philosophical
range: neither ascending, from the less significant to the more
significant, nor descending. In fact, there is a more basic principle of order, which reveals itself quite readily and serves at
once to explain the order of selection of the biographies and to
generate a more impressive conception of Diogenes as a student of the history of philosophy. This principle, which is
actually two basic principles underlying the merely biographical
sequence, involves a deeper understanding of that history and

its problems than is involved in any simple biographical roll call.

First, there is a regional principle, involving a distinction within philosophy deriving from its geographical origin. The chief division here is between the philosophy of the eastern portion of the Mediterranean, with a dual center in Ionia and in archepelagic Greece, and that of the western portion of the Mediterranean basin, with its center in the area that had been colonized by the Greeks: Sicily and the lower portions of the Italian peninsula that together formed Magna Graecia. Second, superimposed on the order induced in the material, or discovered in it, at a deeper level by this principle is the order induced by the principle of the "successions."

It has become customary to speak of philosophical *schools.* The concept of *successions,* however, is more congenial to Diogenes, as he frequently acknowledges, through his citations of other authors (some of whom are lost to us save by way of his citations). Some critics and historians exhibit a tendency to identify the successions with the regional divisions.[2] But this would seem to be a mistake, since members of the successions are geographically distributed across the regions mentioned above. Some critics also think of the succession as being identical with the more modern notion: school. Indeed, between what we would understand as the school and the succession there *is* a close relation, but not a simple one. At first, it seems possible to say that the school represents the doctrinal or methodological principle of identity and continuity, and that the succession represents the registration of the men who in turn represented this doctrinal or methodological element over a span of time, enjoying a certain representative and authoritative position among all those who adhere to those doctrines. But, though not entirely incorrect, this line of thought yields not the notion of succession but the notion of the Scholarchs. The line of descent among Scholarchs bears resemblance to the lines of dynastic succession in the political order. The notion of the succession, on the other hand, embraces both the notion of school and the idea of the Scholarachs and their order but adds

[2]Ibid., Vol. I, pp. XVIII sqq.

something of importance to both. The succession seems to order both the school and the sequence of the Scholarchs in a dual movement of ideal and temporal sequence. It indicates, in the first place, the doctrinal continuity and unity and order of the representative thinkers who served both to maintain the unity and continuity of the school, through their teachings and, through the same means, to advance it.

An understanding of the notion of the succession (always remembering that it does not supersede but both includes and modifies the actions of the school and the Scholarch) makes the actual order of treatment in the *Lives* comprehensible. Contrary to the opinion that the successions lead to an arbitrary separation of thinkers who ought, on some abstract ground, to be treated together, the succession is precisely an attempt to order thinkers upon an actual historical basis that is both temporal and ideal. Thus, the Pre-Socratics, as they would be called (by divisions that have become so conventional as to go unexamined, not to say unchallenged), instead of being treated together, as though representing some kind of monolitihic unity (an impression or, perhaps more accurately, prejudice that is rapidly dissipated by even a cursory examination of Diels's anthology or some other source of the same character), are treated distributively over four books (I, II, VII, IX) while the Pythagoreans and Eleatics, instead of being placed at the very outset of the work, are held over to a place more in conformity with this principle. It would seem, finally, that the understanding of the principle of the succession is necessary not only to grasp the order of this book but also to understand that a pretty firm notion of the history of philosophy controls its organization. Once this principle is grasped, moreover, the justification for placing any of the thinkers in the exact positions in which Diogenes does place them proves remarkably sound and astute.

The succession governs the order of the book as a whole (with due animadversion to the roles of the school and the Scholarch), but something needs to be said also about the organization of the individual entries. Although a large proportion of the lives are individual in content, a certain structure does prevail in all. This structure reveals the points that Diogenes thinks it important should be known about each thinker or philosopher. Needless to say, some of these points would today hardly be considered necessary in any history, or for that matter monograph, of philosophy. But this only proves the difference that exists in the conception of the philosopher and of philosophy itself between his day and ours.

The first of the points that consistently appear in each individual biography involves the details that we would call strictly biographical: birth, place of origin, place of greatest activity, and death. Included in this portion also is the name of the teacher of the philosopher under consideration, included so as to place him at once in the threefold points of reference mentioned above: regional, school, and succession. The philosopher's position in the school is also frequently mentioned, whether, that is, he must be accounted a Scholarch or one who, though he never attained that distinction, is still of sufficient importance on some other ground to merit treatment.

Next, the points that today would seem a bit unusual to us are noted. Thus, a rich store of anecdote, frequently closely associated with the maxims or sayings of the philosopher, is included in many of the lives. Today, it might seem strange to include these in any such history. Today, though, philosophy has become somewhat professionalized, like the sciences, and therefore capable of being treated in "objective" terms, that is, apart from the immediate life of the thinker. Today, his "words" of wisdom would hardly form part of his contribution to philosophy, demanding a place in its objective history. But to Diogenes the *philosopher* is still central, in contrast to the idea that *doctrine* is objective science. The philosopher, moreover, is still one who not only speculates but also follows a *way*, who is still the "wise man," the "Sage," and his philosophy and his life are one. This is true, too, not only (though, to be sure, especially) of the moral philosophers, whose concern is man and the good life, but even of the "physicists," those whose speculations concerned the physical universe. In addition, this latter study conferred on a man a status that would hardly belong to his modern counterpart, a status that is, in the case of the physicists, due in part to the manner in which knowledge of the heavens entered into the conduct of human life and was involved in religion. The character of the philosopher, the Sage, the wise man, is revealed by recalling his ways of doing things and the maxims in which he enshrined his view. The first could be conveyed only by recounting his anecdotes, but these are never, it is safe to say, included as mere objects of curiosity. The anecdotes invariably have some reference to his wisdom, which they illustrate in a diversity of circumstances. The wise saying, finally, rather than being strange, represented to a great extent the typical form in which the wisdom was conveyed. To conclude, the form of these sayings varies. Some are descriptive statements; others are performative. But without them, not only would the account of each philosopher be incomplete; it would, in Diogenes's economy, be incorrect and would leave the very heart of his role and his wisdom untouched. A further point in the typical life is a list of the subject's composition; needless to say, these lists have a certain value in themselves, for they serve as inventories by comparison with which what has come down to us may be, at least in part, determined. Finally, there comes the heart of each treatment: what we could consider the doctrine.

With respect to the doctrine, certain points are to be considered. In the first place, Diogenes tends to take no responsibility for the accounts he gives. Here his diffidence (on the basis of which it has been concluded that he was, in truth, no philosopher) shows most clearly. He is concerned to make the weight of responsibility rest upon some other authority than himself. In this regard, he calls upon an amazing repertory of authorities, and it is in this connection that we owe to him some traces of the work of ancient scholars whose very names would otherwise be lost. Whether he was actually master of these authorities, or whether he had access to them only through some compilation now lost to us, is matter of dispute. In any case, the importance of the point at issue may be made a matter of dispute. It may be argued whether direct access to original sources would have insured any superiority of treatment over that possible simply through compilations, which may have been the works of scholars of greater competence than Diogenes. But Diogenes, himself, put something of a *quietus* on the argument; for, whenever it is possible, he prefers to present the doctrine of a thinker directly in that thinker's own words, as, for example, in the letters of Epicurus that form the substance of his life of that philosopher. In such cases, Diogenes not only permits the philosopher to speak for himself, he does posterity the further service of preserving documents that have an immediate intrinsic interest and that later historians have not hesitated to utilize.

The individual life sometimes closes with an interesting paragraph listing other persons of greater or lesser note who have borne the same name as the biographee. In this Diogenes may have been paying some kind of deference to a book of which he makes mention, Demetrius's *Poets and Prose Writers of the Same Name*. Finally, it is a rare occasion when he does not bring the treatment to a close by quoting an epigraph of his own, much to the dismay of some of his critics who bemoan their quality and aptness.

The inner economy of the work as a whole should not pass without some notice. Certainly, it offers aspects that surprise us today and that, therefore, demand some accounting. The first relevant observation, perhaps, would be with regard to the scope of the entire work. As it exists, the *Lives* must be considered a fragment, mutilated or truncated from its originally intended scope by circumstances, a full account of which, perhaps, will never be known to us. That its original proportions would have swelled it considerably in comparison to what has come down to us touches primarily the scope of Book VII and is indicated by the index of the original work, known as P, that was prefixed by a scribe to the manuscript of the work. The list agrees with the index of the work as it has come down to us save for Book VII. The Paris scribe mentions twenty-two philosophers as appearing in Book VII but lives of only three are extant. Those lost include persons an account of whom would have been precious indeed by any count: Panetius, Posidonius, Apollodorus. Either these philosophers' lives were deliberately excised by someone using his own judgment of their worth, or they were lost as a result of causes that cannot be determined.

The second point that deserves to be noted relative to the overall structure concerns the relative proportions of the treatments of various philosophers. That a considerable disproportion does exist, and one that is calculated to surprise modern judgment, is manifest. The most striking, perhaps, is the disproportion between the treatments of Plato and of Epicurus. It has been asserted that this disproportion is due not so much to an increase in basic material but to the addition of supplementary material in the case of Epicurus. This judgment seems strange, for it means considering the three letters of Epicurus, as well as the anthology of his *Sovereign Maxims,* as supplementary, and it cannot by any stretch of the imagination be vindicated. Indeed, this judgment is directly oppugned by the universal recognition of the fact that these extracts from the writings of Epicurus constitute one of the most precious parts in the whole work. Moreover, the treatment of Plato, though it occupies a whole book (Book III), presents certain features that arouse puzzlement. It is made up, first, of an introduction to the philosophy of Plato, and, second, of a summary of Platonic doctrine. The two parts exhibit a certain unequalness—indeed, even points of inconsistency. Whether, therefore, the whole matter reflects an evaluation of the two figures different from our own, or represents merely the availability of materials, or even, finally, a difference of familiarity and hence of confidence in dealing with each philosopher on the part of Diogenes is an issue on which no certain conclusion can be reached.

But this is not the only instance of such disproportionate treatment. The treatment accorded Socrates and Aristotle surely must prove disappointing, and in the case of the latter, perfunctory and jejune, in no sense proportionate to the pivotal position of the former or the immense influence the latter eventually wielded. Consultation of valuable sources lends a certain value to the treatment of Pythagoras and Empedocles; the authority consulted with respect to the latter was the Sicilian historian, Timaeus, with regard to the former, Alexander Polyhistor.

Some of the lives possess a literary quality and charm that is independent of the intrinsic philosophical interest of their subjects; instances on which this is the consensus of opinion are the lives of Crates, Arcesileus, Lyco, Pyrrho, and Timon. This finding lends support to the view that Diogenes had a primarily literary interest in all this material (though a purely literary interest in so thorny a field as philosophy is difficult to imagine). Moreover, what little literary merit the quality of these lives engenders is more than counterbalanced negatively by the wholly unworthy treatment given such figures as Heraclitus, Parmenides (perhaps the most important thinker in our whole tradition, from the metaphysical point of view), Zeno of Elea, and Democritus.

For these truncations, omissions, and perfunctory treatments, many exonerating circumstances have been adduced. A favorite one is that the book as it stands is not complete, that it represents only a portion of what the author intended and hence would have been filled up to full measure with time and the consultation of sources. It has even been suggested that the project as originally conceived had been abandoned because of the withdrawal of patronage from a noble lady, who has been conjectured to be no less a personage than Julia Domna, the wife of the Emperor Septimius Severus, the restorer of Leptis Magna. The allegation of incompleteness, however, goes against the author's own assertion that he had now brought his work to completion by citing the *Sovereign Maxims* of Epicurus. Whether this is to be construed as applying only to the life of Epicurus is a matter of debate, but the charge of incompleteness would, on the whole, seem a weak conjecture, given the position of the remark and the emphasis placed by the author on the notion of completion and termination.

The strength of the work, it has readily been recognized, does not rest in its originality; nor does the author, for his part, lay any great claim to such originality. On the contrary, he is most generous in quotation of his authorities and most deferential to them — so much so, that his whole role has been characterized, by no less a figure than Nietzsche, in his role as Greek scholar and critic, as a mere copyist for one of his most frequently cited sources, Diocles. This fact certainly makes it obligatory to mention briefly some of the authorities whom Diogenes most frequently calls to witness, especially since, in the case of a number of them, his citation constitutes their one tie to history. The questions of the history of philosophy as a discipline and of the concern to which the pursuit of philosophy itself has always been closely attached also enter here; for in its most serious aspect the *Lives* must be considered a contribution to this field.

A chief source, recognized by Diogenes himself in numerous citations, was Antigonus of Carystus (c. 290-239 B.C.), considered by some a trailblazer in the field of biography and the history of philosophy. Antigonus was himself the author of the lives of a number of philosophers more or less contemporaneous with himself, and traces of his style, critics hold, are to be discerned in many of the biographies in Diogenes, especially those of Arcesilaus, Crates, Zeno, and others. Another name frequently on the tip of Diogenes's pen for acknowledgment of indebtedness is Sotion of Alexandria. Between 200-170 B.C., Sotion produced his important work *Successions,* to which the allusions of Diogenes are frequent. Hermippus of Smyrna, a pupil of that Callimachus whose epigraph Diogenes preserves, is quoted even more frequently than Sotion and only a little less so than Antigonus. Hermippus composed a book of *Lives* that, while not limited to philosophers, gave considerable prominence to them in their guise as men of letters. His lives were noted for their plentiful details and especially for the lists of writings, a point in which Diogenes profited from him very much. Satyrus is cited by Diogenes some nine times and is the source of the story, from which Diogenes draws a moral favorable to the character of the philosopher, that Socrates had two wives. Two other authors of *Diodoxai,* Heraclides Lembus (c. 181-146 B.C.) and Sosicrates of Rhodes, are frequently called upon for testimony, while the name of Apollodorus of Athens, whose *Chronicles* dates from about 140 B.C., recurs through the pages of Diogenes like the response of a litany. We have already mentioned the name of the writer whose influence on Diogenes seemed so great to Nietzsche that he was willing to make of Diogenes his faithful, or at least assiduous, copyist, Diocles. Diocles composed a *Compendium of the History of Philosophy* and is cited most frequently by Diogenes in connection with the Cynic philosophy — which leads to the conclusion that he possessed a particular authority in this area. Finally, no such list as the present, however brief and unpretentious, could fail to mention Favorinus, who was accounted the most eminent Sophist of his day, a writer much admired and the intimate of such other writers as Plutarch, Herodes Atticus, and Aulus Gellius. Diogenes cites with great frequency Favorinus's *Miscellaneous Histories* and his *Memorabilia.* The allegation of slavish imitation made against Diogenes with reference to Diocles has been made with reference to Favorinus, but Wilamowitz Moellendorf lays this charge to rest in a definitive manner with a famous remark that common sense seems unable to challenge "qua tandem de causa totiens Favorini nomen posuit, si omnia ex eo sumpsit?"[3] On the whole, it should be noted that Diogenes, although heavily reliant on his sources, is slavishly beholden to none and is liberal in acknowledgment to all. More than this can be demanded of no one whose project encompasses as vast a scope as his.

It remains to note only a few particulars about the present selection and translation. The selection has been guided by one consideration: What names would the student most desire to see considered that are treated with some degree of fullness, though not in every case of equal fullness, by Diogenes. In this way a fairly representative selection, from both points of view — the student's and the author's — has been secured. The translation is based on the recent edition, H. S. Long's two-volume *Diogenes Laertius: Vitae philosophorum, Recognovit brevique adnotatione critica instruxit* (H.S. Long, Oxonii, E. Typographeo Clarendonliano, 1965). Needless to say, other translations have been consulted and compared, but on the whole the translation presented here may be said to be a fresh translation, insofar as such a term is meaningful, since there is always the norm to which one must adhere: what Diogenes says and one's interpretation of it. Two aims have consistently guided the translation: faithfulness to the text and English readability. Over-literal faithfulness, *as literam,* as Augustine would have said, has in the past issued in unreadable English, and such faithfulness seems pedantic, while the ancients would have been the first to apply the criterion of contemporary readability and comprehension.

[3]*Quoted with reference,* ibid., *Vol. I, pp. XXIX*

Prologue

Sᴏᴍᴇ authorities say that the study of philosophy began among the barbarians. They argue that the Persians have had their Magi, the Babylonians or Assyrians their Chaldeans, and the Indians their Gymnosophists. Among the Celts and Gauls, moreover, there are persons called Druids or Holy Ones. As authorities, they cite the *Magicus* of Aristotle and Sotion in the twenty-third book of his *Succession of Philosophers*. They also say that Mochus was a Phoenician, Zamolxis a Thracian, and Atlas a Libyan.

The Egyptians hold that Hephaestus was the son of the Nile, and that philosophy began with him; priests and prophets were its chief proponents. Hephaestus lived 48,863 years before Alexander of Macedon, and in the interval there occurred 373 solar and 832 lunar eclipses.

Hermodorus the Platonist in his work on mathematics says that the date of the Magians, beginning with Zoroaster the Persian, was five thousand years before the fall of Troy; Xanthus the Lydian, however, reckons six thousand years from Zoroaster to the expedition of Xerxes, and after that event he places a long succession of Magians bearing the names of Ostanas, Astrampsychos, Gobryas, and Pazatas, down to the conquest of Persia by Alexander.

These writers seem to forget that the achievements which they attribute to the barbarians belong to the Greeks, with whom not only philosophy but the human race itself began. For instance, Musaeus is claimed by Athens, Linus by Thebes.

1

The former, the son of Eumolphus, is said to have been the first to compose a genealogy of the gods and to construct a sphere; he also maintained that all things proceed from unity and are resolved again into unity. He died at Phalerum, and this is his epitaph:

> *Musaeus, to his sire Eumolphus dear,*
> *In Phalerian soil lies buried here;*

and the Eumolpidae at Athens get their name from the father of Musaeus.

Linus, it is said, was the son of Hermes and the Muse Urania. He composed a poem which describes the creation of the world, the courses of the sun and moon, and the growth of animals and plants. It begins with the line: "Time was when all things grew up at once"; and Anaxagoras borrowed this idea when he said that all things were originally together until Mind came and ordered them.

Linus died in Euboea, slain by the arrow of Apollo, and this is his epitaph:

> *Here Theban Linus, whom Urania bore,*
> *The fair-crowned Muse, sleeps on a foreign shore.*

Thus philosophy took its rise from the Greeks: its very name resists translation into any alien tongue.

Those, however, who attribute its discovery to barbarians cite Orpheus the Thracian, calling him a philosopher of whose antiquity no one can doubt. Now, considering the sort of things he said about the gods, I doubt whether he should be called a philosopher; for what are we to think of one who does not hesitate to blame the gods for all human suffering, and even for the foul crimes committed by speech amongst some of mankind? He is said to have met his death at the hands of women. According to the epitaph at Dium in Macedonia, however, he was slain by a thunderbolt. The epitaph runs as follows:

Here have the Muses laid their minstrel true,
The Thracian Orpheus whom Jove's thunder slew.

The advocates of the theory that philosophy took its rise among the barbarians go on to explain the different forms it took in various countries. We are told that the Gymnosophists and Druids uttered their philosophy in riddles, admonishing men to reverence the gods, abstain from wrongdoing, and exercise courage. Clitarchus in his twelfth book says that the Gymnosophists despise even death itself. He also says that the Chaldaeans study astronomy and foretell the future, while the Magi spend their time in the worship of the gods, in sacrifices and in prayers, implying that only they have the ear of the gods. They express their opinions concerning the existence and origin of the gods, whom they consider to be fire, earth, and water; they condemn the use of images, and especially the error of attributing difference of sex to the gods. They discourse about justice and consider the practice of cremation impious; they see no impiety, however, in marriage with a mother or daughter, as Sotion states in his twenty-third book. They practice divination and foretell the future, claiming that the gods appear to them in visible form. They say that the air is full of shapes which stream forth like vapor and enter the eyes of keen-sighted seers. They forbid personal ornament and the wearing of gold. Their dress is white; they make their bed on the ground; and their food is vegetables, cheese, and coarse bread. Their staff is a reed, and their custom is, we are told, to plunge it into the cheese and so take up the part they eat.

They were wholly ignorant of the art of magic, according to Aristotle in his *Magicus* and Dinon in the fifth book of his *History*. Dinon says that the name Zoroaster, literally interpreted, means "star-worshiper,"[1] and Hermodorus concurs. Aristotle, in the first book of his dialogue *On Philosophy*, claims that the Magi are more ancient than the Egyptians; also, that they believe in two principles, a good spirit and an evil spirit, called Zeus or Oromasdes and Hades or Arimanius, respective-

---

[1] *An erroneous etymology, because his name was in reality Zarathustra.*

ly. This is confirmed by Hermippus in his first book about the Magi, Eudoxus in his *Voyage Around the World,* and Theopompus in the eighth book of his *Philippica.* The last-named writer says that, according to the Magi, men will enjoy a future life and be immortal, and that the world will endure through their prayers. This is again confirmed by Eudemus of Rhodes. But Hecataeus holds that they the gods are subject to birth. Clearchus of Soli in his tract *On Education,* makes the Gymnosophists descendants of the Magi; some also tract the Jews to the same origin. Those who have written about the Magi criticize Herodotus. They argue that Xerxes would never have cast javelins at the sun nor have let down fetters into the sea, since in the beliefs of the Magi the sun and the sea are gods. It seems natural enough, however, that Xerxes should destroy the statues of the gods.

The philosophy of the Egyptians as it touches on the gods and on justice is described as follows. They hold that matter was the first principle, next the four elements were derived from matter, and thus living things of every species were produced. The sun and the moon are gods bearing the names of Osiris and Isis, respectively. They employ the beetle, the dragon, the hawk, and other creatures as symbols of godhead, according to Manetho in his *Epitome of Physical Doctrines,* and Hecataeus in the first book of his work *On Egyptian Philosophy.* They also erect statues and temples to these sacred animals because they are ignorant of the true form of the deity. They hold that the universe is created and perishable and is spherical in shape. The stars consist of fire, and events on earth occur according to the mixture of fire in them. The moon is eclipsed when it falls into the earth's shadow, and the soul survives death and passes into other bodies. Rain is caused by alteration in the atmosphere, and they give physical explanations for all other phenomena, as Hecataeus and Aristagoras record. They also lay down laws on the subject of justice, which they ascribe to Hermes, and they consider as gods those animals which are serviceable to man. They claim to have invented geometry, astronomy, and arithmetic. So much about the discovery of philosophy.

The first man to use the term "philosophy," and to call himself a philosopher or lover of wisdom, was Pythagoras. Heraclides of Pontus in his *De mortua* says that at Sicyon, in conversation with Leon, who was the prince of that city or of Phlius, Pythagoras held that no man, but only God, *is* wise. Very soon the study was called wisdom and its professor a sage, implying that he had achieved mental perfection; the student who followed this study was a philosopher or *lover* of wisdom. Sophists was another name for the wise men, not for philosophers only, but for poets as well. Therefore Cratinus, praising Homer and Hesiod in his *Archilochi*, assigns them the title *Sophist*.

The men commonly regarded as Sages were the following: Thales, Solon, Periander, Cleobulus, Chilon, Bias, Pittacus. To these are joined Anacharsis the Scythian, Myson of Chen, Pherecydes of Syros, Epimenides the Cretan, some even add Pisistratus the tyrant. So much for the Sages or Wise Men.

Philosophy, the pursuit of wisdom, has had a double origin: on the one hand, with Anaximander, on the other, with Pythagoras. The former was a pupil of Thales; Pythagoras was taught by Pherecydes. The one school was called Ionian, because Thales, a Milesian and therefore an Ionian, instructed Anaximander; the other school was called Italian, from Pythagoras, who worked for the most part in Italy. The one school, the Ionian, ends with Clitomachus and Chrysippus and Theophrastus; the Italian ends with Epicurus. The succession passes from Thales through Anaximander, Anaximenes, Anaxagoras, Archelaus, to Socrates, who introduced ethics or moral philosophy; from Socrates it passes to his pupils, the Socratics, and especially to Plato, who founded the Old Academy; from Plato, through Speusippus and Xenocrates, the succession passes to Polemo, Crantor, Crates, Arcesilaus, founder of the Middle Academy, Lacydes, founder of the New Academy, Carneades, and Clitomachus. This order of succession brings us to Clitomachus.

Another order of succession ends with Chrysippus, that is to say, by passing from Socrates to Antisthenes, then to Diogenes the Cynic, Crates of Thebes, Zeno of Citium, Cleanthes, Chrysippus. Still another ends with Theophrastus, from Plato passing to Aristotle, and from Aristotle to Theophrastus. In this manner the school of Ionia comes to an end.

In the Italian school the order of succession is as follows: first, Pherecydes, next, Pythagoras, next, his son, Telauges, then, Xenophanes, Parmenides, Zeno of Elea, Leucippus, Democritus, who had many pupils, in particular Nausiphanes and Naucydes, who were teachers of Epicurus.

Philosophers may be divided into dogmatics and skeptics: all those who make assertions about things, assuming that they can be known, are dogmatics; all who suspend judgment, on the ground that things are unknowable, are skeptics. Again, some philosophers left writings, others wrote nothing at all; for example, according to some authorites, Socrates, Stilpo, Philippus, Menedemus, Pyrrho, Theodorus, Carneades, Bryson. Some add Pythagoras and Aristo of Chios, save for a few letters. Others wrote only one treatise each, such as Melissus, Parmenides, Anaxagoras. Many works were written by Zeno, more by Xenophanes, more by Democritus, more by Aristotle, more by Epicurus, and still more by Chrysippus.

Some schools were named for cities, for example, the Elians and the Megarians, the Eretrians and the Cyrenaics; others from places, as the Academics and the Stoics; others from accidental characteristics such as the Peripatetics; others had derisive nicknames, as the Cynics; others were named from their temperaments, such as the Eudaemonists or Happiness School; others from some conceit they maintained, as Truthlovers, Refutationists, and Reasoners from Analogy; still others from their teachers, as Socratics, Epicureans, and the like; some finally take the name of Physicists from their investigation of nature, others that of Moralists because they discuss morals, while those who are occupied with verbal analysis are styled Dialecticians.

Philosophy has three divisions: physics, ethics, and dialectic or logic. Physics is the part which concerns the universe and all that it contains; ethics that which concerns life and all that has to do with us men; the processes of reasoning employed by both form the province of dialectic. Physics flourished until the time of Archelaus; ethics, as has been noted, started with Socrates; dialectic is traced as far back as Zeno of Elea. There have been ten schools in ethics: the Academic, the Cyrenaic, the Elian, the Megarian, the Cynic, the Eretrian, the Dealectic, the Peripatetic, the Stoic, and the Epicurean.

The founders of these schools were: Plato of the Old Academy; Arcesilaus of the Middle Academy; Lacydes of the New Academy; Aristippus of Cyrene of the Cyrenaic; Phaedo of Elis of the Elian; Euclides of Megara of the Megarian; Antisthenes of Athens of the Cynic, Menedemus of Eretria of the Eretrian; Clitomachus of Carthage of the Dialectical school; Aristotle of Stagira of the Peripatetic; Zeno of Citium of the Stoic; while the Epicurean school took its name from Epicurus himself.

Hippobotus in his work *On Philosophical Sects* states that there are nine sects or schools and gives them in this order: (1) Megarian, (2) Eretrian, (3) Cyrenaic, (4) Epicurean, (5) Annicerean, (6) Theodorean, (7) Zenonian or Stoic, (8) Old Academic, (9) Peripatetic. He passes over the Cynic, Elian, and Dialectical schools. As for the Pyrrhonians, so indefinite are their conclusions that hardly any authorities recognize them as a sect; some allow their claim in certain respects but not in others. They would seem, however, to be a sect, because we use the term for those who in their attitude follow or seem to follow some principle. And on this ground we are justified in calling the Skeptics a sect. If however, we understand by "sect" a tendency to or preference for coherent positive doctrines, they could not be called a sect, for they have no positive doctrines. So much for the beginnings of philosophy, its order of developments, its different parts, and the number of the philosophic sects.

A final word: not long ago an Eclectic school was introduced by Potamo of Alexandria, who made a selection from the tenets of all the existing sects. As he himself states in his *Elements of Philosophy*, he takes as criteria of truth (1) that by which the judgment is formed, namely, the ruling principle of the soul; (2) the instrument used, for instance, the most accurate perception. His universal principles are matter and the efficient cause, quality, and place; for that out of which and that by which a thing is made, as well as the quality with which and the place in which it is made, are principles. The end to which he refers all actions is, life perfect in all virtue; natural advantages of body and environment are indispensable to its achievement.

It remains to speak of the philosophers themselves, and first of all of Thales.

I

SOLON

Solon, the son of Execestides, was born at Salamis. His first great work was the Law of Release, which he introduced at Athens; its purpose was the release of persons and property. People borrowed money on personal security, and were thus compelled to become serfs or day-laborers from poverty and debt. Solon renounced his claim to a debt of seven talents which was owed to his father and urged others to follow his example.

Thereafter, he proceeded to formulate the rest of his laws (which would take time to enumerate) and inscribed them on the revolving pillars.

His greatest service lay in this: Megara and Athens both claimed his birthplace, Salamis. After a number of reverses, the Athenians passed a decree punishing with death any man who should propose to renew the Salaminian war.

Solon, pretending to be mad, rushed into the Agora with a wreath on his head; there he caused his poem on Salamis to be read to the Athenians by the herald, arousing them to fury. They reopened the war against the Megarians and, thanks to Solon, were victorious. These were the lines which did more than anything else to inflame the Athenians:

> *Would I were citizen of some mean isle*
> *Far in the Sporades! For men shall smile*
> *And mock me for Athenian: "Who is this!*
> *An Attic slave who gave up Salamis."*

9

and

> *Then let us fight for Salamis and fair fame,*
> *Win the beloved isle, and purge our shame!*

He also persuaded the Athenians to seize the Thracian Cherso-
nese. So that it would not be thought that he had acquired
Salamis by force only and not by right, he opened certain
graves to show that the dead were buried with their faces to the
east, according to the burial custom of the Athenians; further,
that the tombs, too, faced east, and that the inscriptions carved
on them named the deceased by their demes, a procedure
peculiarly Athenian. Some authors assert that in Homer's catalogue of the ships after the line, "Ajax twelve ships from Salamis commands,"[1] Solon inserted one of his own, "And fixed
their station next the Athenian bands."

   The people admired Solon for all these things and would
have been happy to have had him rule them as tyrant; he
refused, however, and, detecting the plan of his kinsman, Pisistratus (as we are told by Sosicrates), did his best to impede it.
He rushed into the Assembly armed with spear and shield,
warned it of the plans of Pisistratus, and, even more, offered
his assistance with these words: "Athenians, I am wiser than
some of you and braver than others: wiser than those who fail
to perceive the plot of Pisistratus, more courageous than those
who, though they understand it, keep silence through fear."
The members of the council, who were allies of Pisistratus,
called him mad – which evoked from him these lines:

> *A little while, and the event will show*
> *To all the world if I be mad or no.*

A passage from one of his poems proves that he foresaw the
tyranny of Pisistratus:

> *On splendid lightning, thunder follows straight,*
> *Clouds the soft snow and flashing hailstones bring;*

[1]Iliad, *II, 557.*

> *So from proud men comes ruin, and their state*
> *Falls unaware to slavery and a king.*

After Pisistratus had seized power, Solon, helpless to arouse the people, stacked his arms in front of the generals' quarters, and cried, "My country, I have served thee with my word and sword!" Then he sailed off to Egypt and Cyprus, and from there to the court of Croesus. Croesus asked him, "Whom do you consider happy?" and Solon replied, "Tell us of Athens, and Cleobis and Biton," and went on in words too well-known to need quoting here.

A story relates that Croesus seated himself in magnificent garments upon his throne and asked Solon whether he had ever seen anything more beautiful. "Yes," was the answer, "cocks and pheasants and peacocks; for they glow in nature's colors, which are ten thousand times more beautiful." Leaving Croesus's court, Solon took up residence in Cilicia, where he founded a city which he named Soli after himself. In it, he settled a few Athenians who in the course of time corrupted the purity of the Attic tongue and so were said to "solecize." The people of this town, it is to be noted, are called Solenses, while those of Soli in Cyprus are called Solii. When he learned that Pisistratus had by this time established himself as tyrant, he wrote to the Athenians in this wise:

> If you have suffered sadly through your own wickedness, do not blame the gods. For it is you yourselves who gave pledges to your foes and made them great; this is why you carry the mark of slavery. Every one of you walks in the footsteps of the fox, on the whole mass you have little sense. You listen to the speech and fair words of a flatterer, but pay no regard to any practical result.

So said Solon. After he had gone into exile Pisistratus wrote to him as follows:

Pisistratus to Solon

I am not the only man who sought to establish a tyranny in Greece, nor am I, a descendant of Codrus, incompetent for the role. I take up again the privileges which the Athenians promised to give to Codrus and his family, although later they withdrew them. In all other matters, I offend neither God nor man; rather I leave to the Athenians the conduct of their affairs according to the ordinances which you set up. They are governed better than they would be under a democracy; for I allow no one to expand his rights, and though I am tyrant, I take to myself no undue share of reputation and honor, but merely such clearly stated privileges as belonged to the kings in former times. Every citizen pays a tax of his property, not to me, but to a fund to pay for public sacrifices or any other expenses of the state or the cost of any war which may befall us.

I do not blame you for making my designs known; you did so out of loyalty to the city, not through any enmity against me, not knowing what kind of rule I intended to set up. If you had known, you might have accepted me and not gone into exile. Therefore, come home, trusting in my word, even if not given in oath, that Solon will come to no harm from Pisistratus. No other enemy of mine has suffered; of that you may be sure. If you choose to become one of my friends, you will take your place with the foremost, because I see no treachery in you, nothing to awaken mistrust; or if you wish to live at Athens on other terms, you have my permission. Do not on my account cut your ties to your country.

So far the words of Pisistratus. To return to Solon, one of his sayings is that seventy years are the term of man's life.

Solon seems to have enacted some admirable laws; for instance, if a man fails to provide for his parents, he shall lose his status as citizen. A like penalty awaits one who dissipates his patrimony. To have no settled occupation is a crime for which the offender may be deleted. But Lysias, in his speech against Nicias, assigns this law to Draco, while ascribing to Solon another which strips open profligates of the right to speak in the Assembly. He limited the honors accorded to athletes who took part in the games, fixing the allowance of an Olympic victor at five hundred drachmas, of an Isthmian victor at one hundred drachmas, and in proportion in all other cases. It was against decency, he argued, to increase the rewards of these victors while ignoring the claims of men killed in battle, whose sons deserved to be maintained and educated at state expense.

As a result, many tried to prove themselves gallant soldiers in battle, such as Polyzelus, Cynegirus, Callimachus, and all who fought at Marathon, or such as Harmodius, Aristogiton, Miltiades, and thousands more. Athletes, on the other hand, cost the state heavily while being trained; when successful, only do injury; and receive the crown for victory, not over their enemies, but over their own people. Finally, in the words of Euripides, they "Are worn threadbare, cloaks that have lost their nap."[2] For this reason Solon treated athletes with little regard.

Solon's decree that the guardian of an orphan should not marry the mother of his ward, and that the next heir, who would succeed if the orphan were to die, should be disqualified from acting as the guardian, was also excellent. Good, too, were the decrees that an engraver of seals should not be permitted to retain an impression of the ring which he has sold, and that depriving a one-eyed man of his single eye should be paid for by the loss of both the offender's eyes. Likewise, that a deposit must not be removed except by the depositor himself, on pain of death, and that a magistrate found intoxicated should be punished with death.

Solon provided a fixed succession for the public recitations of Homer: the second reciter must begin from the place where the first left off. Thus, as Dieuchidas says in the fifth book of his *Megarian History*, Solon did more than Pisistratus to illuminate Homer. The specific passage in Homer is that which begins, "Those who dwelt at Athens . . ."[3]

Solon was the first to call the thirtieth day of the month the "Old-and-New" day, and to institute meetings of the nine archons for private conference, as Apollodorus reports in the second book of his work *On Legislators*. When civil conflict broke out, Solon took sides neither with those in the city, nor with those of plain, nor, finally, with coastal factions.

One of his sayings was, "Speech is the mirror of action," and another that the "strongest and most capable are kin." He likened laws to spiders' webs, which stand firm when any light and yielding object falls upon them while a larger thing breaks through them and disappears. Solon called secrecy the seal of speech, and occasion the seal of secrecy. He used to say that

[2]Autolycus, *Frag. 1, 1.12.*
[3]Iliad, *II, 546.*

those who had influence with tyrants were like the pebbles
employed in calculations; for, as each of the pebbles represented now a large and now a small number, so tyrants could treat
each one of those around them, now as great and important,
again as of little account. When asked why he formulated no
law against parricide, he answered that he hoped it was unnecessary. Asked how crime could be diminished most effectively,
he replied, "Make it bring about as much resentment in those
who are not its victims as in those who are," adding, "Wealth
breeds satiety, satiety outrage." He made the Athenians adopt a
lunar month. He prohibited Thespis from performing tragedies on the ground that fiction was pernicious. When Pisistratus appeared with self-inflicted wounds, Solon said, "This
comes from acting tragedies."

Solon's counsel to men in general is stated by Apollodorus in
his work on the *Philosophic Sects,* as follows. Put more trust in
nobility of character than in an oath. Never lie. Pursue worthy
goals. Do not make friends incautiously, but, once made, do
not abandon them. Learn to obey before you command. In
giving advice to a friend, seek to help him, not to please him.
Submit to reason. Shun bad company. Honor the gods, reverence parents. He is also said to have criticized the couplet of
Mimnermus:

> *Would that by no disease, no cares oppressed,*
> *I in my sixtieth year were laid to rest;*

and to have replied thus:

> *Oh, take a friend's suggestion, blot the line,*
> *Grudge not if my invention better thine;*
> *Surely a wiser wish were thus expressed,*
> *At eighty years let me be laid to rest.*

Of the songs to be sung this is attributed to Solon:

> Watch every man and see whether, hiding hatred in his heart, he
> speaks with friendly countenance, and his tongue rings with double
> speech from a dark soul.

He is undoubtedly the author of the laws which bear his name; of speeches, and of poems in elegiac meter, namely, counsels addressed to himself, on Salamis and on the Athenian constitution, five thousand lines altogether, not to mention poems in iambic meter and epodes.

His statue has the following inscription:

> At Salamis, which crushed the Persian might,
> Solon the legislator first saw light.

Solon flourished, according to Sosicrates, about the 46th Olympiad,[4] in the third year of which he was archon at Athens. It was then that he enacted his laws. He died in Cyprus at the age of eighty. His last commands to his relations were that they should carry his bones to Salamis and, when they had been cremated, scatter them over the soil. This is why Cratinus in his play, *The Chirons*, makes him say:

> This is my island home; my dust, men say,
> Is scattered far and wide o'er Ajax' land.

An epigram of my own also is contained in the collection of *Epigrams in Various Meters* mentioned above, where I discuss all the illustrious dead in all meters and rhythms, in epigrams and lyrics. Here it is:

> Far Cyprian fire his body burnt; his bones,
> Turned into dust, made grain at Salamis:
> Wheel-like, his pillars bore his soul on high;
> So light the burden of his laws on men.

It is said that he was the author of the apophthegm "Nothing too much." Dioscurides relates in his *Memorabilia* that when Solon was weeping for the loss of his son (of whom nothing more is known), and someone said to him, "It is all of no avail," he replied, "That is why I weep, because it is of no avail."

[4]594 B.C.

The following letters are attributed to Solon:

Solon to Periander

You tell me that many people are plotting against you. Lose no time if you want to rid yourself of them all. A conspirator against you may appear in a most unexpected quarter; for example, one who is concerned for his personal safety or one who disdains your apprehension of everything. The gratitude of the city would go to one who found out that you had no suspicion. Best of all would be to resign power, and so be free of the accusation. But if you must, in the face of all dangers, remain tyrant, try to make your band of mercenaries stronger than your fear; then you will need to banish no one.

Solon to Epimenides

It seems that after all it was not my lot to confer much benefit on Athenians by my laws, any more than yours by purifying the city. Religion and legislation are not sufficient in themselves to benefit cities; it can only be achieved by those who lead the multitude where they choose. If things are going well, religion and legislation are beneficial; if not, they avail nothing.

My laws and all my enactments fare no better. The popular leaders did harm to the commonwealth by permitting license and could not prevent Pisistratus from setting up a tyranny. When I warned them, they would not believe me. He found more acceptance when he flattered the people than I when I told them the truth. I laid my arms down before the generals' quarters and told the people that I was wiser than those who did not see that Pisistratus was aiming at tyranny, and more courageous than those who drew back from resisting him. They, however, denounced Solon as mad. At last I protested: "My country, I, Solon, am ready to defend you by word and deed, but some of my countrymen think me mad. Therefore I will go forth from among them as the sole opponent of Pisistratus, and let them, if they like, become his bodyguard." You must know, my friend, that he was extremely ambitious to be tyrant. He began by being a popular leader; his next step was to inflict wounds on himself and appear before the court of the Heliaea, crying out that these wounds had been inflicted by his enemies, and he requested them to give him a guard of four hundred young men. And the people, without listening to me, granted him the men, who were armed with clubs. After that he destroyed the democracy. In vain did I seek to free the poor amongst the Athenians from their condition of serfdom, if now they all have become slaves of one master, Pisistratus.

II
THALES

HERODOTUS, Duris, and Democritus agree that Thales was the son of Examyas and Cleobulina and belonged to the Thelidae,[1] who are Phoenicians, and among the noblest of the descendants of Cadmus and Agenor. As Plato says, he was one of the Seven Sages. He was the first to receive the name of Sage, in the archonship of Damasias[2] at Athens, when the term was applied to all the Seven Sages, as Demetrius of Phalerum mentions in his *Catalogue of Archons*. He became a citizen of Miletus when he came to that town along with Nileos, who had been exiled from Phoenicia. Most writers, however, believe him a native Milesian of distinguished family.

Thales first engaged in political life but then became a student of nature. According to some, he left no writings; for the *Nautical Astronomy* attributed to him is also assigned to Phocus of Samos. Callimachus recognizes him as the discoverer of the Ursa Minor; for he says in his *Iambics:*

> *Who first of men the course made plain*
> *Of those small stars we call the Wain*
> *Whereby Phoenicians sail the main.*

Others say he wrote only two treatises, *On the Solstice* and *On the Equinox,* considering other matters unknowable.

Some accounts make Thales out to be the first to study astronomy, the first to predict eclipses of the sun and to fix the

---

[1] *Ingram Bywater suggests "Nelidae."*
[2] *582* B.C.

17

solstices; thus Eudemus in his *History of Astronomy.* These achievements gained him the admiration of Xenophanes and Herodotus and the attention of Heraclitus and Democritus.

Others, among them Choerilus the poet, say that Thales was the first to hold the immortality of the soul. He was also the first to fix the sun's course from solstice to solstice, and, by some accounts, the first to fix the size of the sun as one seven-hundred-and-twentieth part of the solar cycle and the size of the moon to be the same fraction of the lunar cycle. He was the first to call the last day of the month the thirtieth, and the first to discuss problems of nature, as some aver.

Aristotle[3] and Hippias affirm that, on the basis of the properties of the magnet and of amber, Thales attributed a soul or life even to inanimate objects. Pamphila states that, having learned geometry from the Egyptians, Thales was the first to inscribe a right-angled triangle in a circle, and that in honor of the accomplishment he sacrificed an ox. Others tell this same story about Pythagoras, amongst them Apollodorus the arithmetician. (It was Pythagoras who developed most fully the discoveries attributed by Callimachus, in his *Iambics,* to Euphorbus the Phrygian. I mean "scalene triangles" and everything else having to do with theoretical geometry.)

Thales is also credited with having given excellent political advice. For example, when Croesus sent to Miletus offering terms of alliance, Thales frustrated the plan, and this proved the salvation of the city when Cyrus was victorious. Heraclides makes Thales say that he had always lived alone as a private citizen and kept apart from state affairs. Some authorities say that he married and had a son, Cybisthus; others that he remained a bachelor and adopted his sister's son, and that when asked why he had no children he replied, "Because I loved children." The story is told that when his mother tried to force him to marry, he replied it was too soon, and when she urged him again, later in life, he replied that it was too late. Hieronymus of Rhodes in the seond book of his *Random Notes*

---

[3]*cf.* DeAnima, *A2, 405, a 19.*

relates that in order to show how easy it is to grow rich, Thales, foreseeing a good season for olives, leased all the oil-presses and thus amassed a fortune.

Thales held that water is the primary substance of all things and that the world is alive and full of gods. He discovered the seasons of the year and divided it into 365 days.

Thales acknowledged no teacher, though he went to Egypt and spent some time there with the priests. Hieronymus tells us that Thales measured the height of the pyramids by the shadow they cast, taking the observation at the hour when our shadow is the same length as our own bodies. He lived with Thrasybulus, the tyrant of Miletus, according to Minyas.

The famous story of the tripod found by the fisherman and sent by the people of Miletus to all the Wise Men in succession runs as follows. When some young Ionian men purchased a catch of fish from some Milesian fishermen, a dispute arose over the tripod, which had been found in the catch. The Milesians referred the question to Delphi, and the oracle responded in this fashion:

> *Who shall possess the tripod? Thus replies*
> *Apollo: "Whosoever is most wise."*

They therefore gave it to Thales, and he to another, and so on till it came to Solon, who, with the remark that the god was the most wise, sent it to Delphi. Callimachus in his *Iambics* gives a different version of the story, which he borrowed from Maeandrius of Miletus. As he died, Bathycles, an Arcadian, bequeathed a bowl with the solemn injunction that it "should be given to him who had done most good by his wisdom." It was given to Thales, went the round of all the Sages, and came back to Thales again. And he sent it to Apollo at Didyma, with this dedication, according to Callimachus:

> *Lord of the folk of Nelius' line,*
> *Thales, of Greeks adjudged most wise,*
> *Brings to thy Didymaean shrine*
> *His offering, a twice-won prize.*

But the prose inscription is: "Thales the Milesian, son of Examyas dedicates this prize to Delphinian Apollo after twice winning it from all the Greeks."

The bowl was carried from place to place by the son of Bathycles, whose name was Thyrion, as Eleusis relates in his work *On Achilles,* as does Alexo the Myndian in the ninth book of his *Legends.*

Eudoxus of Cnidos and Euanthes of Miletus agree that a certain man who was a friend of Croesus received a golden goblet from that king, to be bestowed upon the wisest of the Greeks. This man gave it to Thales, and from him it passed to others, and so to Chilon.

Chilon laid the question, "Who is a wiser man than I?" before the Pythian Apollo, and the god answered, "Myson." We shall have more to say of him presently. (In the list of the Seven Sages given by Eudoxus, Myson replaces Cleobulus; Plato also includes him, omitting Periander.) The answer of the oracle regarding him is as follows:

> *Myson of Chen in Oeta; this is he*
> *Who for wise-heartedness surpasseth thee:*

and it was given in reply to a question put by Anacharsis. Daimachus the Platonist and Clearchus allege that a bowl was sent by Croesus to Pittacus and began the round of the Wise Men from him.

The story as told by Andron in his work on *The Tripod* is that the Argives offered a tripod as a prize of virtue to the wisest of the Greeks; Aristodemus of Sparta was considered the winner but withdrew in favor of Chilon. Aristodemus speaks of Alcaeus thus:

> *Surely no senseless word was this of the Spartan, I deem,*
> *"Wealth is the worth of a man; and poverty void of esteem."*

Some relate that a loaded vessel was dispatched by Periander to Thrasybulus, tyrant of Miletus, and that, when the ship was wrecked in Coan waters, the tripod was thereafter found by some fishermen. However, Phanodicus says it was found in

Athenian waters and brought to Athens. An assembly was held and it was sent to Bias; the reason will be clarified in our life of Bias.

Yet another version holds that it was a work of Hephaestus given by that god to Pelops on the latter's marriage. From him it passed to Menelaus and was carried off by Paris along with Helen and was thrown by her into the Coan Sea, for she feared it would be a cause of strife. In the course of time some people of Lebedus, having purchased a catch of fish in that region, came into possession of the tripod and, quarreling with the fishermen about it, put in at Cos. When they could not settle the dispute, they reported the fact to Miletus, their native city. When their embassies were disregarded, the Milesians made war upon Cos. Many fell on both sides, and an oracle decreed that the tripod should be given to the wisest. Both parties to the dispute agreed upon Thales. After it had gone the round of the Sages, Thales dedicated it to Apollo of Didyma. The oracle which the Coans received is as follows:

> Hephaestus cast the tripod in the sea;
> Until it leaves the city there will be
> No end to strife, until it reach the seer
> Whose wisdom makes past, present, future clear.

The oracle of the Milesians beginning "Who shall possess the tripod?" had been quoted above. So much for this version of the story.

Hermippus in his *Lives,* assigns to Thales the story which is told by some about Socrates, namely, that he used to say there were three blessings for which he was grateful to fortune: "First, that I was born a human being and not a brute; next, that I was born a man and not a woman; third, a Greek and not a barbarian." It is said that once, when he was taken out of doors by an old woman to observe the stars, he fell into a ditch. To his cry for help the old woman retorted, "How can you expect to know all about the heavens, Thales, when you cannot even see what is just before your feet?" Timon, too, refers to him as an astronomer, and praises him in the *Silli,* where he says: "Thales among the Seven the Sage astronomer."

His writings are said by Lobon of Argos to have amounted to some two hundred lines. His statue is said to bear this inscription:

> *Pride of Miletus and Ionian lands,*
> *Wisest astronomer, here Thales stands.*

Of songs which are still sung these verses belong to him:

> *Many words do not declare an understanding heart.*
> *Seek one sole wisdom.*
> *Choose one sole good.*
> *For thou wilt check the tongues of chatterers prating without end.*

Here too are certain current apophthegms ascribed to him:

Of all things that are, the most ancient is God, for he is uncreated.
The most beautiful is the universe, for it is God's workmanship.
The greatest is space, for it holds all things.
The swiftest is mind, for it speeds everywhere.
The strongest, necessity, for it masters all.
The wisest, time, for it brings everything to light.

Thales held there was no difference between life and death. "Why then," someone asked, "do you die?" "Because," he replied, "there is no difference." Asked which is older, day or night, he replied: "Night is the older by one day." Someone asked him whether a man could hide an evil deed from the gods. "No," he replied, "not even an evil thought." To the adulterer who inquired if he should deny the charge upon oath, he replied that perjury was no worse than adultery. Being asked what is difficult, he replied, "To know oneself." "What is easy?" "To give advice to another." "What is most pleasant?" "Success." "What is the divine?" "That which has neither beginning nor end." Asked what was the strangest thing he had ever seen, his answer was, "An aged tyrant." "How can one best bear adversity?" "By seeing one's enemies in worse plight." "How shall we lead the best and most righteous life?" "By refraining from doing what we blame in others." "Which man is happy?" "The one who has a healthy body, a resourceful mind, and a docile nature." He tells us to remember friends, whether present or absent, not to take pride upon outward appearance, but to try to be beautiful in character. "Avoid ill-gotten gains," he says. "Let not idle words prejudice you against those who have shared your confidence. However you have provided for your parents, the same may you expect from your children." He explained the flooding of the Nile as due to the winds, which, blowing in the contrary direction, drove the waters upstream.

Apollodorus in his *Chronology* places Thales's birth in the first year of the 35th Olympiad.[4] He died at the age of seventy-eight (or, according to Sosicrates, of ninety). He died in the 58th Olympiad. He was a contemporary of Croesus, whom he undertook to transport across the Halys without building a bridge, by diverting the river.

Five other men have borne the name of Thales, according to the *Dictionary of Men of the Same Name* of Demetrius of Magnesia: (1) a rhetorician of Callatia, with an affected style, (2) a painter of Sicyon, of great gifts, (3) a contemporary of Hesiod, Homer, and Lycurgus, in very early times, (4) a person mentioned by Duris in his work *On Painting,* (5) an obscure person in more recent times who is mentioned by Dionysius in his *Critical Writings.*

Thales the Sage died as he was watching an athletic contest, from the heat, thirst, and the weakness incident to advanced age. And the inscription on his tomb is:

> *Here in a narrow tomb great Thales lies:*
> *Yet his renown for wisdom reached the skies.*

I may also cite one of my own, from my first book, *Epigrams in Various Meters:*

> *As Thales watched the games one festive day*
> *The fierce sun smote him, and he passed away;*
> *Zeus, thou didst well to raise him; his dim eyes*
> *Could not from earth behold the starry skies.*

[4] *640* B.C.

To Thales belongs the proverb "Know thyself," which Antisthenes in his *Successions of Philosophers* attributes to Phemonoe, though admitting that it had been appropriated by Chilon.

This seems a good place to say something in general about the Seven Sages, of whom many accounts, of which the following is one, exist. Damon of Cyrene in his *History of the Philosophers* criticizes all Sages, and especially the Seven. Anaximenes notes that they all applied themselves to poetry; Dicaearchus that they were neither sages nor philosophers, but merely shrewd men with a turn for legislation. Archetimus of Syracuse describes their meeting at the court of Cypselus, when he himself happened to be present, while Ephorus speaks of a meeting, without Thales, at the court of Croesus. Some make them meet at the Pan-Ionian festival, at Corinth, and at Delphi. Their utterances are variously reported, and are attributed now to one now to the other; for example the following:

> *Chilon of Lacedaemon's words are true:*
> *Nothing too much; good comes from measure due.*

Nor is there any agreement as to how the number was determined, for Maeandrius, in place of Cleobulus and Myson, includes Leophantus, son of Gorgiadas, of Lebedus or Ephesus, and Epimenides the Cretan in the list; Plato in his *Protagoras* lists Myson but leaves out Periander; Ephorus substitutes Anacharsis for Myson; others add Pythagoras to the Seven. Dicaearchus hands down four names which are recognized by all: Thales, Bias, Pittacus, and Solon. He adds the names of six others, from whom he selects three: Aristodemus, Pemphylus, Chilon the Lacedaemonian, Cleobulus, Anacharsis, Periander. Others add Acusilaus, son of Cabas or Scabras, of Argos. Hermippus in his work *On the Sages* counts seventeen; from this number different people make different selections of seven. They are: Solon, Thales, Pittacus, Bias, Chilon, Myson, Cleobulus, Periander, Anacharsis, Acusilaus, Epimenides, Leophantus, Pherecydes, Aristodemus, Pythagoras, Lasos, son of Charmantides or Sisymbrinus or, according to Aristoxenus, of Chabrinus, born at Hermione, Anaxagoras. Hippobotus in his

List of Philosophers enumerates: Orpheus, Linus, Solon, Periander, Anacharsis, Cleobulus, Myson, Thales, Bias, Pittacus, Epicharmus, Pythagoras.

Here follow the extant letters of Thales.

Thales to Pherecydes

I hear that you intend to be the first Ionian to explain theology to the Greeks. Perhaps it was a wise decision to make the book common property without taking advice, instead of entrusting it to any particular persons, a course without advantages. However, if it would please you, I am quite willing to discuss the subject of your book with you, and if you ask me to come to Syros, I will. Surely Solon of Athens and I would scarcely be sane if, after having sailed to Crete to pursue our inquiries there, and to Egypt to confer with the priests and astronomers, we hesitated to come to you. Solon too will come, with your permission. You, however, are so fond of home that you seldom visit Ionia and have no longing to see strangers, but, as I hope, apply yourself to one thing, namely, writing, while we, who never write anything, travel all over Hellas and Asia.

Thales to Solon

If you leave Athens, it seems to me that you could most conveniently take up residence at Miletus, which is an Athenian colony; for there you would incur no risk. If you are annoyed at the thought that we are governed by a tyrant, hating, as you do, all absolute rulers, you would at least enjoy the society of your friends. Bias wrote inviting you to Priene; if you choose the town of Priene as a residence, I myself will come and live with you.

III
ANAXIMENES

ANAXIMENES, the son of Eurystratus and a native of Miletus, was a pupil of Anaximander. Some say he was also a pupil of Parmenides. He held that the first principle is air or the unlimited. The stars, he said, move around the earth but not under it. He wrote simply and directly in the Ionic dialect.

According to Apollodorus, Anaximenes was contemporary with the capture of Sardis and died in the 63rd Olympiad.[1]

There have been two other men called Anaximenes, both of Lampsacus: one was a rhetorician who wrote on the exploits of Alexander; the other, the nephew of this rhetorician, was a historian.

Anaximenes the philosopher wrote the following letters:

Anaximenes to Pythagoras

Thales, the son of Examyas, has met a harsh fate in his old age. He left the court of his house at night, as he was wont, with his maidservant to view the stars, and as he gazed, forgetting where he was, he came to the edge of a steep slope and fell over. Thus the Milesians lost their astronomer. Let us who were his pupils cherish his memory; and let it be cherished by our children and pupils; and let us not cease to entertain one another with his words. Let all our discourse begin with a reference to Thales.

[1] 528-525 B.C.

And again:

Anaximenes to Pythagoras

You were better advised than we others when you left Samos for Croton, where you live in peace. The sons of Aeaces do mischief incessantly, and Miletus is never without tyrants. The king of the Medes is another terrorizer, though not so long as we are willing to pay tribute. The Ionians are about to go to war with the Medes to secure their common freedom, and once we are at war we can hope for safety no more. How can Anaximenes think any longer of studying the heavens when destruction or slavery threatens? Meanwhile, you are accepted favorably by the people of Croton and the other Greeks in Italy. Pupils come to you from as far as Sicily.

IV
PYTHAGORAS

Now that we have completed our account of the philosophy of Ionia, starting with Thales, and of its chief representatives, let us examine the philosophy of Italy, which was initiated by Pythagoras, son of the gem engraver Mnesarchus. According to Hermippus, Pythagoras was a Samian or, according to Aristoxenus, a Tyrrhenian from one of those islands which the Athenians held after driving out their Tyrrhenian inhabitants. Some claim that he was descended through Euthyphro, Hippasas, and Marmacus from Clenymus, who was exiled from Philus, and that, because Marmacus lived in Samos, Pythagoras was called a Samian. From Samos Pythagoras went, it is said, to Lesbos with an introduction from his uncle Zoilus, to study under Pherecydes. Pythagoras had three silver flagons made and took them as presents to each of the priests of Egypt. He had brothers, of these Eunomus was the elder and Tyrrhenus the second. He also had a slave, Zamolxis, who is worshiped, by the Getans as Cronos, so says Herodotus. Pythagoras was a pupil, as already stated, of Pherecydes of Syros; on the death of Pherecydes, Pythagoras went to Samos and became the pupil of Hermodamas, Creophlus's descendant, a man already of advanced years. While still young, Pythagoras was so eager for knowledge that he left his own country and became initiated into all the mysteries and rites, not only of Greece, but of foreign countries as well.

Pythagoras was in Egypt when Polycrates sent him a letter of introduction to Amasis; he learned the Egyptian language, as

Antiphon says in his book *On Men of Outstanding Merit,* and he also journeyed among the Chaldaeans and Magi. While in Crete Pythagoras descended into the cave of Ida with Epimenides; he also entered the Egyptian Sanctuaries and learned their secret doctrines about the gods. Returning to Samos, Pythagoras found his country under the tyrant Polycrates, so he departed for Croton in Italy, where he established a constitution for the Greeks living in Italy. There he and his followers were held in great esteem, because, being nearly three hundred in number, they governed the state so well that its constitution was a true aristocracy (government by the *best*).

Heraclides of Pontus reports that Pythagoras used to say of himself that he had once been Aethalides and was accounted to be Hermes's son. Hermes told Aethalides that he could choose any gift he wished except immortality, so he asked to retain through life and death a memory of his experiences. Consequently, during his lifetime Aethalides had absolute recall of everything he had experienced, and when he died he still retained the same memories. Afterward, in course of time, Aethalides's soul entered into Euphorbus, who was wounded by Menelaus. Euphorbus used to say that he had once been Aethalides and had obtained this gift from Hermes, and then he recounted the wanderings of his soul, its migrations, the many plants and animals into which it had entered, all that it suffered in Hades, and all that the other souls there have to endure. When Euphorbus died, his soul passed into Hermotimus. Desiring to prove the story, Hermotimus went to the temple of Apollo at Branchidae, where he identified the shield that Menelaus, on his voyage home from Troy, had dedicated to Apollo. The shield was now so decayed that only the ivory facing was left. When Hermotimus died, he became Pyrrhus, a fisherman of Delos, and again he remembered everything: how he was first Aethalides, then Euphorbus, then Hermotimus, and then Pyrrhus. But when Pyrrhus died, he became Pythagoras and still remembered all the facts recounted.

There are some who claim, absurdly, that Pythagoras left no writings whatever. In any event, Heraclitus the physicist loudly proclaims: "Pythagoras, son of Mnesarchus, pursued investigation more than all other men, and in this selection of his writings made himself a wisdom of his own, showing much learning but poor workmanship." This remark provoked the opening words of Pythagoras's treatise *On Nature,* "Nay, I swear by the air I breathe, I swear by the water I drink, I will never suffer censure on account of this work." Pythagoras in fact wrote three books, *On Education, On Statesmanship,* and *On Nature.* The book which passes as the work of Pythagoras is by Lysis of Tarentum, a Pythagorean, who fled to Thebes and taught Epaminondas. Heraclides, the son of Serapion, in his *Epitome of Sotion,* says that he also wrote a poem *On the Universe,* and a second poem, the *Sacred Poem,* which begins,

> Young men, come revere in silence
> All these my words.

On the Soul, Of Piety, Helothales the Father of Epicharmus of Cos, Croton, and other works as well are from his pen. The same authority holds that the poem *On the Mysteries* was written by Hippasus to denigrate Pythagoras, and that many others, written by Aston of Croton, were ascribed to Pythagoras. Aristoxenus says that Pythagoras got most of his moral doctrines from the Delphic priestess Themistoclea. According to Ion of Chios, in his *Triagmi,* Pythagoras ascribed some poems, which he himself had composed, to Orpheus. Also attributed to him is the *Scopiads,* which begins thus: "Be not shameless, before any man."

Sosicrates in his *Successions of the Philosophers* says that when Leon the tyrant of Phlius asked Pythagoras who he was, he said, "A philosopher," and that Pythagoras compared life to the Great Games, where some went to compete for the prize, others went to sell their wares, but the best went as spectators; similarly in life, some grow up with servile natures, greedy for fame and gain, but the philosopher seeks truth.

The general contents of the three treatises of Pythagoras mentioned above are as follows. Pythagoras forbids us to pray for ourselves, because we do not know what is good for us. He calls drinking a trap and frowns on all excess, holding that no one should go beyond due measure either in drinking or in eating. He says of sexual indulgence, "Keep the winter for sexual pleasures, but in summer abstain; they are less harmful in autumn and spring, but they are harmful at all times and not conducive to health." Once asked when a man should consort with a woman, he replied, "When you want to lose the strength you have."

He divides man's life into four phases: "Twenty years a boy, twenty years a youth, twenty years a young man, twenty years an old man, and these four periods correspond to the four seasons, the boy to spring, the youth to summer, the young man to autumn, and the old man to winter," meaning by youth one not yet grown up, and by a young man, a man of mature age. According to Timaeus, Pythagoras was the first to say, "Friends have all things in common," and, "Friendship is equality." His disciples proved this by putting all their possessions into a common pool. They had to keep silence for five whole years, merely listening to his discourses without seeing him, until they passed an examination; thereafter, they were admitted to his house and allowed to see him. The disciples of Pythagoras would never use coffins of cypress, because the scepter of Zeus was made of it, as we are told by Hermippus in his second book *On Pythagoras*.

Pythagoras's bearing is said to have been most dignified, and his disciples held the opinion that he was Apollo come down from the far north. A story circulates that once, when he was disrobed, his thigh was seen to be of gold, and when he crossed the river Nessus, many people claim they heard it greet him. According to Timaeus, in the tenth book of his *History*, Pythagoras remarked that the consorts of men bore divine names, being called first Virgins, then Brides, and then Mothers. He brought geometry to perfection, though it was Moeris who first discovered its elements; Anticlides, in his second book *On Alexander* affirms this and adds that Pythagoras devoted most of his time to the arithmetical side of geometry. He also discovered the musical intervals on the monochord. Neither did Pythagoras neglect medicine. We are told by Apollodorus the arithmetician that upon discovering that in a right-angled triangle the square of the hypotenuse is equal to the squares on the sides containing the right angle, Pythagoras offered a sacrifice of oxen. There is an epigram running as follows:

> *What time Pythagoras that famed figure found,*
> *For which the noble offering he brought.*

Pythagoras is also said to have been the first to put athletes on a diet of meat, experimenting first with Eurymenes – so we learn from Favorinus in the third book of his *Memorabilia*. Previously, athletes had trained on dried figs, cheese, and even on oatmeal, as Favorinus says in the eighth book of his *Miscellaneous History*. Some say it was another Pythagoras, a trainer, and not our subject who instituted this diet, forbidding even the killing, to say nothing of the eating, of animals that, like humans, enjoy the privilege of having a soul. This was the argument advanced, but his real reason for forbidding an animal diet was to exercise people and make them accustomed to a simple way of life, so that they could live on things readily available, spreading their tables with uncooked foods and drinking only pure water. This, Pythagoras taught, was the way to a healthy body and a keen mind. Of course, the only altar at which he worshiped was that of Apollo the Giver of Life, behind the Altar of Horns at Delos. Then, Pythagoras set flour and meal cakes, using no fire, offering no animal victim, as Aristotle recalls in his *Constitution of Delos*.

Pythagoras first declared that the soul, bound now in this creature, now in that one, follows a necessary cycle. He was also, according to Aristoxenus the musician, the first to introduce weights and measures in Greece. He first declared that the evening and morning stars are the same, as Parmenides maintains. So greatly was Pythagoras admired that his disciples used to be called "prophets proclaiming the voice of God," and he himself says in a written work that "after two hundred and seven years in Hades he has returned to the land of the living." For this reason his disciples remained his firm adherents, and men came from afar to hear his words – Lucanians, Peucetians, Messapians, and Romans.

Until the time of Philolaus it was not possible to learn any Pythagorean doctrine, and only Philolaus brought out those three celebrated books for which Plato paid a hundred minas. No fewer than six hundred persons attended Pythagoras's evening lectures. Those who were privileged to see him wrote to their friends congratulating themselves on their great good fortune. Moreover, the Metapontines named his house the "Temple of Demeter" and his porch the "Museum," as may be learned from Favorinus in his *Miscellaneous History*. The other Pythagoreans used to say that not all of his doctrines were for all men to hear; our authority for this is Aristoxenus, in the tenth book of his *Rules of Pedagogy*, where we also are told that a member of the school, Xenophilus by name, when asked by a certain man how he could best educate his son, replied, "By making him the citizen of a well-governed state." Throughout Italy, Pythagoras made friends of many good men as well as of notable men such as the lawgivers Zaleucus and Charondas. Pythagoras had a great gift for friendship; he especially would be attracted to anyone who adopted his aphorisms and would befriend him.

The following were the aphorisms or precepts of Pythagoras. Do not stir the fire with a knife; do not step over the beam of a balance; do not sit down on your bushel; do not eat your heart; do not relieve a man of his burden, but help him carry it; always fold your bedclothes; do not put God's image on the circle of a ring; do not leave the pan's impress on the ashes; do not wipe up a mess with a torch; do not commit a nuisance toward the sun; do not walk on the highway; do not shake hands too readily; do not have swallows under your own roof; do not keep birds with hooked claws; do not make water on or stand upon your nail and hair trimmings; turn the sharp blade away; when you go abroad, do not turn around at the frontier.

The meaning of these sayings is as follows. Do not stir the fire with a knife: do not stir the passions or the swelling pride of the great. Do not step over the beam of a balance: do not overstep the bounds of equity and justice. Do not sit down on your bushel; have the same care for today and the future, a bushel signifying the day's ration. By not eating your heart, he meant not wasting your life in troubles and pains. By saying do not turn around when you go abroad, he meant to advise those who are departing this life not to set their hearts' desire on living or to be too much attracted by the pleasures of this life. The explanations of the rest are similar but would take too long to recount.

Above all, Pythagoras forbade red mullet and blacktail as food, and he counseled abstinence from the hearts of animals and from beans, and sometimes, according to Aristotle, even from tripe and gizzards. Pythagoras is said to have contented himself with a bit of honey, honeycomb, or bread, never touching wine during the day, taking greens, boiled or raw, as dainties, and eating fish only on rare occasions. His robe was white and spotless, his quilts of white wool, for linen was not yet known in those parts. He was never known to overeat, to behave loosely, or to be drunk. He avoided laughter and all pandering to tastes by insulting jests and vulgar tales. He would punish neither slave nor free man when he was angry. He used to call counseling "setting to rights." He practiced divination by sounds or voices and by auguries, never by burned offerings, except for frankincense. His offerings were always inanimate; some, however, claim that he offered cocks, suckling goats, and pigs, but never lambs. Aristoxenus, however, holds that he permitted the eating of all other animals and abstained only from plowing oxen and rams.

The same writer, we have seen, says that Pythagoras derived his teaching from the Delphic priestess Themistoclea. Hieronymus, however, says that when Pythagoras had descended into Hades, he saw the soul of Hesiod bound fast to a bronze pillar and gibbering and the soul of Homer suspended from a tree with serpents writhing about it. In this manner, they were being punished for the things they had said about the gods. He also witnessed the torture of those who had been unfaithful to their wives. This, says our authority, is the reason Pythagoras was honored by the citizens of Croton. Aristippus of Cyrene in his work *On the Physicists* says that he was named Pythagoras because he spoke the truth as unfailingly as the Pythian oracle.

Pythagoras is said to have counseled his disciples in the following way. Always to say on entering their own doors:

Where did I trespass? What did I achieve?
And what duties did I leave unfulfilled?

Not to let victims be sacrificed to the gods, and to worship only at an altar which was not stained with blood. Not to call the gods to witness, for it is man's obligation to try to make his own word convincing. To honor their elders, on the principle that to have preceded in time imposes a greater claim to respect; as, in the world, sunrise precedes sunset, so, in human life, the beginning precedes the end, and, in all organic life, birth comes before death. Pythagoras bade them further to honor gods before demi-gods, heroes before men, and, among men, their parents first. To act toward one another in a way which would not turn friends into enemies but, rather, enemies into friends. To consider nothing their own property, to uphold the law, and to wage war on lawlessness. Never to kill or injure trees that are not wild, or any animal that does no injury to man. That it is becoming and fitting neither to indulge in unbridled laughter nor to look sullen. To avoid excess of flesh; on a journey to let exertion and slackening alternate; to cultivate the memory; to restrain one's hand and tongue when angry; to respect all divination; to sing to the lyre and, by hymns, to show fitting gratitude to gods and to good men. Not to eat beans, because they generate flatulence and share most in the spirit; moreover, it is better for the stomach if they are not eaten, and such abstinence will make our dreams smooth and tranquil.

Alexander in his *Successions of the Philosophers* says that in the Pythagorean memoirs he found also the following teachings. The principle of all things is the monad or unit; arising from this monad the undefined dyad or two serves as material substratum to the monad, which is cause; from the monad and the undefined dyad spring numbers; from numbers, points; from points, lines; from lines, plane figures; from plane figures, solid figures; from solid figures, sensible bodies, the elements of which are four — fire, water, earth, and air. The elements interchange and turn into one another without residue; they also generate a universe which is alive, intelligent, spherical, with the earth at its center. The earth itself is spherical and inhabited on all its surface. There are antipodes, and "down" to us is "up" to them. Light and darkness divide the universe equally, as do hot and cold, dry and moist: if hot dominates, it is summer; if cold, winter; if dry, spring; if moist, late autumn. If all are in equilibrium, we have the best periods of the year, of which the freshness of spring constitutes the healthy season, and the decay of late autumn the unhealthy. Likewise, in the day, freshness belongs to the morning and decay to the evening, and the latter is, therefore, more unhealthy. The air about the earth is inert and unwholesome, and all within it is mortal, but the upper air is in constant motion and hence pure and healthy, and all within it is immortal and therefore divine. The sun, the moon, and the other stars are gods, because heat predominates in them, and heat is the cause of life. The moon is lighted by the sun. Gods and men are akin to the degree that man partakes of heat; therefore, God concerns Himself about man. Fate is the cause of things' being ordered in this way, both as a whole and separately. The sun's ray penetrates through the ether, whether cold or dense — the air is cold ether, and the sea and moisture are dense ether — and this ray reaches to the depths and quickens all things. All things live which partake of heat — this is why plants are living things — but not all have soul, which is a separated part of ether, partly the hot and partly the cold, for it shares the cold ether. Soul is distinct from life; it is immortal, since that from which it is derived by separation is immortal. Living creatures are reproduced from others of the same kind by germination; there is no such thing as spontaneous generation from earth. The germ is a clot of brain containing hot vapor within it, and this, when brought to the womb, throws out, from the brain, fluid and blood, and from these are formed flesh, sinews, bones, hair — in a word, the whole body. Soul and sense, however, come from the vapor inside. Congealing in forty days, this mass receives form, and, according to the ratios of "harmony," the mature child is delivered in seven, nine, or, at the most, ten months. The child has all the relations which constitute life; these, forming a continuous series, keep it together according to the ratios of harmony, each appearing at controlled intervals. The senses in general, and sight in particular, are a certain very hot vapor. This is why sight is said to see through air and water, because the hot ether is resisted by the cold; if the vapor in the eyes were cold, it would be dissipated on contact with the air, which is similar to it. Pythagoras in certain places calls the eyes the portals of the sun. He draws similar conclusions concerning hearing and the other senses.

The soul of man, he says, is divided into three parts: intelligence, reason, and passion. Other animals possess intelligence and passion, but only man possesses reason. The soul extends from the heart to the brain; the part of it which is in the heart is passion, while the parts located in the brain are reason and intelligence. The senses are distillations from these. Reason is immortal, everything else mortal. The soul derives nourishment from the blood; the faculties of the soul are winds; they as well as the soul are invisible, as the ether is invisible. The veins, arteries, and sinews are the bonds of the soul. When the soul is strong and concentrated in itself, thoughts and deeds become its bond. When cast out on the earth, the soul wanders in the air like the body. Hermes is the keeper of souls, and for that reason is called Hermes the Escorter, Hermes the Keeper of the Gate, and Hermes of the Underworld, for he conducts the souls from their bodies both by land and sea. The pure are taken into the uppermost region, while the impure are not permitted to approach the pure or each other but are bound by the Furies in adamantine chains. The air is entirely full of souls which are called demons or heroes; these send men dreams and signs of future disease and health – not only to men, but to sheep also and cattle as well. To such men purifications and lustrations, all divination, omens, and the like are addressed. The most important matter in human life is the art of drawing the soul to good or to evil. Those men are blessed who cultivate a good soul. If the soul is evil, men can never be at rest, nor can they maintain a steady course even for two days.

Right has the power of an oath; for this reason Zeus is called the God of Oaths. Virtue is harmony, as are health and all good and God Himself; all things are, therefore, constructed according to the laws of harmony. The love of friends is essentially concord and equality. We should worship gods and heroes equally: the gods constantly, with reverent silence, in white robes and after purification; the heroes only from noon onward. Purification is achieved by cleansing, baptism, and lustration, and by keeping immune from all deaths and births and all pollution, abstaining from meat and flesh of animals that have died, mullets, gurnards, eggs, and animals hatched from eggs, beans, and the other foods prohibited by those who perform mystic rites in the temples. According to Aristotle in his work *On the Pythagoreans,* Pythagoras counseled abstinence from beans, either because they are like the genitals, or because they are like the gates of Hades (because they are unjointed or because they are injurious), or because they are like the form of the universe, or because they belong to oligarchy, since they are used in election by lot. Pythagoras ordered his disciples not to pick up fallen crumbs, either because he wanted to accustom them not to eat immoderately, or because he connected fallen crumbs with a person's death. According to Aristophanes, crumbs belong to the heroes, for in his *Heroes* he says: "Nor taste ye of what falls beneath the board!"

Another of the commandments of Pythagoras forbade eating white cocks, because they are sacred to the month and wear garments like those of suppliants (supplication is included among goods) or are sacred to the month because they announce the time of day. White represents the nature of the good, black the nature of evil. Pythagoras also forbade touching sacred fish, for it is not right that gods and men should share the same things, any more than free men and slaves should. He likewise forbade breaking bread, for at one time friends used to meet over one loaf, as the barbarians do even today; one should not divide bread which brings friends together. Some explain this with reference to the judgment of the dead in Hades; others say that bread makes men cowards in war; still others that the whole world began from bread.

Pythagoras held that the sphere is the most beautiful figure among solids, and the circle among plane figures. Everything that is decreasing may be spoken of in terms of old age, while all that increases may be spoken of in terms of youth. Health means retention of the form, disease its destruction. He said that salt should be brought to the table to remind us of what is right, because salt preserves all that it touches and arises from the purest sources, sun and sea.

This is derived from Alexander's account of what he found in the Pythagorean records. What follows is Aristotle's account.

Pythagoras's great dignity was noted even by Timon; although this author pokes fun at him in his *Silli*, nevertheless, he speaks of:

> *Pythagoras, inclined to witching works and ways,*
> *Man-snarer, fond of noble periphrase.*

Xenophanes confirms the statement about Pythagoras's having been different people at different times, in the elegiacs stanzas which begin: "Now other thoughts, another path, I show." And he goes on to say of Pythagoras:

> *They say that, passing a belabored whelp,*
> *He, full of pity, spake these words of dole:*
> *"Stay, smite not! 'Tis a friend, a human soul;*
> *I knew him straight when I heard him yelp!"*

Thus Xenophanes. But Cratinus lampooned Pythagoras both in the *Pythagorizing Woman* and in *The Tarentines*, where we read:

> *They are wont,*
> *If haply they a foreigner do find,*
> *To hold a cross-examination*
> *Of doctrines' worth, to trouble and confound him*
> *With terms, equations, and antitheses*
> *Brain-bung'd with magnitudes and periphrases.*

Again, Mnesimachus in the *Alcmaeon*:

> *To Loxias we sacrifice: Pythagoras his rite,*
> *Of nothing that is animate we ever take a bite.*

And Aristophon in the *Pythagorist:*

> A. He told how he traveled in Hades and looked on the dwellers below,
> How each of them lives, but how different by far from the lives of the dead
> Were the lives of the Pythagoreans, for these alone, so he said, were suffered to dine with King Pluto, which was for their piety's sake.
> B. What an ill-tempered god for whom such swine, such creatures, good company make;

And later in the *Pythagorist:*

> Their food is just greens, and to wet it pure water is all that they drink;
> And the want of a bath, and the vermin, and their old threadbare coats so do not stink
> That none of the rest will come near them.

Pythagoras met his death in the following way. As he sat one day with some acquaintances at the house of Milo, the house was set ablaze, out of jealousy, by one of the people who were considered unworthy to be admitted into his presence (though some say it was perpetrated by some inhabitants of Croton who were anxious to protect themselves against the establishment of a tyranny). Pythagoras was captured as he tried to escape. He fled until he reached a field of beans, where he stopped, declaring that he would prefer to be captured rather than cross it, killed rather than discuss his doctrines. His pursuers cut his throat. More than half of his disciples, about forty, were killed in the same way. A very few escaped, including Archippus of Tarentum and Lysis, already mentioned.

Dicaearchus says that Pythagoras died a fugitive in the temple of the Muses at Metapontum after forty days' starvation. Heraclides in his *Epitome of the Lives of Satyrus* says that after burying Pherecydes at Delos, Pythagoras returned to Italy and, when he found Cylon of Croton giving a luxurious banquet to everyone, retired to Metapontum to end his days there by starvation, for he no longer desired to live. On the other hand, Hermippus relates that when Agrigentum and Syracuse were at war, Pythagoras and his disciples fought in the forefront of the army of the Agrigentines. When their line was turned, Pythagoras was killed by the Syracusans as he tried to avoid crossing the beanfield. The rest of his school, about thirty-five, were burned at the stake in Tarentum because they tried to set up a government in opposition to those in power.

Hermippus gives still another account. When Pythagoras came to Italy, he built a subterranean dwelling and ordered his mother to make a record of all that passed, and at what time, and to send her messages down to him until he should ascend. She did so. Some time later Pythagoras ascended, withered and looking like a skeleton. He entered the Assembly, declared he had been down to Hades, and even recounted his experiences to them. Deeply moved, they wept and wailed and looked upon him as divine, going so far as to send their wives to him in hopes that they would learn some of his doctrines. This is why they were called Pythagorean women. So much for Hermippus's account.

Pythagoras had a wife named Theano who was the daughter of Brontinus of Croton, though some say she was Brontinus's wife and Pythagoras's pupil. He had a daughter Damo, according to the letter of Lysis to Hippasus, which says of Pythagoras:

> I am told by many that you discourse publicly, a thing which Pythagoras deemed unworthy, for certain it is that, when he entrusted his daughter Damo with the custody of his memoirs, he solemnly ordered her never to give them to anyone outside his house. Although she could have sold the writings for a large sum of money, she refused, considering poverty and her father's solemn injunctions more precious than gold, even though she was a woman.

Pythagoras and Theano, also had a son Telauges, who succeeded his father and, according to some, was Empedocles's instructor. In any event, Hippobotus has Empedocles say: "Telauges, famed son of Theano and Pythagoras." Telauges wrote nothing, so far as we know, but his mother Theano wrote a few things. A story is told that when she was asked how many days it was before a woman becomes pure after intercourse, she replied, "With her own husband immediately, with another man never." She advised a woman that when she was with her own husband to put off her modesty with her clothes, and on leaving him to put it on again with them. Asked, "Put on what?" she replied, "What makes me be called a woman."

To return to Pythagoras. According to Heraclides, the son of Serapion, Pythagoras was eighty years old when he died, and this agrees with his own description of the life of man, though most authorities say he was ninety. And there are jesting lines of my own upon him which read:

> *Not thou alone from all things animate*
> *Didst keep, Pythagoras. All food is dead*
> *When boil'd and bak'd and salt-besprinkled;*
> *For then it surely is inanimate.*

Again:

> *So wise was wise Pythagoras that he*
> *Would touch no meats, but called it impious*
> *Bade others eat. Good wisdom: not for us*
> *To do the wrong; let others impious be.*

And again:

> *If thou wouldst know the mind of old Pythagoras,*
> *Look on Euphorbus' buckler and its boss.*
> *He says, "I've lived before," If, when he says he was,*
> *He was not, he was no one when he was.*

And again, of the manner of his death:

> *Woe! Woe! Whence, Pythagoras, this deep reverence*
> *for beans? Why did he fall in the midst of his disciples?*
> *A bean field there was he dared not cross; sooner*
> *than trample on it, he endured to be slain at the*
> *crossroads by the men of Acragas.*

Pythagoras flourished in the 60th Olympiad,[1] and his school lasted nine or ten generations. The last of the Pythagoreans,

[1] 588-584 B.C.

according to Aristoxenus, were Xenophilus from the Thracian Chalcidice, Phantom of Phlius, and Echecrates, and, finally, Diocles, Polymnastus, and Phlius, who were pupils of Philolaus and Eurytus of Tarentum.

Favorinus says that Pythagoras used definitions in mathematics; their use was extended by Socrates and his disciples, and afterward by Aristotle and the Stoics.

We are also told that he was the first to call the heavens the "universe" and the earth "spherical," though Theophrastus says this of Parmenides, and Zeno says the same of Hesiod. It is said that Cylon was a rival of Pythagoras, as Antilochus was of Socrates.

Pythagoras the athlete was also the subject of another epigram, as follows:

> Gone to box with other lads
> Is the lad Pythagoras,
> Gone to the Games Olympian
> Crates' son of Samian.

The philosopher also wrote the following letter:

Pythagoras to Anaximenes

Even you, O most excellent of men, were you no better born and famed than Pythagoras, would have risen and departed from Miletus. But now your ancestral glory has detained you as it would have detained me were I Anaximenes's equal. If you, the best of men, abandon your cities, their good order will perish, and the peril from the Medes will increase. Always to scan the heavens is not well, but more seemly is it to be provident for one's mother country. For I, too, am not to be found completely in my discourses but equally in the wars which the Italians wage among themselves.

Having finished our account of Pythagoras, we must speak next of the noteworthy Pythagoreans; after them will come the philosophers whom some denominate "sporadic" (that is, those belonging to no particular school); and then, in the next place, we will append the succession of all those worthy of notice as far as Epicurus, in the way that we promised. We have already treated of Theano and Telauges; now we have to speak first of Empedocles, for some say he was a pupil of Pythagoras.

V
XENOPHANES

XENOPHANES, a native of Colophon, was the son of Dexius or, according to Apollodorus, of Orthomenes. He is praised by Timon in the following, not unambiguous, terms: "Xenophanes, not overly proud, perverter of Homer, castigator." After he was banished from his native city, he lived at Zancle in Sicily and also resided in Catana. Some say he was self-taught; others believe that he was a pupil of either Boton of Athens or of Archelaus. Sotion places him as a contemporary of Anaximander. His writings, in epic, elegiac, and iambic meters, attack Hesiod and Homer, denouncing what they said about the gods. He used to recite his own poems. He opposed the views of Thales and Pythagoras and attacked Epimenides as well. Xenophanes lived to a very great age, as his own words testify:

> Seven and sixty are now the years that have been tossing my cares up and down the land of Greece, and there were then twenty and five years more from my birth up, if I know how to speak truly about these things.

He holds that existent things are composed of four elements, and that the worlds are unlimited in number but do not overlap in time. Clouds are formed when vapor from the sun is carried upward and lifts the clouds into the surrounding air. The substance of God is spherical in form, resembling man in no way whatsoever. He is all eye and all ear but does not breathe. He is all that is of mind and thought and eternal. Xenophanes was the first to hold that everything that comes into being is doomed to perish, and that the soul is breath.

He also said that the greater number of things do not have thought, and that our contacts with tyrants should be as few, or at any rate as pleasant, as possible. When Empedocles remarked that it is impossible to find a wise man, Xenophanes replied, "Naturally, because it takes a wise man to recognize a wise man." Sotion says that he was the first to hold that all things are unknowable, but Sotion is mistaken.

One of Xenophanes's poems is *The Founding of Colophon,* and another, *The Settlement of a Colony at Elea in Italy,* making two thousand lines in all. He flourished about the 60th Olympiad.[1] Demetrius of Phalerum in his work *On Old Age* says that Xenophanes buried his sons with his own hands as Anaxagoras did, and Panaetius the Stoic in his book *Of Cheerfulness* agrees. Xenophanes is believed to have been sold into slavery by (and to have been set free by) the Pythagoreans Parmeniscus and Orestades, so says Favorinus in the first book of his *Memorabilia.* There was also another Xenophanes, of Lesbos, an iambic poet.

Such were the "sporadic" philosophers.

[1] 540-537 B.C.

VI

HERACLITUS

HERACLITUS, son of Bloson or, according to others, of Heracon, was an Ephesian by birth. The height of his career fell in the 69th Olympiad.[1] Heraclitus was the most high-minded of men, but he was also exceedingly conceited, as appears clear from his book, in which he says: "A great deal of learning does not bring wisdom; if it did it would have instructed Hesiod and Pythagoras, Xenophanes and Hecateaus" – because "this alone is wisdom, to understand thought, as that which rules the entire world." Heraclitus was fond of saying that "Homer deserved to be chased out of the lists and chastised with staves, and Archilochus deserved the same."

He also liked to say, "Insolence must be extinguished more than fire," and "The law must be defended like the city walls." He attacks the Ephesians, too, because they exiled his friend Hermodorus; he says:

All the adult Ephesians ought to end their own lives, and leave the city to the beardless boys, because they drove out Hermodorus, the most worthy man among them, saying, "We do not want one who is the worthiest of men among us; or if there be such a one, let him go somewhere else and pass his life among others."

When the Ephesians asked Heraclitus to write their laws, he rejected the request because their state already lay under a

[1]*504-500* B.C.

47

badly framed constitution. He liked to withdraw to the temple of Artemis and play at dice with the boys; when the Ephesians gathered around to gape, he would say, "You rogues, why are you surprised? Surely this is better than taking part in your civil life."

In the end, Heraclitus became a misanthrope and retired to the mountains, where he passed his days living on a diet of grass and herbs. When this regimen gave him dropsy, he returned to the city and put this riddle to the physicians: Could they create a drought after heavy rain? They could not understand this riddle; thereupon he buried himself in a cow barn, thinking that the offensive damp humor would be drawn from him by the warmth of the dung. Even this failed, however, and he died at the age of sixty.

I wrote the following lines about him:

> I have often wondered how it happened that Heraclitus could endure living in this miserable fashion and then die. A fatal disease inundated his body with water, quenching the light in his eyes and bringing on darkness.

Hermippus recounts that Heraclitus asked the doctors whether anyone could draw off the liquid by emptying his intestines. When they replied that this was impossible, he lay down in the sun and ordered his servants to cover him with cow dung. Stretched out thus, prone, he died the following day and was buried in the marketplace. Neanthes of Cyzicus states that since he was unable to tear off the dung, he remained in the prone position, and that because he was unrecognizable in this condition, he was devoured by dogs.

From his boyhood Heraclitus was exceptional; as a youth he used to protest that he knew nothing, but as a grown man he claimed that he knew everything. He was nobody's pupil, claiming that he "inquired of himself" and learned everything from himself. Others say, however, that he had been a pupil of Xenophanes; we learn this from Sotion, too, who also says that Ariston in his book *On Heraclitus* says that Heraclitus was cured of dropsy and died of another disease. Hippobotus repeats the same story.

The work attributed to Heraclitus is a single treatise: *On Nature,* which is divided into three discourses, one on the universe, another on politics, the third on theology. Heraclitus deposited this book in the temple of Artemis, and, some say, he deliberately made it very obscure so that only initiates could approach it, lest familiarity breed contempt. Timon gives a sketch of our philosopher in these words: "In their midst uprose shrill, cuckoo-like, a mob-reviler, riddling Heraclitus."

Theophrastus gives melancholy as the reason that some parts of the work are half-finished, while other parts make a peculiar potpourri. Antisthenes in his *Successions of Philosophers* cites as a proof of Heraclitus's magnanimity the fact that he gave up his claim to the kingship in favor of his brother. *On Nature* enjoyed such fame that a sect was founded called the Heracliteans, named after him.

The following is a summary of his doctrines. All things are composed of fire, and they are again resolved into fire; all things are ruled by destiny, and existent things are brought into harmony by the clash of opposing currents. All things are filled with soul and divinities. He gives an account of all the orderly happenings in the universe and claims that the sun is no larger than it appears. Another of his sayings is: "You will never find the limits of soul, not even if you track it along every path; because its cause is so profound." He used to say that self-conceit is an epilepsy, and vision a deceiving sense. Sometimes, however, his utterances are clear and distinct, so that even the dullest person can easily understand and derive elevation of soul from them. His exposition is incomparable for brevity and weightiness.

We may summarize his specific doctrines in the following statements. Fire is the element; all things are transformations of fire and are produced by rarefaction and condensation. He does not, however, explain clearly what he means by this. All things are generated by conflict of opposites, and the whole of things flows like a river. Everything that exists is limited and forms a single world. It is born from fire and dissolved again into fire in fixed cycles for all eternity; destiny determines this. Of the opposites, the one that leads to generation is called war and strife, while the one that tends to destruction by fire is called harmony and peace. He called change a pathway up and down; the world is generated according to this path.

By contracting, fire turns to moisture. When moisture condenses, it becomes water. When water congeals, it turns into earth. He calls this process the downward path. The earth is again liquefied and thus generates water, and from water the rest of the series is educed. He reduces nearly everything to exhalation from the sea; this process is the upward path. Exhalations arise both from the earth and from the sea. The exhalations from the sea are bright, pure, those from earth, dark. The bright exhalations feed fire, the others, the moist element. He does not give a clear account of the surrounding element. He does say, however, that in it are bowls that have their concave surfaces turned toward us; in these the bright exhalations are collected and produce flames. These are the stars. The flame of the sun is the brightest and the hottest; the other stars are farther from the earth and therefore shed less light and heat on it. Eclipses of the sun and moon occur when the bowls are turned upward; the monthly phases of the moon are due to the bowl's gradually circulating in position. Various exhalations account for day and night, months, seasons, and years, rains and winds, and other similar phenomena. The bright exhalation, set afire in the hollow orb of the sun, produces day; the opposite exhalation, securing dominance, causes night. An increase of warmth due to the dark exhalation brings about winter. He explains other phenomena in a manner consonant with this. He does not explain the nature of the earth or that of the bowls.

In my *Life of Socrates*, I have mentioned the story that Ariston tells of Socrates's remarks upon inspecting the book of Heraclitus, a gift to him from Euripides. Seleuceus the grammarian, however, says that a certain Croton, in a book called *The Diver*, claims that the work of Heraclitus in question was first brought into Greece by one Crates, and Seleuceus goes on to say that it required a Delian diver not to be drowned in it. Some give its title as *The Muses,* others, *Concerning Nature.* Diodotus calls it an unerring helm for the guidance of life; others "a guide of conduct, the keel of the whole world, for one and all alike." We are told that when asked why he kept silent, Heraclitus replied, "Why, to let you chatter." Darius sought to make his acquaintance and wrote him the following:

King Darius, son of Hystaspes, to Heraclitus the wise man of Ephesus, greeting.

You are the author of a treatise *On Nature* which is difficult to understand and hard to interpret. In certain parts, if it be interpreted word for word, it seems to contain a power of speculation on the whole universe and all that goes on within it, which depends upon a most divine motion. But for the most part judgment is suspended, so that even those who are the most skilled in literature do not know the right interpretation of your work. Accordingly, King Darius, son of Hystaspes, wishes to enjoy your instruction and Greek culture. Come then as quickly as possible to visit me at my palace. The Greeks, as a rule, are not eager to honor their wise men; rather, they neglect their excellent precepts which are good to hear and impart learning. Here at my court, however, you will be assured all privileges, good and worthy conversation daily, and a life according to your counsels.

Heraclitus's answer was as follows:

Heraclitus of Ephesus to King Darius, son of Hystaspes, greeting.

All men upon earth hold aloof from truth and justice, while, by reason of wicked folly, they devote themselves to avarice and thirst for popularity. But I, forgetful of all wickedness and shunning the general satiety which is closely joined with envy, and abhorring splendor, could not come to Persia, since I am content with little, so long as that little is to my liking.

This answer shows how independent Heraclitus was, even when he dealt with a king.

In his book called *Men of the Same Name,* Demetrius says that Heraclitus despised even the Athenians, although they held him in the highest esteem, and that though the Ephesians thought little of him, he preferred his own home. Demetrius of Phalerum, too, mentions him in his *Defense of Socrates.* The commentators on his work are very numerous and include

Antisthenes and Heraclides of Pontus, Cleanthes, Sphaerus the
Stoic, Pausanias – who was called the imitator of Heraclitus – Nicomedes, Dionysius, and Diodotus, among the grammarians. The latter affirms that his work is not a treatise upon
nature but upon government, in which the part devoted to
physics serves only as illustration.

Hieronymus relates that Scythinus the satirical poet undertook to put Heraclitus's work into verse. Heraclitus is the subject of many epigrams, among them the following:

> I am Heraclitus. Why do you drag me up and down, you illiterate
> men? I did not toil for you, but for those who understand me. One
> man in my sight is a match for thirty thousand, but the numberless
> hosts do not make a single one. I proclaim this in the very halls of
> Persephone.

Another runs as follows:

> Do not be in too great a hurry to get to the end of Heraclitus the
> Ephesian's book; the path is hard to travel. Gloom is there and
> darkness, without light. But if an initiate be your guide, the path
> shines brighter than sunlight.

VII

ANAXAGORAS

ANAXAGORAS, the son of Hegesibulus or Eubulus, was a native of Clazomenae. He was a pupil of Anaximenes and was the first to place mind over matter, for at the beginning of his treatise, which is written in pleasing and dignified language, he says, "All things were together; then came Mind and set them in order." This gained Anaxagoras the nickname of "Nous" or Mind, and Timon in his *Silli* writes of him:

> Then, I know, there is Anaxagoras, a strong champion, whom they call Mind, because indeed his was the mind which suddenly woke up and fitted closely together all that had formerly been in confusion.

He was eminent for wealth, noble birth, and greatness of soul, for he gave up his patrimony to his relations. When they charged that he neglected it, he replied, "Why then don't you look after it?" Finally, he retired to engage in investigation of nature without troubling himself about public affairs. When someone inquired, "Have you no care for your native land?" "Easily," he replied, "I am greatly concerned for my fatherland," and pointed to the heavens.

He is said to have been twenty years old at the invasion of Xerxes and to have lived seventy-two years. Apollodorus in his *Chronology* says that he was born in the 70th Olympiad and died

in the first year of the 88th Olympiad.[1] He began the study of
philosophy at Athens in the archonship of Callias when he was
twenty; Demetrius of Phalerum reports this in his list of archon. He remained in Athens for thirty years.

He declared that the sun is a mass of red-hot metal, larger
than the Peloponnesus, though others say this was the view of
Tantalus. He claimed that there are dwellings on the moon,
and hills and valleys as well. He held the principles to be the
homoeomeral or homogeneous molecules. Just as gold consists
of fine particles which are called gold dust, so he taught that
the whole universe is compounded of minute bodies having
homogeneous parts. His moving principle was Mind.

Of bodies, he said, some, such as earth, were heavy, occupying the lower region; others were light, such as fire, occupying
the upper region. Water and air were intermediate. Thus on
the earth, which is flat, the sea sinks when the moisture has
been evaporated by the sun. In the beginning the stars moved
through the sky as though within a revolving dome, so that the
celestial pole, which can always be seen, was directly overhead;
later the pole assumed its inclined position. He thought the
Milky Way is caused by the reflection of the light from the stars
which are not illuminated by the sun, that comets are com-
plexes of planets which send out flames, that shooting stars are
a kind of sparks thrown off by the air. He believed that the
winds spring up when the air is dessicated by the sun's heat,
that thunder is a collision of clouds, lightning their violent
rubbing together, an earthquake the pressure downward of air
into the earth.

Animals are produced from moisture, heat, and earth; later
the species was propagated by generation from each other,
males from the right side, females from the left.

A story is told that he predicted the fall of the meteoric stone
at Aegospotami, foretelling it would fall from the sun. For this
reason, Euripides, who had been his pupil, in his play the
Phaëthon calls the sun a "golden clod." When Anaxagoras went
to Olympia, he took his seat with a sheepskin cloak about him

---

[1]*500-497* B.C. *and 428* B.C., *respectively.*

as though expecting rain — and it rained. When asked whether the hills at Lampsacus would ever be turned into sea, he answered, "Yes, all that is needed is time." Asked why he had been born, he replied, "To study the sun and moon and heavens." To one who asked, "Do you miss the society of the Athenians?" he answered, "Not I, but they do mine." When he saw the tomb of Mausolus, he said, "A costly tomb is an image of an estate turned into stone." To one who complained that he was dying in a foreign land, his answer was, "The descent to Hades is the same no matter where we start."

Favorinus in his *Miscellaneous History* claims that Anaxagoras was the first to hold that Homer in his poems treats of virtue and justice, and that this thesis was supported more extensively by his friend Metrodorus of Lampsacus, who was the first to concern himself with Homer's doctrine about nature. Anaxagoras was also the first man to compose a book with diagrams. Selenus in the first book of his *History* says that the meteoric stone fell in the archonship of Demylus, and that Anaxagoras claimed that the whole heaven is composed of stones, and that since rapid rotation caused it to hold together, it would fall if the rotation slackened.

Various accounts of the trial of Anaxagoras are given. Sotion in his *Succession of the Philosophers* says that Anaxagoras was accused of impiety by Cleon because he said the sun is a mass of incandescent metal. Sotion adds that Pericles, his pupil, defended him, and that he received a fine of five talents and was exiled. Satyrus in his *Lives* says that the prosecutor was Thucydides, the opponent of Pericles, that the charge included treasonable transactions with Persia as well as impiety, and that sentence of death was passed on Anaxagoras by default. When he was told that he was condemned and that his sons were dead, he remarked, about the sentence, "Long ago nature condemned both my judges and myself to death," and about his sons, "I knew that my children were born to die." This story is, however, also told by other writers about Solon and Xenophon. Demetrius of Phalerum in his work *On Old Age* says that Anaxagoras buried his sons with his own hands. Hermippus in his *Lives* says that when Anaxagoras was confined in the prison awaiting his execution, Pericles demanded of the people whether they had found any fault with him in his own public career. When they replied that they had not, "Well," he continued, "I am a pupil of Anaxagoras; do not therefore let slander persuade you to put him to death. Let me, rather, persuade you to release him." Thereupon, Anaxagoras was released, but he could not endure the indignity and committed suicide. Hieronymus in the second book of his *Random Notes* relates that Pericles brought Anaxagoras into court so weak and wasted from illness that he was acquitted, not so much on the merits of the case, as by the sympathy of the judges. So much then on the subject of his trial.

Anaxagoras was at odds with Democritus because the latter would not communicate with him. He retired to Lampsacus, where he died. When the rulers of that place asked whether they could do anything for him, he answered that he would like them to give the boys a holiday once a year in the month in which he died. That custom is maintained in that city to this day. On his death, the citizens of Lampsacus buried him with honor and inscribed the following epitaph on his grave: "Here lies Anaxagoras, who, in seeking truth, scaled the very heavens."

I also have composed an epigram about him;

> Anaxagoras said that the sun is a molten mass. This was his crime, for which he must pay with his life, a fate from which Pericles sought to save him, but too late. Crushed in spirit, he died by his own hand.

Three other men were named Anaxogoras: (1) a rhetorician of the school of Isocrates, (2) a sculptor, who is mentioned by Antigonus, (3) a grammarian, who was a student of Zendotus.

VIII
EMPEDOCLES

Hippobotus relates that Empedocles was the son of Meton and grandson of another Empedocles, and that he was a native of Agrigentum. Timaeus confirms this in the fifteenth book of his *Histories*, adding that Empedocles, the poet's grandfather, had been a man of distinction. Hermippus agrees with Timaeus. Heraclides, too, in his treatise *On Diseases* says that Empedocles came from an illustrious family, and that his grandfather kept a stable of racehorses. Eratosthenes, on the authority of Aristotle, records in his *Olympic Victories* that the father of Meton was a victor in the 71st Olympiad.[1] The grammarian Apollodorus in his *Chronology* tells us that Empedocles

was the son of Meton, and Glaucus says he went to Thurii, which then had only recently been founded.

Further on he adds:

Those who say that, on being exiled from his home, he went to Syracuse and fought in the ranks of the Syracusans against the Athenians seem, in my judgment at least, to be completely mistaken. By that time he was either no longer alive or of a very advanced age, which is inconsistent with the story.

Aristotle and Heraclides both say that Empedocles died at the age of sixty. The victor with the riding horse in the 71st

[1]496 B.C.

57

Olympiad was the man's namesake and grandfather, so that Apollodorus in a single passage states the date as well as the fact.

Satyrus in his *Lives* says that Empedocles was the son of Exaenetus, that he himself left a son named Exanenetus, and that in the Olympiad in question Empedocles was victor in the horse race and his son in wrestling (or, as Heraclides in his *Epitome* tells it, in the footrace). I found in the *Memorabilia* of Favorinus a statement that Empedocles offered a banquet to the sacred ambassadors at which he served a sacrificial ox made of barley meal and honey. He also had a brother named Callicratides. Telauges, the son of Pythagoras, in a letter to Philolaus calls Empedocles the son of Archinomus.

Empedocles himself testifies, at the beginning of his *Purifications,* that he was a native of Agrigentum in Sicily: "My friends, who dwell in the great city sloping down to yellow Acragas, hard by the citadel." So much for his descent.

Timaeus in the ninth book of his *Histories* says Empedocles was a pupil of Pythagoras and adds that, being convicted at the time of stealing his discourses, he, like Plato, was excluded from participation in the discussions of the school. Timaeus says, further, that Empedocles himself mentions Pythagoras in the lines:

> And there lived among them a man of superhuman knowledge, who verily possessed the greatest wealth of wisdom.

Others say that in this passage he is referring to Parmenides.

Neanthes states that to the time of Philolaus and Empedocles all Pythagoreans were admitted to the discussions. When Empedocles himself made them public property by his poem, they declared a law that the discussions should not be imparted to any poet. He says the same thing about Plato, who also was excommunicated. Who among the Pythagoreans had Empedocles for a pupil, however, he did not say. He thought that an epistle commonly attributed to Telauges, which states that Empedocles was the pupil of both Hippasus and Brontinus, was not to be believed.

Theophrastus says that Empedocles was an admirer of Parmenides and imitated him in his verses, because Parmenides also had published his treatise *On Nature* in verse. Hermippus's story is that he was an admirer not so much of Parmenides as of Xenophanes, with whom, in fact, he lived and whose poetry he imitated, and that his meeting with the Pythagoreans came later. Alcidamas tells us in his treatise on *Physics* that Zeno and Empedocles were pupils of Parmenides at about the same time but later left him, and that while Zeno formulated a system of his own, Empedocles became the pupil of Anaxagoras and Pythagoras, emulating the latter in dignity of life and bearing and the former in his investigations of nature.

Aristotle in his *Sophist* calls Empedocles the inventor of rhetoric, just as Zeno was the inventor of dialectic. In his treatise *On Poets,* Aristotle also says that Empedocles belonged to Homer's school and was a master of diction, great in the use metaphors and of all other poetical devices. Aristotle also says that Empedocles wrote other poems, one in particular about the invasion of Xerxes, and a hymn to Apollo, which Empedocles's sister (or, according to Hieronymus, his daughter) later cast into the flames. She destroyed the hymn unintentionally, but the poem on the Persian war deliberately, because it was unfinished. Aristotle also says, without specifying any titles, that Empedocles wrote both tragedies and political discourses. Heraclides, the son of Sarapion, attributes the tragedies to a different author. Hieronymus claims to have seen forty-three of these plays, while Neanthes tells us that Empedocles wrote these tragedies in his youth, and that he, Neanthes, knew seven of them.

Satyrus in his *Lives* says that Empedocles was also a physician and an excellent orator, and that Gorgias of Leontini, a man preeminent in oratory and the author of a treatise on that art, had been his pupil. Apollodorus says in his *Chronology* that Gorgias lived to the age of 109. Satyrus quotes Gorgias as saying that he was personally present when Empedocles performed feats of magic. Even more, he contends that Empedocles in his poems lays claim to this power and to much besides when he says:

And thou shalt learn all the drugs that are a defense to ward off ills and old age, since for thee alone shall I accomplish all this. Thou shalt arrest the violence of the unwearied winds that arise and sweep the earth, laying waste the cornfields with their blasts, and again, if thou so will, thou shalt call back winds in requital. Thou shalt make after the dark rain a seasonable drought for men, and again after the summer drought thou shalt cause tree-nourishing streams to pour from the sky. Thou shalt bring back from Hades a dead man's strength.

Timaeus, also, in the eighteenth book of his *Histories* remarks that Empedocles has been admired for many reasons. For instance, when the etesian winds once began to blow violently and to damage the crops, Empedocles ordered asses to be flayed and bags to be made of their skin. These he stretched out here and there on the hills and headlands to catch the wind, and, because this checked the wind, he was called the "windstopper." Heraclides in his book *On Diseases* says that he furnished Pausanias with the facts about a woman in a trance. This Pausanias, according to Aristippus and Satyrus, was Empedocles's bosom friend, to whom he dedicated his poem *On Nature* in the following words: "Give ear, Pausanias, thou son of Anchitus the wise!" He also wrote an epigram upon him:

The physician Pausanias, rightly so named, son of Anchitus, descendant of Asclepius, was born and bred at Gela. Many a wight pining in fell torments did he bring back from Persephone's inmost shrine.

Heraclides says that the case of the woman in a trance was such that for thirty days Empedocles kept her body without pulsation though she never breathed; for that reason Heraclides called him not merely a physician but a diviner as well, deriving the titles from the following lines:

My friends, who dwell in the great city sloping down to yellow Acragas, hard by the citadel, busied with goodly works, all hail! I go about among you an immortal god, no more a mortal, so honored of all, as is meet, crowned with fillets and flowery garlands. Straightway as soon as I enter with these men and women into flourishing towns, I am reverenced, and tens of thousands follow, to learn the path which leads to welfare, some desirous of oracles, others suffering from all kinds of diseases, desiring to hear a message of healing.

Timaeus explains that Empedocles called Agrigentum great, inasmuch as it had eight hundred thousand inhabitants. Hence Empedocles, he continues, speaking of their luxury, said, "The Agrigentines live delicately as if tomorrow they would die, but they build their houses well as if they thought they would live forever."

It is said that Cleomenes the Rhapsode recited this very poem, the *Purifications,* at Olympia; so Favorinus also states in his *Memorabilia.* Aristotle, too, declares Empedocles to have been a champion of freedom and averse to rule of every kind, for, as Xanthus relates in his account, Empedocles declined the kingship when it was offered to him, obviously preferring a frugal life. Timaeus agrees with this, at the same time giving the reason that Empedocles favored democracy, namely, that having been invited to dine with one of the magistrates, when the dinner had gone on some time and no wine was put on the table, though the other guests kept quiet, he, becoming indignant, ordered wine to be brought. Then the host confessed that he was waiting for the servant of the Senate to appear. When Empedocles arrived, he was made master of the revels, clearly by the arrangement of the host, whose design of making himself tyrant was but thinly veiled, for he ordered guests either to drink wine or to have it poured over their heads. At the time Empedocles was reduced to silence; the next day, however, he impeached both the host and the master of the dinner and brought about their condemnation and execution. This marked the beginning of his political career.

Again, when Acron the physician asked the council for a site on which to build a monument to his father, who had been eminent among physicians, Empedocles came forward and forbade it in a speech in which he dwelt upon equality and, in particular, put the following question: "But what inscription shall we put upon it? Shall it be this? 'Acron, the eminent physician of Agrigentum, son of Acros, is buried beneath the steep eminence of his most eminent native city?'" Others give as the second line: "Is laid in an exalted tomb on a most exalted peak." Some attribute this couplet to Simonides.

Subsequently Empedocles broke up the Assembly of the Thousand, three years after it had been set up — which proves both that he was wealthy and that he favored the popular cause. Timaeus, in his eleventh and twelfth books (for he mentions him more than once), states that at all events Empedocles seems to have held opposite views when in public life and when writing poetry. In some passages one may see that he is boastful and selfish; one may judge by these words: "All hail! I go about among you an immortal god, no more a mortal, etc." At the time that Empedocles visited Olympia he demanded an exaggerated deference, so that wherever friends gathered, no one was discussed as much as Empedocles.

Later, when Agrigentum exiled Empedocles, the descendants of his personal enemies opposed his return home; this was the reason of his going to Peloponnesus, where he died. Timon also spoke of him, in these words:

> Empedocles, too, mouthing tawdry verses; to all that had independent force, he gave a separate existence. And the principles he chose need others to explain them.

Different accounts are given of Empedocles's death. Heraclides, after telling the story of the woman in a trance, when Empedocles became famous because he had sent the dead woman away alive, goes on to say that Empedocles was offering a sacrifice close to the field of Peisianax. Some of his friends had been invited to the sacrifice, including Pausanias. After the feast, the company dispersed and retired to rest, some under the trees in the adjoining field, others wherever they chose, while Empedocles himself remained on the spot where he had reclined at table. At daybreak all got up, and he was the only one missing. A search was made, and they questioned the servants, who said they did not know where he was. Thereupon someone related that in the middle of the night he heard an

exceedingly loud voice calling Empedocles; he arose and be-
held a light in the heavens and a glitter of lamps, but nothing
more. His hearers were amazed at what had occurred, and
Pausanias came down and sent people in search of him. Later
he bade them look no further, for something marvelous, and
beyond expectation, had happened to Empedocles so that it
was their duty to sacrifice to him, since he had become a god.

Hermippus tells us that Empedocles cured Panthea, a woman
of Agrigentum, who had been given up by the physicians, and
this was the reason he was offering sacrifice, and that those
invited were about eighty in number. Hippobotus asserts that
when Empedocles got up, he set out on his way to Etna. When
he had reached it, he plunged into the fiery craters and dis-
appeared, his intention being to confirm the report that he had
become a god. The truth later became known when one of his
slippers was thrown up in the flames; it had been his custom to
wear slippers of bronze. Heraclides makes Pausanias take ex-
ception to this story.

Diodorus of Ephesus, writing of Anaximander, declares that
Empedocles emulated him, displaying theatrical arrogance and
wearing stately robes. We are told that the people of Selinus
suffered from pestilence owing to the noisome smells from the
river nearby, so that the citizens perished and their women
died in childbirth. Empedocles conceived the plan of bringing
two neighboring rivers to the place at his own expense; by this
admixture he sweetened the waters, thus halting the pestilence.
While the Selinuntines were feasting on the river bank, Empedocles appeared. The company rose up and worshiped and
prayed to him as to a god. To confirm this belief he leaped into
the fire. These stories are contradicted by Timaeus, who ex-
pressly says that Empedocles left Sicily for Peloponnesus and
never returned at all; this is how Timaeus accounts for the fact
that the manner of his death is not known. Empedocles replies
to Heraclides, whom he mentions by name in his fourteenth
book. Pisianax, he says, was a citizen of Syracuse and possessed
no land at Agrigentum. Further, if such a story had been in
circulation, Pausanias would have set up a monument to his
friend, as to a god, in the form of a statue or shrine, for he was

a wealthy man. "How came he," adds Timaeus, "to leap into the craters, which he had never once mentioned though they were not far off? He must then have died in the Peloponnesus. It is not at all surprising that his tomb is not found; the same is true of many other men." After arguing thus, Timaeus goes on to say: "But Heraclides is everywhere just such a collector of absurdities, telling us, for instance, that a man dropped down to earth from the moon."

Hippobotus assures us that formerly, in Agrigentum, there was a statue of Empedocles with his head covered, and later another with the head uncovered in front of the Senate House at Rome, which the Romans obviously had moved to that site. Some portrait-statues with inscriptions are still extant. Neanthes of Cyzicus, who treats of the Pythagoreans, relates that after the death of Meton, when the germs of a tyranny began to show themselves, it was Empedocles who persuaded the Agrigentines to put an end to their factions and cultivate equality in politics.

From his own ample means Empedocles gave dowries to many of the maidens of the city who had none. No doubt it was the same means that enabled him to don a purple robe and over it a golden belt, as Favorinus relates in his *Memorabilia,* as well as slipppers of bronze and a Delphic laurel-wreath. Empedocles had thick hair and a train of boy attendants. He himself was always dignified and kept this gravity of demeanor unshaken; thus he would appear in public. When the citizens met him, they recognized in this manner the sign of royalty. Later, as he was going in a carriage to Messina to attend some festival, Empedocles fell and broke his thigh; this brought on an illness which caused his death at the age of seventy-seven. His tomb is in Megara.

Aristotle gives a different account of his age; he makes him sixty years of age when he died; while others make him 109. He flourished in the 84th Olympiad.[2] Demetrius of Troezen in his short treatise *Against the Sophists* said of him, adapting the words of Homer: "He tied a noose that hung aloft from a tall

[2] *444-441* B.C.

cornel tree and thrust his neck into it, and his soul went down to Hades."

In the short letter of Telauges which was mentioned above, it is stated that by reason of his age he stumbled into the sea and was drowned.

There is an epigram of my own on him in my *Pammetros,* in a satirical vein, as follows:

Thou, Empedocles, didst cleanse thy body with nimble flame, fire didst thou drink from everlasting bowls. I will not say that of thine own will thou didst hurl thyself into the stream of Etna; thou didst fall in against thy will when thou wouldst fain not have been found out.

And another:

Verily there is a tale about the death of Empedocles, how that once he fell from a carriage and broke his right thigh. But if he leaped into the bowls of fire and so took a draught of life, how was it his tomb was shown still in Megara?

Empedocles's doctrines were as follows. There are four elements – fire, water, earth, and air – and friendship by which these are united, and strife by which they are separated. These are his words: "Shining Zeus and life-bringing Hera, Aidoneus and Nestis, who lets flow from her tears the source of mortal life." By Zeus he means fire, by Hera earth, by Aidoneus air, and by Nestis water. "And their continuous change," he says, "never ceases," as if this ordering of things were eternal.

At all events, he goes on:

At one time all things uniting in one through Love, at another each carried in a different direction through the hatred born of strife.

He says that the sun is a vast mass of fire and larger than the moon; the moon, he says, is of the shape of a quoit; and the heaven itself, he says, is crystalline. The soul, in turn, assumes all the various forms of animals and plants. He says:

Before now I was born a boy and a maid, a bush and a bird, and a dumb fish leaping out of the sea.

His poems *On Nature* and *Purifications* run to five thousand lines, his *Discourse on Medicine* to six hundred. We have mentioned his tragedies above.

IX
PARMENIDES

Parmenides, a native of Elea, son of Pyres, was a pupil of Xenophanes. Though he was taught by Xenophanes, Parmenides was not his follower. According to Sotion, Parmenides also associated with Ameinias the Pythagorean, who was the son of Diochaetas and a poor but worthy man. Parmenides was more inclined to follow Ameinias, and when he died Parmenides built a shrine to him, because he, Parmenides, was of high birth and very wealthy. Ameinias, not Xenophanes, led Parmenides to adopt the peaceful life of a student.

Parmenides was the first to state that the earth is spherical and situated in the center of the universe. He held that there are two elements, fire and earth: the former is like a craftsman, the latter, his material. Man proceeded from the sun as his first cause; heat and cold, of which all things consist, surpass the sun. Parmenides also held that soul and mind are one and the same, as Theophrastus mentions in his *Physics,* where he sets out the tenets of almost all schools. He divided his philosophy into two parts, one dealing with truth, the other with opinion. Hence Parmenides says:

> Thou must needs learn all things, as well the unshakable heart of well-rounded truth as the opinions of mortals in which there is no sure trust.

Our philosopher, like Hesiod, Xenophanes, and Empedocles, expresses his doctrines in verse. He made reason the norm and said that sensations are unreliable. His words are:

And let not long-practised custom force you to tread this path, to be governed by an aimless eye, an echoing ear, and a tongue, but with understanding bring the much-contested issue to decision.

Hence Timon says of Parmenides: "And the strength of high-souled Parmenides, of no diverse opinions, who introduced thought instead of imagination's deceit." It was about him, too, that Plato wrote a dialogue with the title *Parmenides or Concerning Ideas.*

Parmenides flourished in the 69th Olympiad.[1] He is thought by Favorinus in the fifth book of his *Memorabilia,* to be the first to identify Hesperus, the evening star, and Phosphorus, the morning star, but others attribute this to Pythagoras, while Callimachus holds that the poem in question was not the work of Pythagoras. According to Speusippus in his book *On Philosophers,* Parmenides served his native city as a legislator. Favorinus also says in his *Miscellaneous History* that Parmenides was the first to use the argument known as "Achilles and the tortoise."

There was also another Parmenides, a rhetorician, who composed a treatise on that art.

[1] *504-500* B.C.

X

SOCRATES

We read in the *Theaetetus* of Plato that Socrates was the son of Sophroniscus, a sculptor, and of Phaenarete, a midwife. He was a citizen of Athens of the deme Alopece. It was thought that he helped Euripides write his plays; hence Mnesimachus writes: "This new play of Euripides is *The Phrygians,* and Socrates provides the wood for frying." And again he calls Euripides "an engine riveted by Socrates." And Callias in *The Captives* says:

A. Pray why so solemn, why this lofty air?
B. I've every right; I'm helped by Socrates.

Aristophanes in *The Clouds:*

'Tis he composes for Euripides
Those clever plays, much sound and little sense ...

According to some authors, for example, Alexander in his *Successions of the Philosophers,* Socrates was a pupil of Anaxagoras and also of Damon. When Anaxagoras was condemned, Socrates became a pupil of Archelaus the physicist. Aristoxenus says that Archelaus was very fond of him. Duris claims he was a slave and a stonecutter; some say the draped figures of the "Graces" on the Acropolis are his work. Hence the passage in Timon's *Silli:*

From these diverged the sculptor, a prater about laws, the enchan-
ter of Greece, inventor of subtle arguments, the sneerer who mocked at fine speeches, half-Attic in his mock humility.

He was formidable in public speaking, according to Idomeneus; moreover, as Xenophon tells us, the Thirty prohibited
his teaching the arts of words. And Aristophanes attacks him in
his plays for making the worse appear the better reason. Favorinus in his *Miscellaneous History* says Socrates and his pupil
Aeschines were the first to teach rhetoric; this is repeated by
Idomeneus in his work on the Socratic circle. Socrates was also
the first to discourse on the conduct of life, and the first
philosopher who was tried and put to death. Aristoxenus, the
son of Spintharus, claims that Socrates made money; at any
rate, he would invest sums, collect the interest, and then, when
this was spent, lend the principal again.

Demetrius of Byzantium relates that Crito took Socrates
from his workshop and educated him, impressed by his beauty
of soul, that he discussed moral questions in the workshops and
the marketplace, convinced that the study of nature is no
concern of man, that he claimed that his inquiries embraced
"Whatsoever is good or evil in a house,"[1] and that often, because he was so harsh in discussion, men attacked him with
their fists or pulled out his hair. He was despised and laughed
at, yet bore all this ill-usage patiently. Indeed once, when he
had been kicked, and someone wondered how he could accept
this so meekly, Socrates asked, "Should I have taken a donkey
to court, if he had kicked me?" Thus far Demetrius.

Unlike most philosophers, he felt no need of travel, except
when required to go on an expedition. The rest of his life he
remained at home and engaged zestfully in discussion with
anyone who would converse with him; his purpose was not to
change their opinions but to get at the truth. Euripides gave
him the treatise of Heraclitus and asked his opinion of it; he
replied, "What I understand of it is excellent, and so too is, I
daresay, what I do not understand, but it needs a Delian diver
to get to the bottom of it."

[1] Odyssey, *IV*, 392

He took care to exercise his body and kept in good condition. He served on the expedition to Amphipolis. When, in the battle of Delium, Xenophon fell from his horse, Socrates intervened and saved his life. In the general flight, while the other Athenians fled precipitously, he personally retired with composure, quietly turning round from time to time, ready to defend himself in case of attack. Socrates also served at Potidaea, going there by sea, because land communications were interrupted by the war; there he is said to have remained a whole night without changing his position, winning a citation for valor. He gave it to Alcibiades, whom he loved fondly, according to Aristippus in the fourth book of his treatise *On the Luxury of the Ancients*. Ion of Chios relates that as a young man Socrates visited Samos in the company of Archelaus, while Aristotle says that he went to Delphi. He also went to the Isthmus, according to Favorinus in the first book of his *Memorabilia*.

Socrates's courage and attachment to the democracy are clear from his refusal to yield to Critias and his colleagues when they ordered him to bring the wealthy Leon of Salamis before them for execution, as well as from the fact that he alone voted to acquit the ten generals. These qualities also appear from the fact that when he could have escaped from prison, he refused to do so, chiding his friends for weeping over his fate and while in prison addressing to them his most memorable discourses.

Socrates was a man of great independence and dignity of character. Pamphila in the seventh book of her *Commentaries* tells how Alcibiades once offered Socrates a large site on which to build a house. But he replied, "If I needed shoes and you offered me a whole hide from which to make a pair, would it not be ridiculous to take it? How many things I can do without!" And he liked to recite the lines:

The purple robe and silver's shine
More fit an actor's need than mine.

He showed his contempt for Archelaus of Macedon and Scopas of Cranon and Eurylochus of Larissa by refusing to accept presents from them or attend their courts. He was so orderly in his way of living that on several occasions when the plague broke out in Athens, he was the only man who escaped infection.

Aristotle says that he had two wives. The first wife was Xanthippe, by whom he had a son, Lamprocles; the second wife was Myrto, the daughter of Aristides the Just, whom he married without a dowry. With her he had Sophroniscus and Menexenus. Others say that Myrto was his first wife; while some writers, among them Satyrus and Hieronymus of Rhodes, claim that both were his wives at the same time. Athenians lacked men and, to increase the population, passed a decree which permitted a citizen to marry one Athenian woman and have children by a second. This is what Socrates did.

He could afford to disdain those who mocked him. He was proud of his simple mode of life and never asked a fee of anyone. He said that he most relished food which least needed seasoning and drink which least aroused the desire for some other drink, and that he was nearest to the gods because he had the fewest needs. The Comic poets prove this, for even while they ridicule him, they give him high praise. Thus Aristophanes:

O man that justly desirest great wisdom, how blessed will be thy life amongst Athenians and Greeks, retentive of memory and thinker that thou art, with endurance of toil for thy character; never art thou weary whether standing or walking, never numb with cold, never hungry for breakfast; from wine and from gross feeding and all other frivolities thou dost turn away.[2]

Ameipsias too, when he puts him on the stage wearing a cloak, says:

A. You come to join us, Socrates, worthiest of a small band and emptiest by far! You are a robust fellow. Where can we get you a proper coat?

B. Your sorry plight is an insult to the cobblers.

A. And yet, hungry as he is, this man has never stooped to flatter.

[2]Clouds, *412-417.*

His disdainful, lofty spirit is noted by Aristophanes, who writes: "Because you stalk along the streets, rolling your eyes, and endure, barefoot, many a hardship, and gaze up at us [the clouds]."[3] Sometimes, however, he would put on fine clothes to suit the occasion, as in Plato's *Symposium*, where he is going to Agathon's house.

Socrates showed equal ability both in persuasion and in discussion. Plato says that he sent Theaetus away from a discourse on knowledge, fired with a divine impulse. When Euthyphro had indicted his father for manslaughter, Socrates, conversing with him upon piety, dissuaded him from this purpose. Another time, through exhortation, he transformed Lysis into a virtuous character. He had the art of drawing his arguments from facts. When his son Lamprocles was violently angry with his mother, Socrates made him feel ashamed of himself, as Xenophon, I believe, has told us. When Plato's brother Glaucon wished to engage in politics, Socrates dissuaded him, as Xenophon relates, because he lacked experience. On the other hand, he encouraged Charmides to take up politics because he had a gift for it.

He roused a martial spirit in Iphicrates the general by showing him how the fighting cocks of Midias the barber flapped their wings in defiance of those of Callias. Glauconides demanded that he should be acquired for the state as if he were some pheasant or peacock.

He used to say it was odd that when you asked a man the number of sheep he had, he could readily tell you the exact number, but the same man could not name his friends or their number, because he set so little value on them. Finding Euclid keenly interested in eristic arguments, he said to him: "You will be able to get on with Sophists, Euclid, but not with men," for he saw no use in this sort of hair-splitting, as Plato tells us in the *Euthydemus*.

When Charmides offered him some slaves as a source of income, he declined the offer, and, according to some, he scorned the beauty of Alcibiades. He extolled leisure as the best

[3]Ibid., *362*.

of possessions, according to Xenophon in the *Symposium*. He said there is only one good, knowledge, and only one evil, ignorance. Wealth and good birth do not bring their possessors dignity, but rather evil. When someone told him that Antisthenes's mother was a Thracian, he replied, "Nay, did you expect a man so noble to have been born of two Athenian parents?" He made Crito ransom Phaedo, who had been taken prisoner in the war and was kept in degrading slavery. In this way he won him for philosophy.

In his old age Socrates learned to play the lyre, saying he saw nothing absurd in learning something new. Xenophon relates in the *Symposium* that Socrates had a habit of dancing, because he thought such exercise helpful in keeping the body fit. He used to say that his "daimon" warned him of the future; that to make a good start was no trifling advantage, but a trifle turned the scale; and that he knew nothing save that he was ignorant. He said that when people paid much for fruit which had ripened early, they must resign the hope of seeing the fruit ripen at the proper season. Once, when asked in what the virtue of a young man consists, he said, "In doing nothing to excess." He held that geometry should be studied to the point at which a man is able to measure the land which he acquires or sells.

On hearing the line of Euripides's play *Auge* in which the poet says of virtue: " 'Tis best to let her roam at will,"[4] he got up and left the theater. He said it was absurd to make a hue and cry about a slave who could not be found while allowing virtue to perish in this way. Someone asked him whether he should marry or not and received the reply, "Whichever you do you will regret it." He used to express his astonishment that the sculptors of marble statues should take pains to make the block of marble into a perfect likeness of a man and should take no pains about themselves lest they prove mere blocks, not men. He recommended the constant use of the mirror to the young so that handsome men might conduct themselves correspondingly, and ugly men learn to conceal their defects through education.

[4]*Cf.* Electra, *379*, Auge is a lost play.

He had invited some rich men to dine, and when Xanthippe said she was ashamed of the dinner, "Never mind," said he, "if they are reasonable men they will tolerate it; if they are not, we shall not trouble ourselves about them." He said the rest of the world lived to eat, but he himself ate to live. Of the mass of men who count for nothing, he said it was as though someone might complain that a single tetradrachm was counterfeit while permitting a whole heap of such pieces to pass as genuine. Aeschines said to him, "I am a poor man and have nothing else to give, but I offer you myself." And Socrates answered, "Do you not see that you are offering me the greatest gift of all?" To one who complained that he was overlooked when the Thirty rose to power, he said, "You do not regret that, do you?" To one who said, "You are condemned by the Athenians to die," he made answer, "So are they, by nature." But some assign these words to Anaxagoras. When his wife said, "You suffer unjustly," he retorted, "Would you want me to suffer justly?" He had a dream that someone said to him: "On the third day thou shalt come to the fertile fields of Phthia."[5] and he told Aeschines, "On the third day I shall die." When Socrates was about to drink the hemlock, Apollodorus offered him a beautiful garment to die in, "What," he said, "is my own good enough to live in but not to die in?" When he was told that a certain man spoke ill of him, he replied, "True, for he has never learned to speak well." When Antisthenes turned his cloak so that the rip in it came into view, "I can see," said he, "your vanity through your cloak." To one who said, "Don't you find so-and-so very offensive?" his reply was, "No, for it takes two to make a quarrel." We ought not to mind, he used to say, being subjects for the Comic poets, for if they satirize our faults they will do us good, and if not, they do not touch us. When Xanthippe first scolded him and then drenched him with water, his rejoinder was, "Did I not say that Xanthippe's thunder would end in rain?" When Alcibiades declared that the scolding of Xanthippe was unbearable, "Nay, I have got used to it," said he, "as to the continued rattle of a windlass. And you do not mind the cackle of geese." "No," replied Alcibiades, "but they

[5]Iliad, *IX, 363; cf.* Crito, *44B.*

furnish me with eggs and goslings." "And Xanthippe," said Socrates, "is the mother of my children." When she tore his coat off his back in the marketplace and his acquaintances advised him to hit back, "Yes, by Zeus," said he, "in order that while we are sparring each of you may join in with 'Go it, Socrates!' 'Well done, Xanthippe!' " He said that he lived with a shrew, but that just as horsemen like high-spirited horses, for "having mastered that kind, they can readily deal with the rest, so I in the company of Xanthippe will learn to adjust myself to the rest of the world."

These were his words and the deeds of his life, to which the Pythian priestess was referring when she gave her famous answer to Chaerephon: "Of all men living Socrates is the wisest." This was the cause of the envy in which he was held, above all because he would challenge those who thought highly of themselves, making them out to be fools, as he treated Anytus, according to Plato in the *Meno*. Anytus could not endure being ridiculed by Socrates, so he stirred Aristophanes and his friends against him. Later Anytus helped persuade Meletus to lodge a charge of impiety and of corrupting the youth against Socrates.

The charge was lodged by Meletus, and the speech was made by Polyeuctus, according to Favorinus in his *Miscellaneous History*. The speech was written by Polycrates the Sophist, according to Hermippus; others say that it was by Anytus. Lycon the demagogue had made all the necessary preparations.

Antisthenes, in his *Successions of the Philosophers* and Plato in his *Apology* say there were three accusers, Anytus, Lycon, and Meletus. Anytus was roused to anger on behalf of the craftsmen and politicians, Lycon on behalf of the rhetoricians, Meletus of the poets, for all three of these classes had felt Socrates's lash. Favorinus in the first book of his *Memorabilia* says that the speech of Polycrates against Socrates is not authentic, because he speaks of the rebuilding of the walls of Conon – which however, did not take place until Socrates had been dead six years. This certainly is the fact.

The indictment in the case, still preserved, says Favorinus in the *Metroön,* stated:

This indictment and affidavit is sworn out by Meletus: the son of Sophroniscus of Alopece, Socrates is guilty of refusing to acknowledge the gods recognized by the state and of introducing new and different gods. He is also guilty of corrupting the youth. The penalty demanded is death.

After Lysias had written a speech in his defense, the philosopher read it and said: "A fine speech, Lysias; however, it does not suit me": it was obviously more forensic than philosophical. Lysias said, "If it is a fine speech, how can it fail to suit you?" "Well," he replied, "Would not fine raiment and fine shoes suit me just as little?"

Justus of Tiberias in his book entitled *The Wreath* says that in the course of the trial Plato mounted the platform and began: "Though I am the youngest, men of Athens, of all who have risen to address you" – whereupon the judges shouted out, "Get down! Get down!" When he was condemned by 281 votes more than those given for acquittal, and when the judges were debating what should be his fine or penalty, Socrates suggested paying twenty-five drachmas. Eubulides, however, says he offered a hundred. When this caused an uproar among the judges, he said, "Considering my services, I think my penalty should be maintenance in the Prytaneum at the public expense."

Sentence of death was passed after eighty new votes against him had been cast. He was put in prison and a few days later drank the hemlock, after the noble discourses which Plato records in the *Phaedo*. According to some, he composed a paean which began:

> All hail, Apollo, Delos' lord!
> Hail, Artemis, ye noble pair!

Dionysodorus denies that he wrote the paean. He also composed a fable of Aesop, not very skillfully, beginning:

> "Judge not, ye men of Corinth," Aesop cried,
> "Of virtue as the jury-courts decide."

Thus did Socrates depart from among men. Not long afterward, the Athenians felt such remorse that they closed the training grounds and gymnasiums. They put Meletus to death and banished his other accusers. They erected a bronze statue of Socrates to honor him; it was the work of Lysippus and was placed in the hall of processions. When Anytus visited Heraclea, the people of that city immediately expelled him. The Athenians repented in this way not only in the case of Socrates but in very many others. They fined Homer, so says Heraclides, fifty drachmas as a madman and claimed Tyrtaeus was beside himself; they honored Astydamas and his brother poets with a bronze statue before they recognized Aeschylus. Euripides criticizes them in his *Palamedes* in this way: "Ye have slain, have slain, the all-wise, the innocent, the Muses' nightingale." This is one account; Philochorus, however, asserts that Euripides died before Socrates.

According to Apollodorus in his *Chronology*, Socrates was born during the archonship of Apsenphion, in the fourth year of the 77th Olympiad,[6] on the sixth day of the month of Thargelion, when the Athenians purify their city, which, according to the Delians, is the birthday of Artemis. He died in the first year of the 95th Olympiad,[7] at the age of seventy. Demetrius of Phalerum agrees with this, but others say he was only sixty at his death.

Both Socrates and Euripides were pupils of Anaxagoras; Euripides was born in the first year of the 75th Olympiad[8] in the archonship of Calliades.

I believe that Socrates discussed physics as well as ethics; for even Xenophon, who says that he discussed only ethics, admits that he held some conversations about providence. Plato, after mentioning Anaxagoras and certain other physicists in the *Apology*, elects to treat themes which Socrates disliked, although putting everything into the mouth of Socrates.

[6]*469-468* B.C.
[7]*400-399* B.C.
[8]*480-479* B.C.

Aristotle relates that a magician came from Syria to Athens and, among other evils with which he threatened him, predicted that Socrates would come to a violent end.

I have written verses about him, too, as follows:

Drink then, being in Zeus's palace, O Socrates; for truly did the God pronounce thee wise, being wisdom himself; for when thou didst frankly take the hemlock at the hands of the Athenians, they themselves drained it as it passed thy lips.

XI

DEMOCRITUS

DEMOCRITUS, the son of Hegesistratus (though some say of Athenocritus, and others of Damasippus), was a native of Abdera or, according to others, of Miletus. As Herodotus states, Democritus was a pupil of certain Magians and Chaldeans whom King Xerxes, when he was entertained by the father of Democritus, left behind. From these men, Democritus, while still a boy, learned theology and astronomy. Later he met Leucippus and, some say, Anaxagoras; Democritus was forty years younger than the latter. However, Favorinus in his *Miscellaneous History* says that Democritus, speaking of Anaxagoras, states that his views about the sun and the moon were not original but very old, and that he had simply purloined them. Out of spite, Democritus also shattered the opinions of Anaxagoras on the origin of the world and on mind, because Anaxagoras did not like him. In that case, how could he have been a pupil of Anaxagoras, as some allege?

According to Demetrius in his book on *Men of the Same Name* and to Antisthenes in his *Successions of Philosophers,* Democritus traveled to Egypt in order to learn geometry from the priests. Later, he also went to Persia to visit the Chaldeans as well as to the Red Sea. It is recorded that he associated with the Gymnosophists in India and went to Ethiopia. As the third son, Democritus is said to have divided the family property. Most writers say he chose the smaller portion, which was in money, because he had needed it to defray the cost of travels: his brothers were sly enough to foresee that this would be his choice. Demetrius estimates that his share amounted to more than one hundred talents, and he spent it all. His love of work, the same author says, was so great that he cut off a little section in the garden around the house and shut himself up there. His father brought an ox to sacrifice and tied it there; Democritus was not aware of it for some time, until his father called him to attend the sacrifice and told him of the ox. Demetrius goes on: "It would seem that he went to Athens where he was not eager to be recognized, for he despised fame. While he knew of Socrates, he was not known to Socrates; his words being, 'I came to Athens and no one knew me.'"

"If the *Rivals* be the work of Plato," says Thrasylus, "Democritus must be the unnamed character, neither Oenopides nor Anaxagoras, who makes his appearance when conversation is going on with Socrates about philosophy, and to whom Socrates says that the philosopher is like the all-competent athlete. As a matter of fact, Democritus was versed in every department of philosophy; he had trained himself both in physics and in ethics, even more, in mathematics and the routine subjects of education, and he was an acknowledged expert in the arts." From him comes the adage, "Speech is the shadow of action." Demetrius of Phalerum in his *Defense of Socrates* affirms that he had never visited Athens. This is to imply that he considered that great city beneath his notice, for he did not care to win fame from a place; rather, he preferred to make a place famous.

His character can also be seen from his writings. "He seemed," says Thrasylus, "to have admired the Pythagoreans. He mentions Pythagoras himself, praising him in a work of his own entitled *Pythagoras*. He seems to have taken all his ideas from him, and if chronology did not stand in the way, he might be thought to have been his pupil." Glaucus of Rhegium says that he was taught by one of the Pythagoreans, and that Glaucus was his contemporary. Apollodorus of Cyzicus asserts that he lived with Philolaus.

Antisthenes says that Democritus trained himself by a variety of means, testing his sense-impressions by retreating into solitude and frequenting tombs. The same authority states that when he returned from his travels, Democritus was reduced to a humble mode of life because he had exhausted his money. He goes on to say that because of his poverty Democritus was supported by his brother Damasus. His reputation increased when he foretold certain future events; after that, the public considered him deserving of the honor paid to a god. There was a law, says Antisthenes, that no one who had squandered his patrimony could be buried in his native city. Democritus, understanding this and fearing that he should be at the mercy of any envious or unscrupulous prosecutors, read aloud to the people his treatise, the *Great Diacosmos,* considered the best of all his works. As a result, he was rewarded with five hundred talents and with bronze statues as well. When he died, he received a public funeral, after a lifetime of more than a century. Demetrius, however, claims that it was not Democritus himself but certain of his relatives who read the *Great Diacosmos,* and that the sum awarded was only a hundred talents. Hippobotus agrees with this account.

Aristoxenus in his *Historical Notes* claims that Plato wished to burn all the writings of Democritus that he could collect, but that Amyclas and Clinias the Pythagoreans prevented him, pointing out that this would be profitless since the books were already widely circulated. Evidence of this is the fact that Plato, who mentions practically all the early philosophers, never once mentions Democritus, not even in those places where it might seem necessary to controvert him. The obvious reason was that he knew he would have to pit himself against the prince of philosophers, whom Timon praises in these words: "Such is the wise Democritus, the guardian of discourse, keen-witted disputant, among the best I ever read."

Democritus relates in the *Lesser Diacosmos* that he was a young man when Anaxagoras was old; he was, in fact, forty years the latter's junior. He says that the *Lesser Diacosmos* was compiled 730 years after the capture of Troy. According to Apollodorus in his *Chronology,* this would place him in the 80th Olympiad.[1] Thrasylus in his pamphlet entitled *Prolegomena to the Reading of*

[1]*460-457* B.C.

the Works of Democritus says that he was born in the third year of the 77th Olympiad,[2] which makes Democritus one year older than Socrates, . Democritus was, then, a contemporary of Archelaus, the pupil of Anaxagoras, and a follower of the school of Oenopides; as a matter of fact, Democritus mentions Oenopides. Democritus also alludes to the doctrine of the One held by Parmenides and Zeno; they obviously were the persons most discussed in his day. He also mentions Protagoras of Abdera, who, it is recognized, was a contemporary of Socrates.

Athenodorus in the eighth book of his *Walks* says that when Hippocrates came to visit Democritus, he ordered milk to be brought for his guest; after Democritus had examined the milk, he announced that it was the milk of a black she-goat that had given birth to her first kid. Hippocrates was amazed by the accuracy of his observation. Hippocrates, accompanied by a maidservant, encountered Democritus. The first day, Democritus greeted her, "Good morning, maiden." The next day, he said, "Good morning, woman." As a matter of fact, the girl had been seduced during the night.

Hermippus gives the following account of the death of Democritus. When he was very old and nearing his end, his sister was annoyed because it seemed likely that he would die during the festival of Thesmophoria, and she would thus be unable to pay fitting worship to the goddess. He told her not to worry and ordered that hot loaves should be brought to him every day. By applying these to his nostrils he contrived to outlive the festival. As soon as the three festival days were passed, he let his life leave him painlessly. He was according to Hipparchus, 109 years old.

In my *Pammetros* I have a piece on him which reads:

> Pray who was so wise, who wrought so vast a work as the omniscient Democritus? When death was near, for three days he remained in his house and maintained himself with the steam of hot loaves.

Such was the life of our philosopher.

[2]*470-469* B.C.

His opinions are the following. The first principles of the universe are atoms and empty space; everything else is merely thought. The worlds are unlimited in number; they come into being and perish. Nothing can come into being from that which is not, or pass away into what is not. Further, the atoms are without limit in size and number and are borne along in the whole universe in a vortex, by which they generate all composite things—fire, water, air, earth. These, too, are conglomerations of given atoms. Atoms are impassive and unalterable because of their solidity. The sun and the moon are composed of such smooth and spherical masses of this kind, that is, atoms, and so, too, is the soul, which is identical with reason. We see by means of the impact of images upon our eyes.

All things happen through necessity, for the vortex is the cause of the creation of all things, and Democritus calls the vortex necessity. The end of action is tranquillity, which is not the same as pleasure, as some have mistaken him to mean, but a state in which the soul continues calm and strong, undisturbed by fear, superstition, or any other emotion. He calls this state well-being and many other names. The qualities of things exist only by convention; in nature there are only atoms and void space.

Of his works Thrasylus has made an ordered catalogue, arranging them in fours, as he also arranged Plato's works.

The ethical works are the following:

I.   Pythagoras
      Of the Disposition of the Wise Man
      Of Those in Hades
      Tritogeneia (so called because three things, on which all mortal life depends, come from her)
II.   Of Manly Excellence, or of Virtue
      Amalthea's Horn (The Horn of Plenty)
      Of Tranquillity
      Ethical Commentaries (the Work on Well-being is not to be found)

So much for the ethical works.

The physical works are these:

III.   The Great Diacosmos (which the school of Theophrastus attribute to Leucippus)
        The Lesser Diacosmos
        Description of the World
        On the Planets
IV.   Of Nature, one book
        Of the Nature of Man, or Of Flesh, (a second book on Nature)
        Of Reason
        Of the Senses (some editors combine these two under the title Of the Soul)
V.   Of Flavors
        Of Colors
        Of the Different Shapes (of Atoms)
        Of Changes of Shape
VI.   Confirmations (summaries of the aforesaid works)
        On Images, or On Foreknowledge of the Future
        On Logic, or Criterion of Thought, three books
            Problems

So much for the physical works.
    The following fall under no head:

Causes of Celestial Phenomena
Causes of Phenomena in the Air
Causes on the Earth's Surface
Causes Concerned with Fire and Things in Fire
Causes Concerned with Sounds
Causes Concerned with Seeds, Plants, and Fruits
Causes Concerned with Animals, three books
Miscellaneous Causes
Concerning the Magnet

These works have not been arranged.
    The mathematical works are these:

VII.   On a Difference in an Angle, or On Contact with the Circle or the Sphere

On Geometry
Gemotrica
Numbers
VIII. On Irrational Lines and Solids, two books
Extensions (Projections)
The Great Year, or Astronomy, Calendar
Contention of the Water Clock (and the Heaven)
IX. Description of the Heaven
Geography
Description of the Pole
Description of Rays of Light

These are the mathematical works.
The literary and musical works are these:

X. On Rhythms and Harmony
On Poetry
On Beauty of Verses
On Euphonious and Cacophonous Letters
XI. Concerning Homer, or On Correct Epic Diction, and On
Glosses
Of Song
On Words
A Vocabulary

So much for the works on literature and music.
The works on the arts are these:

XII. Prognostication
Of Diet, or Dietetics
Medical Regimen
Causes Concerned with Things Seasonable and Unseasonable
XIII. Of Agriculture, or Concerning Land Measurements
Of Painting
Treatise on Tactics
On Fighting in Armor

So much for these works.
Some include as separate items in the list the following works
taken from his notes:

Of the Sacred Writings in Babylon
Of Those in Meroe
A Voyage Around the Ocean
Of (the Right Use of) History
A Chaldean Treatise
A Phrygian Treatise
Concerning Fever and Those Whose Malady Makes Them
  Cough
Legal Causes and Effects
Problems Wrought by Hand

Other works attributed to Democritus prove either to be compilations from his writings or not his. This is all about his books and their number.

Six persons have borne the name Democritus: (1) our philosopher, (2) a contemporary of his, a musician of Chios, (3) a sculptor, mentioned by Antigonus, (4) an author who wrote on the temple at Ephesus and the state of Samothrace, (5) an epigrammist whose style is clear and richly ornamented, (6) a native of Pergamum who became famous for his rhetorical speeches.

XII
LEUCIPPUS

Leucippus was born at Elea, though others say at Abdea and still others, Miletus. He was a pupil of Zeno, and the following were his opinions. Things are without number, and all change one into another. The All embraces the void as well as the full. The worlds take form when atoms fall into the void and become entangled with one another; the substance of the stars arises from their motion as they increase in size. The sun revolves around the moon in a larger circle. The earth is steady and is moved about its center; it has the shape of a drum. Leucippus was the first to identify atoms as first principles. This is a general review of his opinions; his views on particular points are as follows.

He believes the All to be unlimited, as already stated; the All is part full and part empty, and he calls elements the void and the full. The worlds, unlimited in number, emerge from them and are resolved into them again. The following is the manner in which the worlds are formed. In a given area many atoms of different shapes are born from the unlimited into the vast empty space. Together these form a single vortex, in which they hurtle against one another. Swirling about in every possible direction, they become separate entities, separate off, like atoms joining like. Since the atoms are so numerous that they can no longer circle in equilibrium, the light atoms flow into the empty space without, as by a sifting process. Those that remain cling together and, becoming entangled, circle together to form a basic spherical system. This basic sphere separates, like a shell, disclosing within it atoms of all varieties. As these are twirled about by centrifugal force, the enclosing shell becomes thinner, and the atoms that are contiguous combine as they touch the vortex. The earth is formed by parts that cohere to the center. The outer shell grows larger by the accretion of atoms from outside; as it is borne about in the vortex, it takes to itself any atoms it may touch. Some portions lock together to form a mass, which at first is damp and muddy; they dry, however, as they revolve with the universal vortex, taking fire to form the matter of the stars.

The orbit of the sun is farthest from the earth, that of the moon nearest. The orbits of the other celestial bodies fall between. The fire of all the stars is kindled by the speed of their motion; the fire of the sun is fed by the stars. The moon is only slightly inflamed. The sun and the moon are eclipsed when the circles of the stars are oblique as a result of the earth's inclination being toward the south. The regions to the north are always covered by mist and are extremely cold and frozen. Eclipses of the sun are rare; eclipses of the moon occur frequently, because their orbits are unequal. Just as the world is born, so, too, it grows, decays, and perishes by some necessity, the nature of which he does not indicate precisely.

XIII
PLATO

PLATO was the son of Ariston and a citizen of Athens. His mother Perictione (or Potone) was descended from Solon. Solon had a brother, Dropides; he was the father of Critias, the father of Callaeschrus, who was the father of another Critias, one of the Thirty, as well as of Glaucon, who was the father of Charmides and Perictione. Thus Plato, the son of this Perictione and Ariston, was of the sixth generation from Solon. Solon in turn traced his descent to Neleus and Poseidon. His father is said to be in direct line from Codrus, the son of Melanthus, and, according to Thrasylus, Codrus and Melanthus also trace their descent from Poseidon.

Speusippus in the work entitled *Plato's Funeral Feast*, Clearchus in his *Enomium of Plato*, and Anaxilaides in his second book *On Philosophers*, tell us that there was a story in Athens that Ariston violently wooed Perictione, then at the height of her youth, and failed to win her, and that, when he ceased his violence, Apollo appeared to him in a dream, whereupon he left her untouched until her child was born.

Plato was born, according to Apollodorus in his *Chronology*, in the 88th Olympiad[1] on the seventh day of the month Thargelion, the same day on which the Delians say that Apollo himself was born. Hermippus wrote that he died at a wedding feast in the first year of the 108th Olympiad,[2] in his eighty-first year.

[1] *427* B.C.
[2] *347* B.C.

Neanthes, however, says he died at the age of eighty-four. He was, therefore, six years the junior of Isocrates. Isocrates was born in the archonship of Lysimachus, Plato in that of Ameinias, the year of Pericles's death.[3] He belonged to the deme Collytus, as Antileon states in his second book, *On Dates*. He was born, according to some, in Aegina, in the house of Phidiades, the son of Thales, as Favorinus states in his *Miscellaneous History*. His father had been sent, along with other people, to Aegina to settle on the island but returned to Athens when the Athenians were expelled by the Lacedaemonians, who championed the Aeginetan cause. Athenodorus in the eighth book of a work entitled *Walks* states that Plato acted as *choregus* at Athens, the cost being borne by Dion. He had two brothers, Adeimantus and Glaucon, and a sister, Potone, the mother of Speusippus.

Plato learned his letters in the school of Dionysius, whom he mentions in the *Rivals*. He learned gymnastics under Ariston, the Argive wrestler, and received the name of Plato from him because of his robust physique. He was originally named Aristocles, after his grandfather, as Alexander records in his *Successions of the Philosophers*. By another account, he got the name Plato from the sweep of his style, or from the breadth of his forehead, as Neanthes suggests. It is said that he wrestled in the Isthmian Games — so Dicaearchus says, in the first book of his work, *On Lives* — and that he both painted and wrote poems, first dithyrambs, and later lyrics and tragedies. He is reported to have had a weak voice; this is confirmed by Timotheus the Athenian in his book *Biographies*. The story goes that Socrates saw, in a dream, a cygnet, on its knees, suddenly put forth plumage and, after uttering a loud sweet note, fly off. The next day Plato was introduced to Socrates as a prospective pupil, and Socrates recognized him as the swan he had seen in his dream.

Plato studied philosophy first in the Academy, and later in the garden at Colonus, as Alexander relates in his *Successions of the Philosophers*, as a follower of Heraclitus. He was about to compete for the prize with a tragedy when he heard Socrates in front of the theater of Dionysus. He consigned his poems to the flames, with the words: "Come hither, O fire god, Plato now has need of thee."

From that time onward — his twentieth year (so it is said) — he became the pupil of Socrates. When Socrates died, he attached himself to Cratylus the Heraclitean, and to Hermogenes who professed the philosophy of Parmenides. At the age of twenty-eight, accroding to Hermodorus, he withdrew with a number of Socrates's disciples to Megara to listen to Euclid. Thence he went on to Cyrene on a visit to Theodorus the mathematician, and to Italy to see the Pythagorean philosophers Philolaus and Eurytus, and finally to Egypt to see those who read the auspices. Euripides is said to have gone there with him. In Egypt, he fell sick and was cured by the priests, by a treatment with seawater, and for this he liked to quote the line: "The sea doth wash away all human ills."[4]

He also said, quoting Homer,[5] that the Egyptians were more skilled in healing than all other men. Plato also wanted to make the acquaintance of the Magians, but the wars in Asia prevented him. On his return to Athens, he lived in the Academy, which is a gymnasium outside the walls, in a grove named after a certain hero, Hecademus, as is stated by Eupolis in his play entitled *Shirkers*: "In the shady walks of the divine Hecademus."

Some verses of Timon also refer to Plato:

> Amongst all of them Plato was the leader, a big fish, but a sweet-voiced speaker, musical in prose as the cicada who, perched on the trees of Heccademus, pours forth a strain as delicate as a lily.[6]

Thus the original name of the place was Hecademy, spelled with an aspirated "e". Plato became a friend of Isocrates. Praxiphanes reports that they conversed about poets at a country seat where Plato was entertaining Isocrates. Aristoxenus asserts that he went on embassy three times, first to Tanagra, second

---

[4]*Euripides*, Iphegnia in Tauris, *1193.*
[5]*Odyssey IV, 231.*
[6]*Diels*, Frag. der Vorsok, *30.*

to Corinth, and third to Delium, where also he obtained a prize. He combined doctrines of Heraclitus, the Pythagoreans, and Socrates. His doctrine on sensible things derives from Heraclitus, his doctrine of the intelligible from Pythagoras, his political philosophy from Socrates.

Some authorities, amongst them Satyrus, say that he wrote to Dion in Sicily instructing him to purchase three Pythagorean books from Philolaus for one hundred minas. He was reputed to have been wealthy, having received over eighty talents from Dionysius. Onetor states this is an essay on the theme "Whether a wise man will make money." He further derived great assistance from Epicharmus the comic poet, for he transcribed a great deal from him, as Alcimus says in the four essays dedicated to Amyntas. In the first he writes thus:

It is evident that Plato often employs the words of Epicharmus. Consider the following: Plato asserts that the object of sense is that which never abides in quality or quantity, but is always in flux and changing. When number is taken away from things they are no longer equal or of a certain kind or of a certain quantity or quality. These are the things to which becoming always, but being never, belongs. The object of thought is something constant from which nothing is subtracted, to which nothing is added. This is the nature of the eternal things, the character of which is to be ever alike and the same. Epicharmus had expressed himself plainly about objects of sense and objects of thought.

A. But gods always were; never at any time were they absent while things in this world are always alike, and are brought about through the same agencies.

B. Nevertheless, the first born of the gods is said to be Chaos.

A. How is that possible? Since there was nothing out of which, or into which, it could come first.

B. Indeed! Then did nothing come first?

A. No, by Zeus, nor second either, at least of the things which we are talking about now; on the contrary, they existed from all eternity . . .

But suppose someone chooses to add a single pebble to a heap containing either an odd or an even number, whichever you please, or to take away one of those already there; do you think the number of pebbles would remain the same?

B. I do not.

A. Again, if one chooses to add another length, to a cu-
bit-measure, or cut off some of what was there already, would the
original measure still exist?

B. Of course not.

A. Think of mankind in this same way. One man grows, and
another shrinks; and they are all always undergoing change. Now
something which naturally changes and never remains in the
same state must ever be different from that which has thus
changed. And even so you and I were one pair of men yesterday,
are another today, and again will be another tomorrow, and will
never remain ourselves, by this same argument.

Again, Alcimus makes this further statement: "The wise men
say that there are some things which the soul perceives through
the body, by seeing and hearing; there are other things which it
perceives by itself without the aid of the body." Hence it follows
that some things are objects of sense and others objects of
thought. Plato therefore said that if we wish to take in at a
glance the principles underlying the universe, we must first
distinguish the ideas by themselves, for example, likeness, unity, and plurality, magnitude, rest, and motion; next, we must
assume the existence of beauty, goodness, justice, and the like,
each existing in and for itself; in the third place, we must see
how many of the ideas are relative to other ideas, as are knowledge, magnitude, ownership, remembering that the things
within our experience have the same names as those ideas
because they partake of them — namely, things which partake
of justice are just, things which partake of beauty are beautiful.
Each one of the ideas is eternal, a notion, incapable of changing. Plato therefore calls them archetypes in nature, and says
that all other things bear a resemblance to the ideas because
they are copies of these archetypes. Now here are the words of
Epicharmus about the good and about the ideas:

A. Is flute-playing a thing?

B. Most certainly.

A. Is man flute-playing?

B. By no means.

A. Come, let me see, what is a flute-player? How do you identify him? Isn't he a man?

B. Indeed, he is.

A. Well, don't you think the same would be the case with the good? Is not the good in itself a thing? And does not he who has learned that thing and knows it at once become good? For, just as he becomes a flute-player by learning flute-playing, or a dancer when he has learned dancing, or a plaiter when he has learned plaiting, in the same way, if he has learned anything of the sort, whatever you like, he would not be one with the craft but he would be the craftsman.

Plato in formulating his theory of ideas says that since there is such a thing as memory, there must be ideas present in things, because memory refers to something stable and permanent, and only the ideas are permanent. "For how," he says, "could animals have survived unless they had apprehended the idea and had been endowed by nature with intelligence for that purpose? They remember similarities and what their food is like, which shows that animals have the innate power of perceiving what is similar. And hence they perceive others of their own kind."

How then does Epicharmus put it?

Wisdom is not confined, Eumaeus, to one kind alone, but all living creatures likewise have understanding. For, if you will study intently the hen among poultry, she does not bring forth her chicks alive, but sits clucking on the eggs and wakens life in them. As for this wisdom of hers, the true state of the case is known to nature alone, for the hen has learned it from herself.

And in another place:

It is no wonder then that we talk thus and are pleased with ourselves and think we are fine folk. For a dog appears the fairest of things to a dog, an ox to an ox, an ass to an ass, and verily a pig to a pig.

Alcimus notes these and similar instances throughout four books, pointing out the assistance derived by Plato from Epicharmus. That Epicharmus himself was fully conscious of his wisdom can also be seen from the lines in which he foretells that he will have an imitator:

> And as I think—for when I think anything I know it full well—that my words will some day be remembered; someone will take them and free them from the meter in which they are now set, nay, will give them instead a purple robe, embroidering it with fine phrases, and, being invincible, he will make everyone else an easy prey.

Plato first brought the mimes of Sophron, which had been neglected, to Athens, to depict characters in Sophron's style; a copy of the mimes, they say, was actually found under his pillow. He made three voyages to Sicily, the first time to view the island and the craters of Etna. At that time Dionysius, the son of Hermocrates, was king and forced Plato to be intimate with him. When Plato discoursed on tyranny and argued that the interest of the ruler alone was not the highest good of the state unless the ruler were also a man of exceptional virtue, Dionysius exclaimed in a rage, "You talk like an old fool." "And you talk like a tyrant," Plato replied. The tyrant became so angry that he was at first intent on putting Plato to death. When Dionysius had been dissuaded from this by Dion and Aristomenes, he handed Plato over to Pollis the Lacedaemonian, who had just then arrived on an embassy, with orders to sell him into slavery. Pollis took him to Aegina and offered him for sale there. Then Charmandrus, the son of Charmandrides, indicted Plato on a capital charge according to the law in force among the Aeginetans, which ordered that the first Athenian to set foot upon the island should be executed without a trial. This law had been established by the prosecutor himself, as Favorinus says in his *Miscellaneous History*. When some one pointed out, jestingly, that the accused was a philosopher, the court acquitted him. Another version states that he was brought before the assembly and, being kept under close scrutiny, maintained an absolute silence and awaited the issue with confidence. The assembly decided not to execute him but to sell him as they would a prisoner of war.

Anniceris the Cyrenaic, who was present at the time, ransomed him for twenty minas (others say thirty minas) and sent him to his friends at Athens, who immediately repaid the money. Anniceris declined it, however, saying that the Athenians were not the only people worthy of the honor of providing for Plato. Others say that it was Dion who sent the money and that Anniceris would not take it, but instead bought the little garden, which is in the Academy, for Plato. Pollis, however, is said to have been defeated by Chabrias and later to have drowned at Helice, because his treatment of the philosopher provoked the wrath of heaven, as Favorinus says in the first book of his *Memorabilia*. Dionysius, could not restrain himself. On learning the facts, he wrote and begged Plato not to speak evil of him. Plato replied that he was too busy to think of Dionysius.

Plato visited the younger Dionysius a second time and asked him for lands and settlers to set up his republic. Dionysius promised them to him but did not keep his word. Plato was in great danger because he was suspected of abetting Dion and Theodotas in a plot to free the whole island. On this occasion Archytas the Pythagorean wrote to Dionysius, secured Plato's pardon, and had him borne safe to Athens. The letter runs as follows:

Archytas to Dionysius, wishing him health! We, being all of us friends of Plato, have sent Lamiscus and Photidas to you to take the philosopher away by the terms of our agreement with you. You will do well to recall the zeal with which you urged us all to bring Plato to Sicily, how determined you were to persuade him and to assume, amongst other things, responsibility for his safety as long as he stayed with you and on his return. Also remember that you expected much from his coming, and from that time you esteemed him more than any of those at your court. If he has not offended you, you ought to behave with humanity and restore him safely to us. By so doing you will satisfy justice and at the same time put us under an obligation.

The third time Plato went in order to reconcile Dion and Dionysius. When he failed in this effort, he returned to his own country. At home he declined to enter politics, though his writings show that he was a statesman. His reason was that the people had already become used to laws and institutions different from those he approved. Pamphila in the twenty-fifth book of her *Memorabilia* says that the Arcadians and Thebans, on the founding of Megalopolis, invited Plato to become their lawgiver. When, however, he discovered that they were opposed to equality of possessions, he refused.

There is a story that when the general, Chabrias, was on trial for his life, Plato pleaded for him although no one else at Athens would do so. On this occasion, as he was climbing the Acropolis with Chabrias, Crobylus the informer met him and said, "What, have you come to speak for the defense? Don't you know that the hemlock of Socrates awaits you?" Plato replied, "I faced dangers when serving in the cause of my country, and I will face them now in the cause of duty toward a friend."

Plato was the first to introduce argument by means of question and answer, says Favorinus in the eighth book of his *Miscellaneous History*. He also was the first to explain to Leodamas of Thasos the method of solving problems by analysis, and the first to employ in philosophical discussion, such terms as *antipodes, element, dialectic, quality, oblong number* and, among boundaries, the *plane superficies*. He also introduced divine providence.

Plato, also, was the first philosopher to challenge the speech of Lysias, the son of Cephalus, quoting it literally and extensively. He also was the first to study the significance of grammar. Because he was the first to attack the views of almost all his predecessors, the question arose as to why he does not mention Democritus. Neanthes of Cyzicus says that, on Plato's going to Olympia, the eyes of all the Greeks were turned toward him; it was there he met Dion, who was about to lead his expedition against Dionysius. In the first book of the *Memorabilia* of Favorinus, there is a statement that Mithradates the Persian set up a statue of Plato in the Academy and inscribed upon it these words: "Mithradates the Persian, the son of

Orontobates, dedicated to the Muses a likeness of Plato made by Silanion."

Heraclides declares that in his youth Plato was so modest and orderly that he was never seen to laugh aloud. Nevertheless, he, too, was ridiculed by the Comic poets. At any rate Theopompus in his *Hedychares* says: "There is nothing that is truly one, even the number two is not one, according to Plato." Moreover, Anaxandrides in his *Theseus* says: "He was eating olives exatly like Plato." Timon puns on his name thus: "As Plato placed strange platitudes." Alexis again, in the *Meropis:* "You have come just in time. I am at my wits' end and walking up and down, like Plato, and yet have discovered no wise plan but only wearied my legs." And in the *Ancylion:* "You don't know what you are talking about; run about with Plato, and you'll learn all about soap and onions." Amphis, too, in the *Amphicrates,* says:

> A. And as for the good, whatever that is, that you are likely to get on her account, I know no more about it,
> B. Just attend.

And in the *Dexidemides:* "O Plato, all you know is how to frown with eyebrows lifted high like a snail." Cratinus, too, in *The False Changeling:*

> A. Clearly you are a man and have a soul.
> B. In Plato's words, I am not sure but I suspect that I have.

And Alexis, in the *Olympiodorus:*

> A. My mortal body withered up, my immortal part sped into the air.
> B. Is not this a saying of Plato's?

And in the *Parasite:* "Or, to converse with Plato alone." Anaxilas, again, in the *Botrylion,* and in *Circe* and in *Rich Women,* has a joke at his expense: Aristippus in his fourth book *On the Luxury of the Ancients,* says that he loved a youth called Aster, who joined him in the study of astronomy; he was also attached to Dion, mentioned above, and, some say, to Phaedrus, as well. His passionate affection appears in the following epigrams which he is said to have written upon them:

> Star-gazing Aster, would I were the skies,
> To gaze upon thee with a thousand eyes.

And another:

> Among the living once the Morning Star,
> Thou shin'st, now dead, like Hesper from afar.

And he wrote thus upon Dion:

> Tears from their birth the lot had been
> Of Ilium's daughters and their queen.
> By thee, O Dion, great deeds done
> New hopes and larger promise won.
> Now here thou liest gloriously,
> How deeply loved, how mourned by me.

These lines were inscribed upon the tomb of Dion at Syracuse.

To Alexis and Phaedrus, of whom he was also enamored, as mentioned before, he composed the following lines:

Now, when Alexis is of no account, I have said no more than this. He is fair to see, and everywhere all eyes are turned upon him. Why, my heart, do you show the dogs a bone? And then will you smart for this hereafter? Was it not thus that we lost Phaedrus?

He is also said to have had a mistress, Archeanassa, about whom he wrote the following: "I have a mistress, fair Archeanassa of Colophon, on whose very wrinkles sits hot love. O hapless ye who met such beauty on its first voyage, what a flame must have been kindled in you!" There is another upon Agathon: "While kissing Agathon, my soul leaped to my lips, as if it would pass over to him." And another:

I throw an apple to you and, if indeed you are willing to love me, then receive it and let me taste your virgin charms. But if you are otherwise minded (heaven forbid), take this very apple and see how short-lived all beauty is.

And another: "An apple am I, thrown by one who loves you. Nay, Xanthippe, give consent, for you and I are both born to decay."

He also wrote the epigram on the Eretrians, who were driven out of the country: "We are Eretrians by race, from Euboea, and lie near Susa. How far, alas, from our native land!" And again:

> Thus Venus to the Muses spoke:
> Damsels, submit to Venus' yoke,
>   Or dread my Cupid's arms.
> Those threats, the virgins nine replied,
> May weigh with Mars, but we deride
>   Love's wrongs, or darts, or charms.

And again:

> A certain person found some gold,
> Carried it off and, in its stead,
> Left a strong halter, neatly rolled.
> The owner found his treasure fled,
> And, dismayed by his fortune's wreck,
> Fitted the halter to his neck.

Molon, his enemy, said, "It is no wonder that Dionysius should be in Corinth, but rather a wonder that Plato should be in Sicily." Plato does not seem to have been on good terms with Xenophon. They have written similar pieces, however, as though in competition with each other, namely, a *Symposium*, a *Defense of Socrates*, and their moral treaties or *Memorabilia*. Then one wrote the *Republic*, the other *Cyropaedia*. In the *Laws*, Plato calls the story of the education of Cyrus a fiction, because Cyrus was not at all as described there. Both wrote of Socrates, but neither mentions the other, except in one passage in book three of Xenophon's *Memorabilia*, in which he mentions Plato. Antisthenes, intending to read one of his compositions in public, asked Plato to attend. When Plato asked what was to be read, Antisthenes replied that it was a piece about the impossibility of contradiction. "How then," said Plato, "can you write on this subject?" pointing out that the argument contradicts itself. Antisthenes wrote a dialogue against Plato and entitled it *Sathon,* and from that time they were at odds. Hearing Plato read the *Lysis,* Socrates is said to have exclaimed, "By Heracles, what a number of lies this young man is telling about me!" because Plato included in the dialogue many things which Socrates did not say.

Plato was also on unfriendly terms with Aristippus. In the dialogue *Of the Soul,* he denigrates Aristippus by saying that he was not present at the death of Socrates, though sojourning as near as Aegina. He was jealous of Aeschines, because the latter enjoyed the favor of Dionysius. When Aeschines arrived at the court, Plato showed contempt for his poverty, while Aristippus assisted him. Idomeneus claims that the arguments used by Crito while in the prison, urging Socrates to escape, are really those of Aeschines, and he says that Plato put them in the mouth of Crito because of his jealousy of Aeschines.

Plato never mentions himself by name in his writings, except in the dialogue *On the Soul* and in the *Apology.* Aristotle says that the style of the dialogues falls halfway between poetry and prose. Favorinus says that when Plato read the dialogue *On the Soul,* only Aristotle stayed to hear the end; the others in the audience left. Philippus of Opus is said to have transcribed the *Laws,* which were left upon tablets of wax; he is also said to be the author of the *Epinomis.* Euphorion and Penaetius state that the opening portion of the *Republic* was found in several revised and rewritten forms, while Aristoxenux claims that practically all of the *Republic* is to be found in the *Controversies* of Protagoras. The *Phaedrus* is called Plato's first dialogue, because the subject has the freshness of youth. But Dicaearchus thought its style vulgar.

Plato once saw a man playing at dice and chided him. When the man replied that he was playing for a small sum, Plato answered, "But the habit is not a small thing." Asked whether any monuments of him would be erected as they had been of his predecessors, he replied, "If a man makes a name, he will never lack for monuments." One day Plato asked Xenocrates, who had just arrived, to chastize his slave; because Plato was angry, he did not want to do it himself. He once said to one of his slaves, "I would have whipped you, but I was angry." Once, while riding horseback, he dismounted quickly, saying he was afraid he would become guilty of horse-pride. He thought that people who got drunk should look in a mirror; they would surely stop a habit which made them so ugly. One might fittingly drink to excess, he used to say, only at the festivals of the god who was the giver of wine. He also disapproved of oversleeping. In the *Laws,* he states that "a man asleep is good for nothing." He also said that the most pleasant sound of all is the truth. Another version of this saying is that to speak the truth is the pleasantest of all things. He speaks of truth in the *Laws* in the following way: "Truth, O stranger, is a fair and lasting thing. It is, however, a thing of which it is hard to persuade men." His greatest wish was to leave a memorial of himself, either in the hearts of his friends or in his books. Some writers say that, personally, he liked solitude.

His death, the circumstanes of which have already been described, took place in the thirteenth year of the reign of King Philip, as Favorinus states in the third book of his *Memorabilia.* According to Theopompus, honors were paid him at his death by Philip. Byronianus in his *Parallels,* however, says that Philo mentions some sayings that went about concerning Plato's lice, implying his death was due to this cause. He was buried in the Academy, where he had passed the greatest part of his life in philosophical study. The school of which he was the founder was called the *Academic* school. All his students walked in the funeral procession. His will read as follows:

These things have been left and devised by Plato: the estate in Iphistiadae, bounded on the north by the road from the temple at Cephisia, on the south by the temple of Heracles in Iphistiadae, on the east by the property of Archestratus of Phrearrhi, on the west by that of Philippus of Chollidae: this no one may legally sell or alienate, but it shall be the property of the boy Adeimantus free of all conditions; the estate in Eiresidae which I bought from Calli-machus, bounded on the north by the property of Eurymedon of Myrrhinus, on the south by the property of Demostratus of Xypete, on the east by that of Eurymedon of Myrrhinus, and on the west by the Cephisus; three minas of silver; a silver vessel weighing 165 drachmas; a cup weighing 45 drachmas; a gold signet ring and earring together weighing four drachmas and three obols. Euclides the lapidary owes me three minas. I set Artemis free. I leave four household servants, Tychon, Dictas, Apollonides, and Dionysius. Household furniture, as set down in the inventory of which De-metrius possesses a copy. I owe no one anything. My executors are Leosthenes, Speusippus, Demetrius, Hegias, Eurymedon, Calli-machus, and Thrasippus.

Such were the items of his will. The following two epitaphs were inscribed upon his tomb:

Here lies the godlike man Aristocles, eminent among men for temperance and the justice of his character. He, if anyone, had the greatest praise for wisdom, and was too great for envy.

Earth in her bosom here hides Plato's body, but his soul has its immortal station with the blest, Ariston's son, whom every good man, even if he dwell afar off, honors because he discerned the divine life.

And a third of later date:

A. Eagle, why fly you o'er this tomb? Say, is your gaze fixed upon the starry house of one of the immortals?
B. I am the image of the soul of Plato, which has soared to Olympus, while his earth-born body rests in Attic soil.

I also wrote an epitaph, which is as follows:

If Phoebus did not cause Plato to be born in Greece, how happens it that he healed the minds of men by letters? As the god's son Asclepius is a healer of the body, so is Plato of the immortal soul.

And another on the manner of his death:

Phoebus gave to mortals Asclepius and Plato, the one to save their souls, the other to save their bodies. From a wedding banquet he has passed to that city which he had founded for himself and planted in the sky.

His disciples were Speusippus of Athens, Xenocrates of Chalcedon, Aristotle of Stagira, Philippus of Opus, Hestiaeus of Perinthus, Dion of Syracuse, Amyclus of Heraclea, Erastus and Coriscus of Scepsus, Timolaus of Cyzicus, Euaeon of Lampsacus, Python and Heraclides of Aenus, Hippothales and Callippus of Athens, Demetrius of Amphipolis, Heraclides of Pontus, and many others, among them two women, Lastheneia of Mantinea and Axiothea of Phlius, who is reported by Dicaearchus to have worn men's garments. Some say that Theophrastus, too, attended his lectures. Chamaeleon adds Hyperides the orator and Lycurgus, and Polemo agrees. Sabinus makes Demosthenes his pupil, quoting, in the fourth book of his *Materials For Criticism*, Mnesistratus of Thasos as his authority. This is plausible.

Since you are a lover of Plato with justification—since you inquire into that philosopher's doctrines more intently than into those of any other—I have thought it necessary to give an account of the true character of his discourses, of the arrangement of the dialogues, and of his inductive method of proceeding—as far as I can in a simple manner and in their chief traits—so that the facts I have collected concerning his life may not prove insufficient because his doctrines have been neglected. As the proverb says, it would be taking owls to Athens, to give you, especially, a full account.

Zeno the Eleatic was the first to write dialogues. According to Favorinus, however, in his *Memorabilia*, Aristotle, in the first book of his dialogue *On Poets* maintains that it was Alexamenus of Styra or Teos. In my opinion Plato, who perfected this form of writing, ought to be credited with its invention as well as with its adornment. A dialogue is a discourse, in the form of question and answer, on some philosophical or political subject, with due concern given to the characters of the persons taking part and the elegance of the diction. Dialectic is the art of discourse by which we either refute or establish some proposition by means of question and answer through the interlocutors.

There are two general types of Platonic dialogues, the one directed to instruction, and the other to inquiry. The former type is further divided into two parts, the theoretical and the practical. The theoretical is further divided into the physical and logical, while the practical is divided into the ethical and political. The dialogue directed to inquiry also has two main divisions, one of which aims at training the mind and the other at victory in controversy. Again, the part which aims at training the mind has two subdivisions, the one like the midwife's art, the other merely probing. That suited to controversy is also subdivided into one part which raises critical objections and another which attacks the main position directly.

I am aware that other writers classify the dialogues differently. Some dialogues are called dramatic, others narrative, and still others a mixture of these two. These terms seem better suited to the stage than to philosophy. Physics is represented by the *Timaeus,* logic by the *Statesman, Cratylus, Parmenides* and *Sophist,* ethics by the *Apology, Crito, Phaedo, Phaedrus,* and *Symposium,* as well as by the *Menexenus, Clitophon,* the *Epistles, Philebus, Hipparchus,* and the *Rivals,* and, lastly, politics by the *Republic,* the *Laws, Minos, Epinomis,* and the dialogue concerning Atlantis. To the category of mental obstetrics belong the two *Alcibiades, Theages, Lysis* and *Laches,* while the *Euthyphro, Meno, Io, Charmides,* and *Theaetetus* exemplify the probing method. The *Protagoras* illustrates the method of critical objections while the *Euthydemus, Gorgias,* and the two dialogues entitled *Hippias* illustrate that of subversive argument. These remarks define the dialogue and indicate its varieties.

Since there is great difference of opinion between those who affirm and those who deny that Plato was a dogmatist, I shall take up this question. A dogmatist in philosophy lays down positive dogmas, just as a legislator lays down laws. Under dogma, moreover, two things are included, the matter about which an opinion is formed and the opinion itself.

The former is a proposition, the latter a conception. When on firm ground, Plato expounds his own view and refutes the false one; if the subject is obscure, he suspends judgment. His own views are expounded by four persons, Socrates, Timaeus, the Athenian Stranger, and the Eleatic Stranger. These strangers are not, as some hold, Plato and Parmenides, but imaginary characters without names, for, even when Socrates and Timaeus are the speakers, it is Plato's doctrines that are stated. For the refutation of false opinions, he introduces Thrasymachus, Callicles, Polus, Gorgias, Protagoras, or again Hippias, Euthydemus, and others.

In formulating his proofs, Plato uses induction for the most part, not always in the same way, and chiefly under two forms. Induction is an argument from true premises properly inferring a truth resembling those premises. Induction is of two kinds, the first proceeds by way of contradiction, the second by agreement. In that which proceeds by means of contradiction, the answer given to every question will of necessity be the contrary of the respondent's position, for example, "My father is either other than or the same as your father. If your father is other than my father, by being other than my father he will not be my father. But if he is the same as my father, then by being the same as my father he will be my father." And again: "If man is not an animal, he will be either a stick or a stone. But he is not a stick or a stone; for he is animate and self-moved. Therefore he is an animal. But if he is an animal, and if a dog or an ox is also an animal, then man by being an animal will be a dog and an ox as well." This is the kind of induction that proceeds by contradiction and dispute. Plato used it, not for laying down positive doctrines, but to repute other positions. The other kind, induction by agreement, appears in two forms, the one proving the particular conclusion under discussion from a particular, the other proceeding by way of the universal (by means of many particular facts). The former is suited to rhetoric, the latter to dialectic. For instance, under the first form the question is raised, "Did so-and-so commit a murder?" The proof is that he was found at the time with stains of blood on him. This is the rhetorical form of induction, since rhetoric is concerned with particular facts and not with universals. It does not inquire about justice in the abstract, but about particular cases of justice. The other kind, where the general proposition is established from particular facts, is the induction of dialectic. To illustrate, the question put is whether the soul is immortal, and whether the living come back from the dead. This is proved in the dialogue *On the Soul* by means of a certain general proposition: that opposites proceed from opposites. The general proposition itself is established by means of propositions that are particular, such as that sleep comes from waking and vice versa, the greater from the less and vice versa. This is the form which he employed to establish his own views.

Long ago, the chorus was the sole actor in tragedy; later, in order to afford the chorus a respite, Thespis introduced one actor, Aeschylus a second, and Sophocles a third, bringing tragedy to completion. Something similar happened in philosophy. At first it discussed only one topic, physics; Socrates added a second subject, ethics, and Plato a third, dialectics; and in this way philosophy, too, reached completion. Thrasylus says that Plato grouped his dialogues in tetralogies, on the model of the tragic poets. At the Dionysia, the Lenaea, the Panathenaea and the festival of Chytri, the contest involved four plays, of which the last was a satiric drama. The four together were called a tetralogy.

Thrasylus also holds that the genuine dialogues are fifty-six in number, if the *Republic* be counted as ten and the *Laws* as twelve. Favorinus, however, in the second book of his *Miscellaneous History* claims the *Republic* is to be found almost entire in a work of Protagoras entitled *Controversies*. This makes nine tetralogies, if the *Republic* counts as one single work and the *Laws* as another. Plato's first tetralogy has a common plan underlying it, for he wishes to depict the life of the philosopher. To each of the works Thrasylus affixes a double title, the one taken from the name of the interlocutor, the other from the subject. This first tetralogy begins with the *Euthyphro* or *On Piety* and is a tentative dialogue; the *Apology of Socrates*, an ethical dialogue, is second; the third, *Crito* or *On What is to be Done*, is ethical; the fourth, Phaedo or *On the Soul*, also ethical.

The second tetralogy begins with *Cratylus* or *On Correctness of Names*, a logical dialogue, followed by *Theaetetus or* or *On Knowledge*, tentative, the *Sophist* or *On Being*, logical, the *Statesman* or *On Monarchy*, also logical. The third tetralogy includes, first, *Parmenides* or *On Ideas*, which is logical, next are *Philebus* or *On Pleasure*, an ethical dialogue, the *Banquet* or *On the Good*, ethical, and *Phaedrus* or *On Love*, also ethical.

The fourth tetralogy starts with *Alcibiades* or *On the Nature of Man*, an obstetric dialogue; this is followed by the second *Alcibiades* or *On Prayer*, also obstetric; then comes *Hipparchus* or *The Lover of Gain*, which is ethical, and *The Rivals* or *On Philosophy*, also ethical. The fifth tetralogy includes, first, *Theages* or *On Philosophy*, an obstetric dialogue, then *Charmides* or *On Temperance*, which is tentative, *Laches* or *On Courage*, obstetric, and *Lysis* or *On Friendship*, also obstetric. The sixth tetralogy starts with *Euthydemus* or *The Eristic*, a refutative dialogue, which is followed by *Protagoras* or *Sophists*, critical, *Gorgias* or *On Rhetoric*, refutative, and *Meno* or *On Virtue*, which also is tentative. The seventh tetralogy contains, first, two dialogues entitled *Hippias*, the former *On Beauty*, the latter *On Falsehood*, both refutative; next are *Ion* or *On the Iliad*, which is tentative, and *Menexenus* or *The Funeral Oration*, which is ethical. The eighth tetralogy starts with *Clitophon* or *Introduction*, which is ethical, and is followed by the *Republic* or *On Justice*, political, *Timaeus* or *On Nature*, a physical treatise, and *Critias* or *Story of Atlantis*, which is ethical. The ninth tetralogy starts with *Minos* or *On Law*, a political dialogue, followed by the *Laws* or *On Legislation*, also political, *Epinomis* or *Nocturnal Council* or *Philosopher*, political, and lastly the *Epistles*, thirteen in number, which are ethical. In these epistles his heading was "Welfare," as that of Epicurus was "A Good Life," and that of Cleon "All Joy." Included are: one to Aristodemus, two to Archytas, four to Dionysius, one to Hermias, Erastus and Coriscus, one each to Leodamas, Dion and Perdiccas, and two to Dion's friends. This is the division adopted by Thrasylus and other editors.

Aristophanes the grammarian as well as some other editors arrange the dialogues aribtrarily in trilogies. In the first trilogy they place the *Republic*, *Timaeus*, and *Critias;* in the second the

Sophist, the *Statesman,* and *Cratylus;* in the third the *Laws, Minos,* and *Epinomis;* in the fourth *Theaetetus, Euthyphro,* and the *Apology;* in the fifth *Crito, Phaedo,* and the *Epistles.* The rest follow as separate compositions in no rigid order. Still other critics put the *Republic* first, while others start with the greater *Alcibiades,* and others again with the *Theages;* some begin with the *Euthyphro,* others with the *Clitphon;* some with the *Timaeus,* others with the *Phaedrus;* others again with the *Theatetus,* while many begin with the *Apology.* The following dialogues are recognized as spurious: the *Midon* or *Horsebreeder,* the *Eryxias* or *Erasistratus,* the *Alcyon,* the *Acephali* or *Sisyphus,* the *Axiochus,* the *Phaeagians,* the *Demodocus,* the *Chelidon,* the *Seventh Day,* the *Epimenides.* Of these the *Alcyon* is thought to be the work of a certain Leon, according to Favorinus in the fifth book of his *Memorabilia.*

Plato has employed many different terms so that his ideas might be less intelligible to the uninformed. Specifically, he thinks of wisdom as the science of those things which are at once objects of thought and really exist, the science which, he says, considers God and the soul as separate from the body. By wisdom he means especially philosophy, which is a hunger for divine wisdom. In a wide sense he calls all experience wisdom, for example, as when he calls a craftsman wise. He also applies the same terms with very different meanings. For instance, the word for slight or plain is employed by him in the sense of "simple" or "honest," just as it is applied to Heracles in the Licymnius of Euripides in the following passage: "Plain, unaccomplished, staunch to do great deeds, unversed in talk, with all his store of wisdom curtailed to action."

But sometimes Plato uses this same word to mean what is bad, and at other times what is small or petty. Conversely, he often uses different terms to express the same thing. For instance, he calls the idea form, genus, archetype, principle, and cause. Sometimes he uses opposite expressions for the same thing. Thus he calls the sensible thing both existent and nonexistent, existent inasmuch as it comes into being, nonexistent because it is continually changing. He also says the idea is neither in motion nor at rest, that it is the same and yet both one and many. He does this habitually in many other cases.

To interpret his dialogues three things must be considered: first, the meaning of every statement must be explained; next, its purpose, that is it must be discovered whether it is made for a basic reason or is illustrative, to establish his own doctrines or to refute those of his opponent; in the third place, its truth must be examined.

Plato held the following doctrines. The soul is immortal; by transmigration it passes through many bodies. Its first principle is numerical, while that of the body is geometrical. Soul is the idea of vital breath blown in all directions. It is self-moved and tripartite: the rational part has its seat in the head, the passionate part about the heart, the appetitive part its locus in the region of the navel and the liver.

From the center outward the soul encloses the body on all sides in a circle; it is made up of elements and, being divided at harmonic intervals, forms two circles which touch one another at two points. The interior circle is cut six times, making seven circles in all. This interior circle moves across to the left, the other circle to the right. Hence the one is supreme, because it is a single circle, for the other, the interior circle, is divided. The former is the circle of the Same, the latter that of the Other, by which he means to say that the motion of the soul is the motion of the universe together with the revolutions of the planets.

When the division from the center to the circumference, which thus is in harmony with the soul, is determined in this way, the soul knows what is and adjusts proportionately because it has the elements proportionately disposed in itself. When the circle of the Other revolves correctly, the result is opinion. From the harmonic motion of the circle of the Same comes knowledge. There are two universal principles: God and matter. He calls God mind and cause. Matter is without form and limit, and composite things arise out of it. Matter was once in unordered motion, but because God preferred order to disorder, he brought matter together in one place. Thus substance, Plato says, is converted into the four elements—fire, water, air, and earth—of which the world itself and all that is in it are formed. Of these elements only earth is not subject to change, by reason of the special character of its constituent triangles. In all the other elements the figure employed is the same, the scalene triangle, whereas a triangle of special shape is employed for earth. The element of fire is a pyramid, of air an octahedron, of water an icosahedron, of earth a cube. This is the reason that earth is not transmuted into the other three elements, and these are not transmuted into earth.

Each element does not occupy its own region of the universe because revolving motion brings together their minute particles, forcing and compressing them toward the center, at the same time as it separates the larger masses. Therefore, they alter the regions they occupy as they change their shapes.

There is only one created universe—that perceptible to sense—and it has been made by God. This universe is alive because the soul is superior to the inanimate. This universe is the work of a supremely good cause. It is one and finite because the form on which it was patterned was one. It is spherical because its maker is spherical. The maker embraces the other living things, and this universe embraces the shapes of them all. It is smooth and has no organ surrounding because it has no need of organs. The universe is imperishable because it does not dissolve into the Deity. The whole created universe is caused by God, because the good is beneficient, and the created universe has the highest good for its cause. The most beautiful of created things is due to the best of intelligible causes; because God is the best, the universe is like the best in its perfect beauty. It will not be like any created thing, but like God alone.

The universe is composed of fire, water, air, and earth; fire renders it visible; earth solid; water and air, proportional. The powers represented by solids are connected by two mean proportions in such a way as to secure the complete unity of the whole. The universe was made of all the elements so as to be complete and indestructible.

Time was created as an image of eternity. Eternity is forever at rest, while time is the motion of the universe. Night and day and month and the like are all parts of time; hence, time has no reality apart from the nature of the universe. Time comes to be with the coming to be of the universe.

The sun, moon, and planets were created to make possible

the creation of time. God kindled the light of the sun so that seasons might be definite in number and the animals might be numbered. The moon is in the circle immediately above the earth, and the sun in the next beyond, and the planets are in the other circles. The universe is a living being, and it is held fast in animate movement. All other animals were created so that the universe which had been created in the likeness of the intelligible living creature might be complete. Since the model of the universe must have them, it contains many gods whose nature is fire; the others are of three kinds, winged, aquatic, and terrestrial. The earth is the oldest of all the gods in heaven. It was fashioned to make night and day, and since it is at the center it moves around its center. Since there are two causes, Plato says, some things are due to reason, while others have a necessary cause, either air, fire, earth, or water; these are not elements but rather receptacles of form. They are composed of triangles and are resolved into triangles. Their constituent elements are the scalene triangle and the isosceles triangle.

The principles and the causes are the two mentioned earlier; of these, God and matter are the exemplars. Matter of necessity is without form, as are the other receptacles of form. All have a necessary cause. Matter in some way or another receives the ideas, thus generating substances. It moves because its power is not uniform. Since it is in motion, it sets in motion those things which are generated from it. These were at first in irrational and irregular motion, but after they began to frame the universe, God made them, as far as possible, symmetrical and regular. The two causes existed even before the world was made, as did becoming; they were not distinct, for only traces of them were found and those were in disorder. When the world was made, they too acquired order. The universe was fashioned out of all the bodies there are. Plato holds that God, like the soul, is incorporeal and thus exempt from change and decay. The ideas are causes and principles whereby the world of natural objects is such as it is.

His discussion of good and evil took the following line. The end is assimilation to God; virtue itself is sufficient for happiness, but it also needs as instruments for use, first, bodily advantages such as health and strength, sound senses, and the like, and, second, external aids such as wealth, good birth, and reputation. The wise man, however, will be happy even though he is without these things. The wise person will engage in public affairs, marry, and refrain from breaking the established laws. He will legislate for his own country unless by reason of the extreme corruption of the people the state of affairs justifies his complete abstention. He believes that the gods concern themselves with human life and that superhuman beings exist. Plato was the first to define the good as that which is bound up with whatever is praiseworthy, rational, useful, proper, and becoming. These are all related to what is consistent and in accord with nature.

Plato discusses the suitability of names. He was the first to frame the science of rightly putting and answering questions, and he himself employed it, perhaps to excess. In the dialogues he identified righteousness as the law of God because it is more powerful in inclining men to do righteous acts, so that malefactors may not be punished even after death. To some, consequently, he appeared too fond of myths. He introduces these narratives into his works in order to deter men from wickedness, by calling to mind how little they know of what awaits them after death. These, then, are the doctrines he advocated.

According to Aristotle, Plato used to divide things in the following manner. Goods are of the mind or of the body, or external. Justice, prudence, courage, temperance, and other qualities of this kind are in the mind; beauty, a good constitution, health, and strength are in the body; friends, the welfare of one's country, and riches are among external things.

Three kinds of goods emerge: goods of the mind, goods of the body, and external goods. There are three kinds of friendship: one is natural, another social, the third hospitable. Natural friendship is the affection which parents have for their children and relatives for each other. Other animals besides man exhibit this form. Social friendship arises from intimacy and has nothing to do with kinship; an example is offered by the friendship of Pylades and Orestes. The friendship of hospitality is that extended to strangers on presentation of an introduction or recommendation. Friendship is, therefore, natural or social or hispitable. A fourth kind, love, may be added.

There are five forms of civil government: democratic, aristocratic, oligarchic, monarchical, and tyrannical. In the democratic form the people are in control and choose magistrates and laws alike. In the aristocratic form the state is guided neither by the rich, nor by the poor, nor by the nobles, but by the best. Oligarchy is the form in which a property qualification limits access to office, for the rich are fewer than the poor. Monarchy is either regulated by law or is hereditary. In Carthage the kingship is regulated by law and offered for sale. In Lacedaemon and Macedonia the monarchy is hereditary; the king is selected from a given family. A tyranny is that form in which an individual rules the citizens either by fraud or by force. Civil government is, therefore, democratic, aristocratic, oligarchic, monarchical, or tyrannical.

Justice is of three kinds. One relates to gods, another to men, and the third to the dead. Those who offer sacrifice, as the laws enjoin, and care for the temples are pious toward the gods. Those who repay loans and restore what they have received in trust act justly toward men. Finally, those who honor tombs are obviously just toward the dead. For this reason, justice relates to the gods, to men, and to the dead.

There are three kinds of knowledge or science: one practical, one productive, and one theoretical. Architecture and shipbuilding are productive arts, because they have visible products. Politics, flute-playing, harp-playing, and other such arts are practical; although they produce nothing visible, they *do* or *perform* something—in the latter case the artist plays the flute or the harp, in the former the politician engages in political activity. Geometry, harmonics, and astronomy are theoretical sciences; they neither perform nor produce. The geometer considers the relation of lines to each other; the student of harmony investigates sounds; and the astronomer observes the stars and the universe. Hence some sciences are theoretical, others are practical, and others are productive.

There are five varieties of medicine: the first is pharmacy, the second, surgery, the third deals with diet and regimen, the fourth with diagnosis, and fifth with remedies. Pharmacy cures sickness by drugs; surgery, by the knife and cautery. The species concerned with diet prescribes a regimen for the cure of disease. That concerned with diagnosis determines the nature of the ailment, and that concerned with remedies prescribes for the relief of pain. The kinds of medicine, then, are pharmacy, surgery, diet and regimen, diagnosis, and prescription of remedies.

There are two divisions of law: the written and the unwritten. Written law is that under which we live in different cities, but the law which emerges out of custom is called unwritten law; for example, not to appear in the marketplace undressed or in women's attire. No statute forbids such conduct; nevertheless we refrain from it, because it is prohibited by an unwritten law. Law, then, is either written or unwritten.

There are five kinds of speech. One is the speech politicians employ in the assemblies and is called political speech. A second is that which the rhetors employ in written compositions, whether composed for display, praise, blame, or indictment; this is termed rhetorical. A third division is that of private persons' conversing with one another; this is called the mode of speech of ordinary life. Another species is the language of those who converse by means of short questions and answers; this kind is called dialectical. The fifth species is the speech of craftsmen when talking about their own crafts; this is technical language. Thus speech is either political, rhetorical, ordinary conversation, dialectical, or technical.

Music has three divisions. One employs the mouth alone, such as singing. The second employs both the mouth and the hands, as in the case of the harpist who sings to his own accompaniment. The third employs the hands alone; for instance, playing the harp. Thus music employs either the mouth alone, or the mouth and the hands, or the hands alone.

Nobility has four divisions. First, when the ancestors are wellbred, handsome, and just, their descendants are said to be noble. Second, the descendants of ancestors who have been princes or magistrates are called noble. The third kind of nobility is derived from ancestors who have been illustrious, for the exercise of military command or the attainment of success in the national games, for example. The last division includes the man who is personally generous and high-minded; he too, is said to be noble, and his is the highest form of nobility. Therefore, one kind of nobility depends on excellent ancestors, another on princely ancestors, a third on illustrious ancestors, while the fourth is due to the individual's own beauty and worth.

Beauty has three divisions. The first is the object of praise, as a form fair to look upon. Another is serviceable; thus an instrument, a house, and other similar things, are beautiful because they are useful. Other things relating to customs and pursuits and the like are beautiful because beneficial. Beauty, then, is a matter for praise, another is for use, and another for the benefit it brings.

The soul has three divisions. One part of it is rational, another appetitive, and a third irascible. The rational part is the agent of purpose, reflection, understanding, and the like. The appetitive part is the cause of desire for eating, sexual activity, and the like, while the irascible part is the cause of courage, pleasure, pain, and anger. Thus one part of the soul is rational, another appetitive, and a third irascible.

There are four species of perfect virtue: prudence, justice, courage, and temperance. Prudence is the cause of right conduct, justice of just dealing in partnerships and commercial transactions. Courage causes a man not to give way but to stand his ground in alarms and dangers. Temperance enables one to control desires, so that one is not the slave of pleasure, but leads instead an ordered life. Thus virtue includes prudence, justice, courage, and temperance.

Rule has five divisions. The first is rule of law, the second, according to nature, another, according to custom, a fourth, by birth, a fifth, by force. Magistrates of cities, if chosen by their fellow citizens, rule according to law. Males are natural rulers, not only among men, but among the other animals as well; males everywhere exert extensive rule over the females. Rule according to custom is illustrated by the authority which servants exercise over children and teachers over their pupils.

Hereditary rule is exemplified by the Lacedaemonian kings, for the office of king is limited to a certain family. The same system obtains in the kingdom of Macedonia; there, too, the office of king is inherited. Power is sometimes acquired by force or fraud, and citizens are governed against their will; this kind of rule is called coercive. Thus rule is either by law, or by nature, or by birth, or by force.

There are six kinds of rhetoric. When speakers urge war or alliance with a neighboring state, the rhetoric they exercise is called persuasion. When they speak against war or alliances, exhorting their hearers to remain at peace, their rhetoric is called dissuasion. When a speaker protests that he is wronged by someone who, he says, has caused him a great deal of injury, this is called accusation. The fourth kind of rhetoric is called defense. The speaker demonstrates that he has done no wrong and that his conduct is in no respect abnormal; defense is the term applied in such a case. A fifth kind of rhetoric is employed when a speaker speaks well of someone and proves him to be worthy and honorable; encomium is the name given to this kind. A sixth kind is employed when the speaker shows that someone is unworthy, and it is called invective. Under rhetoric, then, are included encomium, invective, persuasion, dissuasion, accusation, and defense.

Successful speaking has four divisions. The first consists in speaking to the purpose, the next in due length, the third before a suitable audience, and the fourth at the proper moment. Things are said to be to the purpose when they are likely to be useful or expedient for speaker and hearer. Due length means neither too much nor too little. If speaking to the proper audience means addressing persons older than yourself, the discourse must be made suitable to the condition of the audience as elderly men; if addressing juniors the discourse must be suitable to young men. The proper time of speaking is neither too soon nor too late; otherwise, one will miss the mark and not speak with success.

There are four divisions of conferring benefits. One confers benefits either by giving pecuniary aid or by rendering personal service, by means of knowledge or of speech. Pecuniary aid is given when one assists a man in need, so that he is relieved from concern on the score of money. Personal service is given when men come to the aid of those who are being beaten and rescue them. Those who train, heal, or teach something valuable confer benefit by means of knowledge. When, in a law court, one man appears as advocate for another and delivers an effective speech on his behalf, he benefits him by speech. Thus benefits are conferred by means either of money, of personal service, of knowledge, or of speech.

There are four ways in which things are completed and brought to an end. The first is by legal enactment, such as when a decree is passed and this decree is confirmed by law. The second is in the course of nature, as the day, the year, and the seasons are completed. The third is by the rules of art, as with the builder's art, by which a house is completed, or with shipbuilding, by which vessels are completed. Fourthly, matters are brought to an end by chance or accident, when they turn out otherwise than is expected. Thus the completion of things is due either to law, or to nature, or to art, or to chance.

There are four divisions of power or ability. First, whatever we can do with the mind, namely, calculate or anticipate; next, whatever we can effect with the body, for instance, marching, giving, taking, and the like. Thirdly, whatever we can do by a multitude of soldiers or a plentiful supply of money; hence a king is said to have great power. The fourth division of power or influence is doing or suffering, well or ill; thus we can become ill or be educated, be restored to health, and the like. Power, then, is either in the mind, in the body, in armies and resources, or in acting and being acted upon.

Philanthropy is of three kinds. One is by way of salutations, as when certain people address everyone they meet and, stretching out their hand, give him a hearty greeting. Another mode is seen when one assists everyone in distress; another type of philanthropy makes some people fond of giving dinners. Thus philanthropy is shown either by a courteous address, or by conferring benefits, or by hospitality and the promotion of social intercourse.

Welfare or happiness includes five parts. One part of it is good counsel; a second, soundness of the senses and bodily health; a third, success in one's undertakings; a fourth, good repute among one's fellow men; a fifth, ample resources in money and in whatever else ministers to the end of life. Deliberating well is a result of education and of having experience in many things. Soundness of the senses depends upon the bodily organs. I mean, if one sees with his eyes, hears with his ears, and perceives with his nostrils and his mouth the appropriate objects, then such a condition is soundness of the senses. Success is attained when a man does what he aims at in the right way, as becomes a good man. A man has a good reputation when he is well spoken of. A man has ample resources when he is so supplied for the demands of life that he can afford to benefit his friends and fulfill his public duties with lavish display. If a man has all these things, he is completely happy. Thus of welfare or happiness one part is good counsel, another soundness of senses and bodily health, a third success, a fourth a good reputation, a fifth plentiful resources.

There are three divisions of the arts and crafts. The first division consists of mining and forestry, which are productive arts. The second includes the smith's and carpenter's arts which transform material; for the smith makes weapons out of iron and the carpenter transforms timber into flutes and lyres. The third division is that which uses what is thus made, as horsemanship uses bridles, the art of war uses weapons, and music uses flutes and the lyre. Thus there are three different species of art, as listed above.

Good falls into four kinds. One is the possessor of virtue, whom we say is individually good. Another is virtue itself and justice; these we affirm to be good. A third includes such things as food, suitable exercises, and drugs. The fourth kind of thing we call good includes the arts of flute-playing, acting, and the like. Thus there are four kinds of good: the possession of virtue, virtue itself, food and beneficial exercises, flute-playing, acting, and the poetic art. Anything that is in any sense is either good, bad, or indifferent. We call evil what is capable of invariably doing harm; for instance, bad judgment, folly, injustice, and the like. The contraries of these things are good. The things which can sometimes benefit and sometimes injure—walking, sitting, eating—or which can do neither any benefit nor harm at all are indifferent: neither good nor evil. Thus all things whatever are either good or evil, or neither good nor evil.

Good order in the state is categorized under three headings. First, if the laws are good, we say that there is good government. Second, if the citizens obey the established laws, this, too, we call good government. Third, if, without the aid of laws, the people manage their affairs well under the guidance of customs and institutions, again we call this good government. Thus three forms of good government may exist: when the laws are good, when the existing laws are obeyed, when the people live under salutary customs and institutions.

Disorder in a state has three forms. The first arises when both the laws affecting citizens and strangers are bad, the second when the existing laws are not obeyed, and the third when there is no law at all. Thus the state is badly governed when the laws are bad, or where they are not obeyed, or when there is no law.

Contraries are divided into three species. For instance, we say that good is contrary to evil, as justice to injustice, wisdom to folly, and so forth. Again, evils are contrary to evils: prodigality is contrary to miserliness, to be unjustly tortured is the contrary of being justly tortured, and so with similar evils. Again, heavy is the contrary of light, quick of slow, black of white; these pairs are contraries, while they are neither good nor evil. Thus, of contraries, some are opposed as good to evil, others as evils to evils, and others as things which are neither good nor evil.

There are three kinds of good, that which can be exclusively possessed, that which can be shared with others, and that which simply exists. To the first, namely, that which can be exclusively possessed, belong such things as justice and health. To the next belong all the good which, though it cannot be exclusively possessed, can be shared with others. Thus we cannot possess

the absolute good, but we can participate in it. The mere
existence of worth and justice is good; these things cannot be
shared or had in exclusive possession but must simply exist. Of
good, then, some is possessed exclusively, some shared, and
others merely are.

Counsel is divided into three kinds. One is taken from past
time, one from the future, and the third from the present.
That from past time consists of examples; for instance, what
the Lacedaemonians suffered because they trusted others.
Counsel drawn from the present is to show, for instance, that
the walls are weak, men cowards, and supplies running out.
Counsel from the future is, for example, to urge that we
should not wrong embassies by being suspicious, in order not
to blemish the bright fame of Hellas. Thus counsel is derived
from the past, the present, and the future.

Vocal sound falls into two divisions, animate or inanimate.
The voice of living things is animate sound; notes of instruments and noises are inanimate. Of the animate, part is
articulate, part inarticulate — that of men being articulate
speech, that of the animals inarticulate. Thus vocal sound is
either animate or inanimate.

Everything that exists is either divisible or indivisible. Some
divisible things are divisible into similar parts and others into
dissimilar parts. Those things are indivisible which cannot be
divided and are not compounded of elements — for example,
the unit, the point, and the musical note — whereas those which
have constituent parts, such as syllables, concords in music,
animals, water, and gold are divisible. If they are composed of
similar parts, so that the whole does not differ from the part
except in quantity, as water, gold, and all that is malleable, and
the like, they are called homogeneous. Whatever is composed
of dissimilar parts, such as a house, is termed heterogeneous.
Thus all things whatever are either divisible or indivisible, and
of the divisible some are homogeneous, others heterogeneous.

Some existing things are absolute, and some are said to be
relative. Things said to exist absolutely are those which need
nothing else to explain them, as man, horse, and all other
animals; none of these profits by explanation. All which stand

in need of some explanation are called relative, as what is greater than something or quicker than something, or more beautiful, and so forth. The greater implies a less, and the quicker is quicker than something. Existing things are therefore absolute or relative. According to Aristotle, Plato used to divide the primary conceptions in this way also.

There was also another man named Plato, a philosopher of Rhodes, a pupil of Panaetius, as is stated by Seleucus the grammarian in his first book *On Philosophy;* another a Peripatetic and pupil of Aristotle; another who was a pupil of Praxiphanes; and lastly, there was Plato the poet of the Old Comedy.

XIV
XENOPHON

Xenophon, son of Gryllus, was an Athenian citizen and belonged to the deme Erchia. He was an extremely handsome man, yet possessed an unusual modesty. There is a story that once Socrates on meeting him in a narrow passage stretched out his stick, barring his way, and asked him where different kinds of food might be bought. When Xenophon answered, Socrates asked another question, "And where do men become good and honorable?" Xenophon was too puzzled to reply. "Then follow me," said Socrates, "and learn." Thence forward Xenophon was a pupil of Socrates. He was the first to take notes of the conversation of Socrates and report it to the world, under the title of *Memorabilia*. He also wrote the first history of the philosophers.

Aristippus in the fourth book of his work *On the Luxury of the Ancients* declares that Xenophon was enamored of Clinias, and said of him,

> I prefer to gaze on Clinias than on all the fair sights in the world. I would be satisfied to be blind to all else if I could gaze only on him. I am annoyed by the night and by sleep because I cannot see Clinias, and I am most grateful to the day and to the sun because they show him to me.

He gained the friendship of Cyrus in the following manner. He had a close friend, Proxenus, a Boeotian, a pupil of Gorgias of Leontini and a friend of Cyrus. Proxenus, while living in

Sardis at the court of Cyrus, wrote a letter to Xenophon at Athens, inviting him to come and cultivate the friendship of Cyrus. Xenophon showed this letter to Socrates and asked his advice; Socrates counseled him to go to Delphi and ask the oracle. Xenophon complied and entered the presence of the god. He inquired not whether he should go and seek service with Cyrus but how he should do so. Socrates criticized him for doing this but nevertheless advised him to go. Arriving at the court of Cyrus, he became as deeply devoted to him as Proxenus was. We have his own ample account of all that happened during the expedition and on the march home. He was at odds with Meno of Pharsalus, the mercenary general, throughout the expedition and accused him of having a favorite older than himself. He also criticized a certain Apollonides for having had his ears pierced.

After the expedition and the disasters it endured in Pontus and the betrayal by Seuthes, the king of the Odrysians, Xenophon returned to Asia, after hiring the troops of Cyrus as mercenaries in the service of Agesilaus, the Spartan king, to whom he was very devoted. At this time, too, he was exiled by the Athenians because he took Sparta's side. In Ephesus, Xenophon entrusted one half of a sum of money he possessed to Megabyzus, a priest of Artemis, to keep against his return, or failing his return, to apply to the erection of a statue in honor of the goddess, and sent the other half as votive offerings to Delphi. Later, he came to Greece with Agesilaus, who had been recalled to carry on the war against Thebes. The Lacedaemonians conferred many privileges on him.

Leaving Agesiluas, Xenophon went to Scillus, a place in the vicinity of Elis, not far from that city. Demetrius of Magnesia says he was accompanied by his wife Philesia, and, Dinanhus, in a speech written in defense of the freedman whom Xenophon prosecuted for neglecting his duty, mentions that his two sons, Gryllus and Diodorus, the Dioscuri, as they were called, also went with him. When Megabyzus arrived to attend the festival, Xenophon received the deposit of money from him and bought and dedicated to the goddess an estate with a river running through it which bears the same name, Selinus, as the river at Ephesus. From that time onward he hunted, entertained his friends, and worked at his histories without interruption. Dinarchus, however, says that the Lacedaemonians gave him land and a house.

We are also told that when he was at Scillus, Phylopidas the Spartan sent him a present of captive slaves from Dardanus, and that he disposed of them at his pleasure. We are also told that the Elians marched against Scillus and captured it because the Spartans were so slow. His sons therefore retired to Lepreum with a few of the servants, while Xenophon, who had previously gone to Elis, went to Lepreum to join his sons, making his escape with them from Lepreum to Corinth, where he took up residence. The Athenians, meanwhile, decided to assist Sparta. Xenophon therefore sent his sons to Athens to serve in the army in defense of Sparta. According to Diocles in his *Lives of the Philosophers*, they had been trained in Sparta. Diodorus came through the battle safely, though without performing any distinguished service. He had a son of the same name, Gryllus, as his brother. Gryllus served with the cavalry. In the battle of Mantinea, he fought bravely and died, as Ephorus relates in his twenty-fifth book. Cephisodorus was in command of the cavalry and Hegesilaus was commander-in-chief. Epaminondas also fell in this battle. Xenophon is said to have been sacrificing, with a chaplet on his head. When his son's death was announced, he removed it. Afterward, when he learned that he had fallen gloriously, he replaced the chaplet. Some report that he did not even weep but simply exclaimed, "I knew my son was mortal." Aristotle mentions that there were innumerable authors of epitaphs and eulogies upon Gryllus, many of whom wrote, in part at least, to please his father. Hermippus in his *Life of Theophrastus* also affirms that even Isocrates wrote an encomium on Gryllus. Timon, however, jeers at Xenophon in the lines:

> A feeble pair or triad of works, or even a greater number, such as would come from Xenophon or the might of Aeschines, that not unpersuasive writer.

Such was his life. He flourished in the fourth year of the 94th Olympiad,[1] and he took part in the expedition of Cyrus in the archonship of Xenaenetus in the year before the death of Socrates.

According to Ctesiclides of Athens in his list of archons and Olympic victors, Xenophon died in the first year of the 105th Olympiad,[2] in the archonship of Callidemides, the year in which Philip, the son of Amyntas, came to the throne of Macedon. As Demetrius of Magnesia states, he died at Corinth obviously very advanced in years. He was a worthy man, very fond of horses and hunting, an able tactician as his writings make clear, pious, fond of sacrificing, and expert in augury from the victims. He made Socrates his model.

He wrote some forty books in all, though the list of books given is not always the same, here is the list:

The Anabasis, with a Preface to Each Separate Book
   but None to the Whole Work
Cyropaedia
Hellenica
Memorabilia
Symposium
Oeconomicus
On Horsemanship
On Hunting
On the Duty of a Cavalry General
A Defense of Socrates
On Revenues
Hieron or of Tyranny
Agesilaus
The Constitutions of Athens and Sparta

Demetrius of Magnesia says that the last of these works is not by Xenophon.

Xenophon is said to have made Thucydides famous by publishing his history, till then unknown, and which he might have appropriated to his own use. For the sweet cadence of his

[1]*401-400* B.C.
[2]*360-359* B.C.

narrative he earned the name of the *Attic Muse*. For this reason, Plato and he were jealous of each other, as we shall narrate in the chapter on Plato.

I also have composed about him:

> *Up the steep path to fame toiled Xenophon*
> *In that long march of glorious memories;*
> *In deeds of Greece, how bright his example shone,*
> *How fair was wisdom seen in Socrates.*

Another refers to the circumstances of his death:

> *Albeit the countrymen of Cranaus*
> *and Cecrops condemned you, Xenophon,*
> *to exile because of your friendship with*
> *Cyrus, hospitable Corinth welcomed*
> *you and so well were you pleased*
> *with the delights of that city that*
> *you resolved to take up residence there.*

Other sources state that he flourished, with the other Socratics, in the 89th Olympiad,[3] and Istrus affirms that he was banished by a decree of Eubulus and also recalled by his decree.

---

[3] *424-420* B.C. *This date is an error, but not of Diogenes Laertius.*

XV
DIOGENES

DIOGENES, son of Hicesius, a banker, was a native of Sinope. Diocles relates that Diogenes was exiled because his father, who had been placed in charge of public moneys, had adulterated the coinage. Eubulides, however, in his book *On Diogenes* says that it was Diogenes himself who did this and was exiled; his father accompanied him. Moreover, Diogenes actually acknowledges, in his *Pordalus*, that it was he who adulterated the coinage. Other accounts have it that Diogenes was in charge of the workmen and that they persuaded him to do this, and that he went either to the Delphian or the Delian oracle in his own city to ask Apollo whether he should do what they urged. The god gave him permission to alter the *political* currency, but not understanding what this involved, he adulterated the *state* coinage. When detected, he was, according to some accounts, banished; according to others, he voluntarily left the city to avoid the consequences. One version has it that his father entrusted him with the money and that he debased it. His father, as a consequence, was imprisoned and died; the son fled, came to Delphi, and inquired not whether he should falsify the coinage but what he should do to achieve the greatest reputation. Then it was that he received the oracle.

In Athens he met Antisthenes. Antisthenes at first repulsed him, because he never welcomed pupils; Diogenes overcame him by sheer persistence. Once, when Antisthenes raised his staff as though to strike him, the pupil offered his head, saying, "Strike, for you will find no wood hard enough to keep me

131

away from you, so long as I think you have something to say."
From thence forward, Diogenes became Antisthenes' pupil
and, in exile, determined to live a simple life.

Theophrastus says, in the *Megarian Dialogue*, that Diogenes
discovered the means of adapting himself to circumstances
through watching a mouse running about, not looking for a
place to lie down, nor afraid of the dark, nor seeking any of the
things which are thought to be comforts. Diogenes was the first
to double his cloak because he had to use it to sleep in as well as
to wear; he also carried a wallet to hold his victuals, and he
used any place for any purpose, to breakfast, to sleep, or to
converse. He would say, pointing to the portico of Zeus and the
Hall of Processions, that the Athenians had provided him with
places to live. He did not lean upon a staff until he grew infirm;
thereafter, he carried it everywhere, not, to be sure, within the
city, but when walking along the road. Then he carried it and
his wallet as well. So say Olympiodorus, once a magistrate at
Athens, Polyeuctus the orator, and Lysanias the son of
Aeschrio. Diogenes had written to ask a friend to find a cottage
for him. While the friend dallied over the matter, Diogenes
took up residence in the tub in the Metroon, as he himself
explains in his letters. In summer he used to roll in it over hot
sand, and in winter he used to embrace statues covered with
snow, thus taking every means of accustoming himself to hardship.

Diogenes was a master of vituperation directed at his con-
temporaries. He called the school of Euclid bilious, and Plato's
lectures a waste of time; the performances at the Dionysia were
great diversions for fools, and the demagogues the lackeys of
the mob. He used also to say that when he saw physicians,
philosophers, and pilots at work, he considered man the most
intelligent of all animals, but when, on the other hand, he saw
interpreters of dreams and diviners and those who listened to
them, and those bloated with pride of wealth, he thought no
animal more silly. His favorite statement was that for the conduct of life, we need either right reason or a halter.

One day, at an expensive banquet, Diogenes saw Plato taking
olives. "How does it happen" he said, "that you, the philoso-

pher who sailed to Sicily to find these dishes, here, when they are before you, do not relish them?" "Not so, by the gods, Diogenes," answered Plato, "in Sicily too, I lived almost exclusively on olives and other similar things." "Why then," Diogenes demanded, "did you have to go to Syracuse? Didn't olives grow in Attica at that time?" Favorinus, however, in his *Miscellaneous History* tells this story about Aristippus. On another occasion, while eating dried figs, Diogenes encountered Plato and offered him some. Plato took and ate them, and Diogenes exclaimed, "I said that you should share them, not eat them all up."

On one occasion, when Plato had invited to his house some friends whom Dionysius had recommended to him, Diogenes, who was present, soiled his carpets, saying, "I trample upon Plato's vainglory." Plato's reply was, "How much pride you exhibit, Diogenes, while protesting not to be proud." Another account has it that Diogenes said, "I trample upon the pride of Plato," and the latter retorted, "Yes, Diogenes, with pride of another kind." Sotion, however, in his fourth book makes the Cynic address this remark to Plato himself. Diogenes once asked Plato for wine, and later for some dried figs, too, and Plato sent him a jarful. Then Diogenes said, "If someone asks you how many two and two are, will you say, twenty? So, it seems you neither give as you are requested nor answer as you are questioned." He meant this to imply that Plato talked without end.

Asked where, in Greece, he had seen good men, Diogenes replied, "Good men nowhere, but good boys in Lacedaemon." One day he was lecturing earnestly, but nobody was listening to him; therefore he began to whistle. When people gathered about him in response, he chided them with coming in all haste to hear nonsense, but languidly and with little enthusiasm to hear a serious matter. He would say that men strive to outdo one another in digging and kicking, but no one strives to become a good and true man. He expressed wonder that the grammarians investigate the ills of Odysseus while ignorant of their own; that the musicians should tune the strings of their lyre while leaving the passions of their own souls out of harmony; that the mathematicians should gaze at the sun and the moon but overlook what is close at hand; that orators should rage about justice in their speeches but never practice it; or that the miserly cry out against money while they themselves are inordinately fond of it. He condemned those who praised honest men as being superior to money while they themselves envied the very rich. He was angered because men sacrifice to the gods to ensure health and, while sacrificing, feast to the detriment of their health. He was astonished that slaves watching their gluttonous masters did not steal some of the food. He praised those who were about to marry but did not, those about to go on a voyage who never set sail, those who thought about going into politics but did not, those who, purposing to raise a family, do not do so, and those who get ready to live with the powerful but never approach them. He used to say that we ought to stretch out our hands to our friends with the fingers open and not closed.

Menippus in his *Sale of Diogenes* tells how, when Diogenes was captured and put up for sale, he was asked what he could do. He replied, "Govern men." And he told the auctioneer to make that announcement in case anybody wanted to buy himself a master. When forbidden to sit down, Diogenes said, "It makes no difference, for in whatever position fishes lie, they still find purchasers." He said he was astonished that before we buy a jar or dish, we test whether it rings true, but if it is a man, we are satisfied simply to look at him. To Xeniades, who purchased him, he said: "You must obey me, although I am a slave; for, if a physician or a steersman were in slavery, he would be obeyed." Eubulus in his book called *The Sale of Diogenes* tells us that Diogenes trained the sons of Xeniades in the following way. After their other studies he taught them to ride, to shoot the bow, to sling stones, and to hurl javelins. Later, when they reached the wrestling-school, he would not permit the master to give them full athletic training, but only enough to heighten their color and keep them in good condition.

The boys learned many passages from poets, historians, and the writings of Diogenes himself by heart, and Diogenes exercised them in every shortcut to a good memory. In the house, he taught them to wait upon themselves and to be satisfied with plain food and with water to drink. He used to make them cut their hair short and to wear it without ornaments, and to go lightly clad, barefoot, in silence, and without gaping about them in the streets. He also took them hunting. They held Diogenes in great esteem and made requests of their parents for him. The same Eubulus relates that Diogenes grew old in the household of Xeniades and that after Diogenes's death was buried by his sons. Xeniades once asked him how he wished to be buried. He replied, "On my face." "Why?" inquired the other. "Because," said he, "after a little time down will be converted into up." By this, he referred to the Macedonians, who had at that time achieved supremacy, that is, had risen high from a humble situation. A friend took Diogenes into a splendid palace and warned him not to expectorate; whereupon having cleared his throat, Diogenes discharged the phlegm into the man's face, because, he said, he could find no meaner receptacle. Other writers tell this of Aristippus. One day Diogenes called out for men, and when people collected, he struck out at them with his stick, crying, "I called for men, not scoundrels." Hecato tells this anecdote in the first book of his *Anecdotes*. Alexander is reported to have said, "Were I not Alexander, I should have liked to be Diogenes."

The word "crippled," Diogenes held, ought to be applied not to the deaf or blind but to those who have no wallet.[1] One day he made his way with head half-shaven into a party of young revelers, as Metrocles relates in his *Ancedotes*, and was roughly handled by them. Afterward, he entered on a tablet the names of those who had struck him and went about with the tablet hung round his neck, till he had covered them with ridicule and brought universal criticism and discredit upon them. He called himself a hound such as all men praise, but none of his admirers, he added, would dare go with him. When a victor of the Pythian games boasted that he had vanquished men, Diogenes replied, "Nay, I defeat men; you defeat slaves."

To those who said to him, "You are old; rest," he replied,

---

[1] *A play on the Greek words for "crippled" and "purse."*

"What? If I were running in the stadium, ought I lessen my pace when approaching the goal? Ought I not rather to put on speed?" When invited to dinner, he declared that he wouldn't go, since the last time he went, his host had not been properly grateful. He would walk upon snow barefoot and do the other things mentioned above. Not only that, he even attempted to eat meat raw but could not digest it. He once encountered Demosthenes the orator dining at an inn, and, when Demosthenes retired within, Diogenes said, "All the more you will be inside the tavern." When some strangers expressed a wish to see Demosthenes, pointing his middle finger, Diogenes said, "There goes the demagogue of Athens." A certain man dropped a loaf of bread and, out of shame, would not pick it up; Diogenes, wishing to teach him a lesson, tied a rope to the neck of a wine jar and proceeded to drag it across the Ceramicus.

Diogenes used to say that he followed the example of the trainers of choruses; they, too, set the note a little high, to make sure that the rest would hit the right note. Most people, he would say, are so much alike that a finger makes all the difference. If you go about with your middle finger stretched out, people will think you are mad; if it's the little one, they will not think so. Very valuable things, said he, are bartered for things of no value and vice versa. A statue brings three thousand drachmas, while a quart of barley flour fetches two copper coins.

To Xeniades, who purchased him, he said, "Come, see that you obey orders." When Xeniades quoted the line, "The streams flow backward to their sources,"[2] Diogenes asked, "If you had been ill and had purchased a doctor, would you then, instead of obeying him, have said, 'Backward the streams flow to their founts'?"

Someone wanted to study philosophy with him. Diogenes gave him a tuna fish to carry and told him to follow him. The man, out of shame, threw it away and left him; some time later, on meeting him, Diogenes laughed and said, "The friendship

[2]*Euripides*, Medea, *410*.

between you and me was broken by a tuna fish." Diocles, however, gives the following version of this same story. When someone said to him, "Tell me what to do, Diogenes," he led him away and gave him a cheese to carry, which cost half an obol. When the man refused, Diogenes remarked, "The friendship between you and me is shattered by a little cheese worth half an obol."

One day, seeing a child drinking out of his hands, Diogenes cast away the cup from his wallet with the words, "A child has surpassed me in plain living." He also threw away his bowl when, on a similar occasion, he saw a child, who had broken his plate, scoop up his lentils with a rolled-up morsel of bread. He argued thus: "All things belong to the gods. The wise are friends of the gods, and friends hold things in common. Therefore all things belong to the wise." One day he saw a woman kneeling before the gods in an ungraceful attitude; wishing to rid her of superstition, as the story is told by Zoilus of Perga, he came forward and said, "Are you not afraid, my good woman, that a god may be standing behind you?—for all things are full of gods—and you may be embarrassed." He recommended to Asclepius a thug who, whenever people fell on their faces, used to run up to them and kick them.

All the curses of tragedy, he used to say, had descended upon his head. At all events he was:

> *A homeless exile, to his country dead.*
> *A wanderer who begs his daily bread.*

To fortune however, he could oppose courage, he said, to convention, nature, to passion, reason. Once when Diogenes was sunning himself in the Craneum, Alexander came and stood over him and said, "Ask of me any favor you like." To which he replied, "Stand out of my light." A certain person had been reading aloud for a very long time and, approaching the end of the roll, pointed to a space with no writing on it. "Take heart, men," cried Diogenes, "there's land in sight." To a person who claimed that by pure logic he had conclusively proved that he had horns, Diogenes, touching the man's forehead, said, "Well, I for my part don't see any." When another claimed that there is no such thing as motion, Diogenes got up and walked about. Someone was discoursing on celestial phenomena. "How many days," asked Diogenes, "were you in coming from the sky?" A eunuch of ill repute had written on his door, "Let no evil thing enter." "But how," Diogenes asked, "is the master of the house to get in?" When he had annointed his feet with unguent, Diogenes declared that from his head the unguent passed into the air, but from his feet into his nostrils. The Athenians urged him to become initiated, telling him that in the other world those who have been initiated enjoy a special privilege. "It would be ridiculous," he said, "if Agesilaus and Epaminondas are to dwell in the mire, while certain folk of no account will live in the Isles of the Blest because they have been initiated."

When mice crept on to the table, he addressed them thus, "See now even Diogenes keeps parasites." Once Plato styled him a dog. "Quite true," he said, "for I come back again and again to those who have sold me." As he was leaving the public baths, somebody inquired if many men were bathing. He said, "No." But to another who asked if there was a great crowd of bathers, he said, "Yes." Plato had defined Man as an animal, biped and featherless, and was applauded. Diogenes plucked a fowl and brought it into the lecture room with the words, "Here is Plato's man," following which he added to the definition, "Having broad nails." To one who asked what was the proper hour for dining, he said, "If you are rich, when you will; if poor, when you can."

At Megara Diogenes saw sheep that were protected by leather jackets and children who were uncovered. "It is better, " said he, "to be a Megarian's ram than his son." To one who had brandished a beam at him and then cried, "Look out," he replied, "What, are you intending to strike me again?" He used to call the demagogues the lackeys of the people and the crowns awarded to them the effluence of fame. He lit a lamp in broad daylight and said, as he went about, "I am looking for a man." One day Diogenes got a thorough drenching where he stood; when some bystanders expressed pity, Plato said, referring to Diogenes's vanity that if they really pitied him, they should move away. When someone struck him with his fist, "Heracles," said Diogenes "why do I forget to wear a helmet when I walk out?" Meidias assaulted him and said, "There are three thousand drachmas to your credit." The next day Diogenes put on boxing gloves, gave him a thrashing, and said, "There are three thousand blows to *your* credit." Diogenes was asked by Lysias the druggist whether he believed in the gods, "How can I help believing in them," said he, "when I see a godforsaken wretch like you?" Others ascribe this exchange to Theodorus. Watching a man perform rites of purification, Diogenes said, "Wretched man, don't you know that you can no more get rid of errors of conduct by sprinklings than you can of mistakes in grammar?" He criticized the prayer of men in general, saying that they asked for the things which seemed good to them, not for the things which are truly good. He criticized people who became excited about their dreams, saying they were not concerned about what they did when awake but reserved their interest for the visions seen in their sleep. At Olympia, when the herald proclaimed Dioxippus victor over the men, Diogenes protested, "Nay, he is victorious over slaves, I over men."

Nevertheless, Diogenes was loved by the Athenians. When a boy broke up Diogenes's tube, they flogged the lad and presented Diogenes another. Dionysius the Stoic says that after Chaeronea Diogenes was seized and dragged off to Philip. Asked who he was, Diogenes replied, "A spy upon your insatiable greed." For this answer he was admired and set free.

When, on one occasion, Alexander sent a letter to Antipater at Athens by a certain Athlios, Diogenes, who was present, said: "Graceless son of graceless sire to graceless wight by graceless squire."

When Perdiccas threatened Diogenes with death unless he visited him, "That's nothing wonderful," Diogenes said, "for a beetle or a tarantula would do the same." He would have expected the threat to be instead that Perdiccas would be quite happy without his company. He often insisted loudly that the gods had given men the means of living easily, but that this had been forgotten, because we demand honeyed cakes, unguents, and such things. To a man who was having his shoes put on by his servant, Diogenes said, "You have not reached full happiness yet, unless he wipes your nose too, but that will come, when you have lost the use of your hands."

Once Diogenes saw the officials of a temple leading away someone who had stolen a bowl belonging to the treasurers and said, "The great thieves are leading away the little thief." One day he noticed a boy throwing stones at a gallows."Well done," he said, "you will hit your mark." When some boys gathered around him and said, "Take care he doesn't bite us," he answered, "Never fear, boys, a dog does not eat beetroot." To a man who liked to go around in a lion's skin, he said, "Stop bringing dishonor to the trappings of courage." When some exclaimed about the good fortune of Callisthenes, citing the luxury he shared in the entourage of Alexander, "Not good," said Diogenes, "but rather ill fortune; for he breakfasts and dines when Alexander thinks fit."

When short of money, Diogenes told his friends that he was asking them not for alms but for repayment of what they owed him. When he relieved himself in the marketplace, he said that he wished it were as easy to relieve hunger by rubbing his empty stomach. When he saw a young man setting out to dine with some powerful persons, he reported him to some friends of his and told them to keep close watch over him. When asked a question by a boy dressed in an effeminate mode, he refused to answer until the boy pulled up his robe and showed whether he was man or woman. A youth was playing in the baths. Diogenes said to him, "The better you play, the worse it is for you." At a feast certain people kept throwing all the bones to him as they would have done to a dog. Thereupon he played a dog's trick and sprayed them.

He called rhetoricians and all others who talked for fame "thrice human," meaning "thrice wretched." An ignorant rich man he called "the sheep with the golden fleece." Seeing a "For Sale" notice on the house of a profligate, he said, to the house, "I knew well that after such surfeiting you would throw up the owner." He told a young man who complained of the number

of people who annoyed him with their attentions, "Stop hang-
ing out a sign of invitation." Of a public bath that was dirty he
said, "When people have bathed here, where must they go to
get clean?" There was a stout musician whom everybody de-
preciated and Diogenes alone praised. When asked why, he
said, "Because, though he is so huge, still he sings to his lute
and does not become a thief."

The musician who was always deserted by his audience Diogenes greeted with a "Hail chanticleer," and when asked why he
so addressed him, he replied, "Because your song makes every
one get up." While a young man was delivering a set speech,
Diogenes filled the lap of his garment with lupins and began to
eat them, standing opposite the orator. After he had thus
distracted the assemblage, he said he was greatly surprised that
they would desert the orator to look at him. A very superstitious person said to him, "With one blow I will break your
head." "And I," said Diogenes, "by a sneeze from the left
nostril will make you tremble." When Hegesias asked to borrow
one of his writings, Diogenes said, "You are a simpleton, Hegesias. You do not choose painted figs, but real ones, and yet
you reject true training to follow written rules."

When someone reproached Diogenes with his exile, he replied, "Nay, it was through that, you miserable fellow, that I
came to be a philosopher." Again, when someone reminded
him that the people of Sinope had sentenced him to exile,
"And I them," said he, "to stay home." Once he saw an Olympic victor tending sheep and thus accosted him: "Too quickly,
my good friend, have you left Olympia for Nemea." When
asked why athletes are so stupid, his answer was, "Because they
are built of pork and beef." He once begged alms of a statue;
when asked why, he replied, "To get used to being turned
down." When asking alms (as he did because of his poverty), he
used this form: "If you have already given to anyone else, give
to me also; if not, begin with me."

When asked by a tyrant what bronze is best for a statue, he
replied, "That of which Harmodius and Aristogiton were
molded." Asked how Dionysius treated his friends, "Like purs-
es," he answered, "so long as they are full, he hangs them up,

and when they are empty, he throws them away." A newlywed set up on his door the notice: "The son of Zeus, victorious Heracles, dwells here; let nothing evil enter in." Diogenes added, "After war, alliance." He called the love of money the mother-city of all evils. Seeing a spendthrift eating olives in a tavern, he said, "If you had breakfasted in this fashion, you would not so be dining."   .

Diogenes called good men images of the gods and love the business of the idle. To a question about what is wretched in life he replied, "A destitute old man." Being asked what creature's bite is the worst, he said, "Of those that are wild, a sycophant's; of those that are tame, a flatterer's." Upon seeing two centaurs very badly painted, he asked, "Which of these is Chiron (worse man)?" Ingratiating speech he compared to honey used to choke a person. The stomach he called livelihood's Charybdis. Hearing a report that Didymon the flute player had been caught in adultery, Diogenes's comment was, "His name alone is enough to hang him." To the question as to why gold is pale, his reply was, "Because so many thieves are plotting against it." Seeing a woman being carried in a litter, he remarked that the cage was out of keeping with the quarry.

One day, seeing a runaway slave sitting on the brink of a well, he said, "Take care, my lad, you don't fall in." Seeing a boy taking clothes at the baths, he asked, "Is it for a little unguent or is it for a new cloak?" Seeing some women hanged from an olive tree, he said, "Would that every tree bore similar fruit." On seeing a footpad he accosted him thus:

> *What do you do here, my bravo?*
> *Perhaps you came to rob the dead?*[3]

Being asked whether he had any maid or boy to wait on him, Diogenes said, "No." The person asked, "If you should die, then, who will carry you out to bury you?" "Whoever wants the house," he replied.

Noticing a handsome youth lying exposed, he nudged him and cried, "Up, man, up, lest some foe put a dart into your

[3]Iliad, X, 343,387.

back!" To one who was gorging himself he said: "Short-liv'd thou'lt be, my son, by what thou buy'st."[4] As Plato was conversing about ideas and using the nouns "tablehood" and "cuphood," Diogenes said, "Table and cup I see, but your tablehood and cuphood, Plato, I cannot see at all." "That's readily accounted for," said Plato, "for you have the eyes to see the visible table and cup, but not the understanding by which ideal tablehood and cuphood are discerned."

Somebody asked "What sort of man do you consider Diogenes to be?" "A Socrates gone mad," said Diogenes. Asked the right time to marry, Diogenes replied, "For a young man not yet; for an old man never." Asked what he would take to be soundly cuffed, he replied, "A helmet." Seeing a youth dressing with elaborate care, he said, "If it's for men, you're a fool; if for woman, a knave." One day he detected a youth blushing. "Splendid," he said, "that is the color of virtue." One day, after listening to two lawyers disputing, he condemned them both, saying that the one had no doubt stolen, but that the other had not lost anything. To the question as to what wine he found pleasant to drink, he replied, "That for which other people pay." When he was told that many people laughed at him, Diogenes made answer, "But I am not laughed down."

Hearing someone call life an evil, Diogenes corrected him, saying, "Not life itself, but living ill." When he was advised to pursue his runaway slave, he replied, "It would be absurd, if Manes could live without Diogenes but not Diogenes without Manes." He was breakfasting on olives and found a cake among them; he threw it away, addressing it thus: "Strangers, betake thee from the princes' path."[5] And on another occasion thus: "He lashed an olive."[6] When asked what kind of hound he was, Diogenes replied:

> When hungry, a Maltese; when full, a Molossian — two breeds which most people praise, though for fear of fatigue they do not

[4]Iliad, *V, 40, XVIII, 95.*
[5]*Euripides,* Phoecian Women, *40.*
[6]Iliad, *V, 366, VIII, 45.*

venture out hunting with them. So neither can you live with me, because you are afraid of the discomforts.

Diogenes was asked if the wise eat cakes. "Yes," he said, "cakes of all kinds, just like other men." Asked why people give to beggars but not to philosophers, he said, "Because they think they may one day be lame or blind but never expect to become philosophers." Asking alms of a miserly man who was slow to respond, he said, "My friend, I'm asking for food not for funeral expenses." One day, when reproached with having falsified the currency, Diogenes said, "That was the time when I was such a man as you are now, but such a man as I am now, you will never be." To another person who reproached him for the same offense he made a more scurrilous reply.

On coming to Myndus and finding the gates large but the city very small, he cried, "Men of Myndus, bar your gates, lest the city run away." Seeing a man who had been caught stealing purple, he said: "Fast gripped by purple death and forceful fate."[7] When Craterus wanted him to come and visit him, "No," Diogenes replied, "I would rather live on a few grains of salt at Athens than enjoy sumptuous fare at Craterus's table." He went up to Anaximenes the rhetorician, who was fat, and said, "Let us beggars have something of your paunch; it will be a relief to you and an advantage to us." When the same man was discoursing, Diogenes distracted his audience by bringing some salt fish. This annoyed the lecturer, and Diogenes said, "An obol's worth of salt fish has broken up Anaximenes's lecture class."

Reproached for eating in the marketplace, Diogenes said, "Well, it was in the marketplace that I felt hungry." Some writers say the following anecdotes refer to him: Plato saw him washing lettuce, approached him, and said quietly, "Had you paid court to Dionysius, you wouldn't now be washing lettuce," Diogenes replied with equanimity, "If you had washed lettuce, you wouldn't have paid court to Dionysius." When someone remarked, "Most people laugh at you," his reply was, "And so very likely do the asses at them, but as they don't care for the

[7]Iliad, *V, 83.*

asses, so neither do I care for them." One day, observing a youth studying philosophy, he said, "Well done, Philosophy, that you turn admirers of bodily charms to the real beauty of the soul."

When someone expressed astonishment at the votive offerings in Samothrace, Diogenes's comment was, "There would have been far more, if those who were not saved had set up offerings." Others, however, attribute this remark to Diagoras of Melos. To a handsome youth who was going out to dinner, he said, "You will come back a worse man." When the youth returned the next day, saying, "I went and am none the worse for it," Diogenes said, "Not worse-man (Chiron), but Lax-man (Eurytion)." Once, Diogenes was asking alms of a bad-tempered man, who said, "Yes, if you can persuade me." "If I could persuade you," said Diogenes, "I would persuade you to hang yourself." He was returning from Lacedaemon to Athens, and when someone asked, "Whither and whence?" Diogenes replied, "From the men's apartments to the women's."

He was returning from Olympia, when somebody inquired whether there was a great crowd, "Yes," he said, "a great crowd, but few who could be called men." He compared libertines to fig trees growing upon a cliff: their fruit is not enjoyed by men but is eaten be ravens and vultures. When Phryne set up a golden statue of Aphrodite in Delphi, Diogenes is said to have written upon it: "From the licentiousness of Greece." Alexander once came and stood opposite him, saying, "I am Alexander the great king." "And I," said he, "am Diogenes the Cynic." Being asked what he had done to be called a hound, he said, "I fawn on those who give me anything, I bark at those who refuse, and I fix my teeth in rascals."

While Diogenes was gathering figs, the keeper told him that not long before a man had hanged himself on that very fig tree. "Then," said he, "I will now purify it." Seeing an Olympian victor casting repeated glances at a courtesan, "See," Diogenes said, "that ram raging for battle, but now held fast by the neck by fascination with a common trollop." He would liken beautiful courtesans to a lethal honeyed potion. Once, as he breakfasted in the marketplace, bystanders gathered around him, shouting, "Dog." "It is you who are dogs," cried he, "when you stand around and watch me at my breakfast." When two cowards hid from him, he called out, "Don't be afraid, a hound is not fond of beetroot." After seeing a stupid wrestler practising as a doctor, he inquired of him, "What does this mean? Are you taking revenge on the rivals who formerly beat you?" Seeing the child of a courtesan throw stones at a crowd, he cried out, "Take care you don't hit your father."

A boy showed him a dagger which he had received from an admirer, and Diogenes remarked, "A pretty blade with an ugly handle." When some people praised a man who had given him alms, he broke in, "But you have no praise for me who was worthy to receive it." When someone asked him to give back a cloak, "If it was a gift," replied Diogenes, "I possess it; if it was a loan, I am using it." A superstitious boy told him that he had gold in the pocket of his dress. "True," said Diogenes "and therefore you sleep with it under your pillow." When asked what he had gained from philosophy, he replied, "This at least—if nothing else—to be prepared for every kind of fortune." Asked where he came from, Diogenes said, "I am a citizen of the world." Certain parents were sacrificing to the gods so that a son might be born to them. "Why" said he, "do you not sacrifice to make sure what manner of man he shall turn out to be?" When asked for a subscription toward a club, he said to the president: "Despoil the rest; off Hector keep thy hands."[8]

The mistresses of kings he designated queens; for, said he, they make the kings do their bidding. When the Athenians gave Alexander the title of Dionysus, he said, "Me too you might make Sarapis." When someone criticized him for going into dirty places, he answered that the sun also visits cesspools without being defiled.

Once, he was dining in a temple, and in the course of the meal some soiled loaves were placed on the table. He picked them up and flung them away, saying that nothing unclean should enter a temple. To a man who said to him, "You don't

---

[8]*An uncertain line of Homer: rendered in Pope as* Iliad, *XVI, 86.*

know anything, although you are a philosopher," he replied, "Though I am only a pretender to wisdom, that in itself is philosophy." When someone brought a child to him, praising the child's high gifts and excellent character, "What need then," said Diogenes, "has he of me?" He compared to a harp those who say admirable things but fail to do them; for like them, he said, the harp has neither hearing nor perception. As he entered a theater, he met those who were coming out head-on; asked why he did this, he said, "This is what I practice doing all my life."

Seeing a young man behaving effeminately, he said, "Are you not ashamed that your own intention about yourself should be worse than nature's; for nature made you a man, but you are forcing yourself to play the woman." Observing a fool tuning a recorder, he said, "Are you not ashamed to give this wood harmonious sounds while you fail to harmonize your soul with life?" To one who protested that he was ill adapted for the study of philosophy, Diogenes said, "Why then do you live, if you do not care to live well?" To one who despised his father, "Are you not ashamed," he said, "to despise him to whom you owe the reason that you can so pride yourself?" Noticing a handsome youth chattering in unseemly fashion, "Are you not ashamed," he said "to draw a dagger of lead from an ivory scabbard?"

When reproached with drinking in a tavern, "Why," said he, "I also get my hair cut in a barber's shop." Reproached with accepting a cloak from Antipater, he replied: "The gods' choice gifts are nowise to be spurned."[9]

When someone first shook a beam at him and then shouted, "Look out," Diogenes struck the man with his staff and added, "Look out." To a man who was urgently pressing his suit with a trollop, Diogenes said, "Why, foolish man, are you at such pains to gain your suit, when it would be better for you to lose it?" To one with perfumed hair he said, "Beware lest the sweet scent on your head cause an ill odor in your life." He said that bad men obey their lusts as servants obey their masters.

[9]Iliad, *III, 65.*

When question was raised why footmen are called such, he replied, "Because they have the feet of men, but souls such as you, my questioner, have." He asked a spendthrift for a mina. The man inquired why it was that he asked others for an obol but him for a mina. "Because," said Diogenes, "I expect to receive from others again, but whether I shall ever get anything from you again lies on the knees of the gods." Being reproached for begging when Plato did not beg; "Oh, yes," says Diogenes, "he does, but when he does so, he holds his head down close, that none may hear!"[10] Seeing a bad archer, Diogenes sat down beside the target with the words, "in order not to be hit." Lovers, he declared, derive their pleasures from their misfortune.

Asked whether death was an evil thing, he replied, "How can it be evil, when in its presence we are not aware of it?" One time Alexander stood opposite him and asked, "Are you not afraid of me?" "Why, what are you?" said Diogenes "a good thing or a bad?" Alexander answered, "A good thing." "Who then," said Diogenes, "is afraid of the good?" Education, according to Diogenes, is a controlling grace to the young, consolation to the old, wealth to the poor, and adornment to the rich. Once when Didymon, who was a rake, was treating a girl's eye, "Beware," says Diogenes, "lest the oculist while curing the eye should ruin the pupil." When somebody warned that his own friends were plotting against him, Diogenes exclaimed, "What is one to do then, if you have to treat friends and enemies alike?"

Asked what was the most beautiful thing in the world, he replied, "Freedom of speech." On entering a boys' school, he found there many statues of the Muses but few pupils. "By the help of the gods," said he, "schoolmaster, you have plenty of pupils." It was his habit to do everything in public, the works of Demeter and of Aphrodite alike. He used to draw out the following arguments. "If to breakfast be not absurd, neither is it absurd in the marketplace. But to breakfast is not absurd, therefore it is not absurd to breakfast in the marketplace."

---

[10]Odyssey, *I, 157, IV, 70.*

Once when found behaving indecently in public, he wished, "It were as easy to banish hunger by rubbing the belly." Many other sayings are attributed to him, which it would take long to enumerate.

He asserted that there are two kinds of training, mental and bodily. The latter by constant exercise forms perceptions which secure freedom of movement for virtuous deeds. Either part of this training is incomplete without the other, for good health and strength are counted among things essential for both body and soul. He would cite unanswerable examples showing how easily gymnastic training leads to virtue. In the crafts and arts it can be seen how craftsmen develop amazing manual skill through practice. Again, take the example of flute players and athletes: what extraordinary skill they acquire by their own tireless effort; if they had transferred those efforts to the training of the mind, how their labors would surely have been profitable and effective.

Nothing in life, Diogenes asserted, can succeed without strenuous practice; and practice can overcome anything. Therefore, instead of useless toil men should choose those which nature recommends, which will insure a happy life. But such is the folly of men that they choose to be miserable. Even to despise pleasure is most pleasurable, when we are habituated to it. And just as those accustomed to a life of pleasure feel disgust when they experience the opposite, so those whose training has been of the opposite kind derive more pleasure from despising pleasure than from pleasures themselves. This was the gist of his conversation, and it was plain that he acted accordingly, adulterating currency in very truth, allowing convention no such authority as he allowed natural rights, and asserting that the manner of life he lived was the same as that of Heracles when he preferred liberty to everything else.

Diogenes maintained that everything is the property of the wise and employed such arguments as those cited above. All things belong to the gods. The gods are friends of the wise, and friends share all property in common; therefore, all things are the property of the wise. Pertaining to law, he believed that it is impossible for society to exist without law; for without a city no benefit can be derived from that which is civilized. But the city is civilized, and there is no advantage in law without a city; therefore, law is something civilized. He would ridicule good birth and fame and all such distinctions, calling them showy ornaments of vice. The only true commonwealth, he said, is that which is as wide as the universe. He advocated community of wives, and acknowledged no other marriage than the union of the persuading male with the consenting woman. Consequently, he thought sons should also be held in common.

Neither did Diogenes see anything wrong in stealing from a temple or in eating the flesh of any animal, nor anything impious in touching human flesh; for, he said, this is clear from the custom of some foreign nations. Moreover, according to right reason, as he put it, all elements are contained in all things and pervade everything. Thus meat is a constituent of bread, and bread of vegetables. All other bodies also, by means of certain invisible passages and particles, find their way in and unite with all substances in the form of vapor. This he makes plain in the *Thyestes* (if the tragedies ascribed to him are really his and not the work of his friend Philiscus of Aegina or of Pasiphon, the son of Lucian, who, according to Favorinus in his *Miscellaneous History,* wrote them after the death of Diogenes). He held that we should neglect music, geometry, astronomy, and similar studies, because they were useless and unnecessary.

That Diogenes became very agile in the give and take of verbal debates is evident from what has been said above.

When Diogenes was sold into slavery, he endured it most nobly. On a voyage to Aegina he was captured by pirates under the command of Scirpalus, carried off to Crete, and offered at auction. When the auctioneer asked him what skill he had, he replied, "Ruling men." He then pointed to a certain Corinthian with a wide purple border on his robe, the man named Xeniades whom we mentioned above, and said, "Sell me to this man; he needs a master." This was the way Xeniades came to buy him, take him to Corinth, make him his children's tutor, and entrust him with the management of the whole household. He administered everything so well that Xeniades used to say, "A good genius has entered my house."

Cleomenes in his work entitled *Concerning Pedagogues* says that when the friends of Diogenes offered to ransom him, he called them simpletons; for, said Diogenes, lions are not the slaves of those who feed them, but rather those who feed them are at the mercy of the lions, for fear is the mark of the slave, whereas wild beasts make men afraid of them. Diogenes had a marvelous gift of persuasion and could easily vanquish anyone who opposed him. A certain Onesicritus of Aegina is said to have sent to Athens one of his two sons, the one named Androsthenes; he became a pupil of Diogenes and remained with him. The father then sent the other son called Philiscus, who was the elder, to find the younger. Philiscus, however, also stayed on. When, finally, the father himself arrived, he was just as much attracted to the pursuit of philosophy as his sons had been and joined the circle — so great was the magical spell which the discourses of Diogenes cast on him. Amongst Diogenes's hearers was Phocion, who was called the Honest, and Stilpo the Megarian, and many other men prominent in political life.

Diogenes is said to have been nearly ninety years old when he died. There are several different accounts of his death. One holds that he was seized with colic after eating an octopus raw and so met his end. Another states he died voluntarily by holding his breath. This account was followed by Cercidas of Megalopolis (or of Crete), who in his meliambics writes thus:

> *Not so he who aforetime was a citizen of Sinope,*
> *That famous one who carried a staff, doubled his*
>   *cloak, and lived in the open air.*
> *But he soared aloft with his lip tightly pressed*
>   *against his teeth*
> *And holding his breath withal. For in truth*
>   *he was rightly named.*
> *Diogenes, a true-born son of Zeus, a hound of heaven.*

Another version is that while trying to divide an octopus among the dogs, Diogenes was so severely bitten on the sinew of the foot that he died. His friends, however, according to Antisthenes in his *Successions of the Philosophers*, speculated that it was due to holding his breath. He happened to be living in the Craneum, the gymnasium in front of Corinth. When his friends came, as was their custom, and found him wrapped up in his cloak, they thought that he must be asleep, although he was by no means of a drowsy or somnolent nature. They drew aside his cloak and discovered that he was dead. They took this to have been a deliberate act on his part in order to escape from life.

A quarrel arose among his students as to who should bury him; they even came to blows. However, when their fathers and men of influence arrived, they arranged for his burial beside the gate leading to the Isthmus. Over his grave they erected a pillar with a dog in Parian marble upon it. Later, his fellow citizens honored him with bronze statues, on which these verses were inscribed:

> Time makes even bronze grow old: but your fame, Diogenes, all
> eternity will not destroy. Since you alone pointed out to mortals the
> lesson of self-sufficingness and the easiest path of life.

We too have written on him in the proceleusmatic meter:

> A. Diogenes, come tell what fate took you to the world below?
> B. A dog's savage tooth.

Some say that as he lay dying, Diogenes left instructions that he should be thrown out unburied, so that the wild beasts might feed on him, or thrust into a ditch and a little dust sprinkled over him. According to others, his instructions ordered that he be thrown into the Ilissus so that he might be useful to his brethren.

Demetrius in his work *On Men of the Same Name* asserts that on the same day on which Alexander died in Babylon, Diogenes died in Corinth. He was already an old man in the 113th Olympiad.[11]

The following writings are attributed to Diogenes:

[11] *324-321* B.C.

Dialogues:

Cephalion
Ichthyas
Jackdaw
Pordalus
The Athenian Demos
Republic
Art of Ethics
On Wealth
On Love
Theodorus
Hypsias
Aristarchus
On Death
Letters

Seven Tragedies:

Helen
Thyestes
Heracles
Achilles
Medea
Chrysippus
Oedipus

Sosicrates in the first book of his *Successions* and Satyrus in the fourth book of his *Lives* allege that Diogenes left nothing in writing, and Satyrus adds that the tragedies are by his friend Philiscus the Aeginetan. Sotion in his seventh book declares that only the following are genuine works of Diogenes: *On Virtue, On Good, On Love, A Mendicant, Tolmaeus, Pordalus, Casandrus, Cephalion, Philiscus, Aristarchus, Sisyphus, Ganymedes, Anecdotes, Letters.*

XVI
EUCLID

EUCLID was a native of Megara on the Isthmus, or, according to others, such as Alexander in his *Successions of Philosophers,* of Gala. He studied the writings of Parmenides. His followers were first called *Megarians* after his birthplace, later *Eristics*, and at a still later time *Dialecticians,* a name given them for the first time by Dionysius of Chalcedon, because they put their arguments into "question and answer" form. Hermodorus says that after the death of Socrates Plato and the rest of the philosophers, disturbed at the cruelty of the tyrants, appealed to Euclid. He held that the supreme good is really one, though it has many names, wisdom, God, Mind, and so forth. He rejected all that is contradictory of the good, holding it to be nonexistent.

When he challenged a demonstration, he centered his attack, not on the premises, but on the conclusion. He rejected the argument from analogy, declaring that it must be based either on similarities or on dissimilarities. If from similars, it is with these and not with their analogies that their arguments should deal; if from dissimilars, it is gratuitous to set them side by side. For this reason Timon, with a veiled aside at the other Socratics, says:

I dislike these babblers, and all others, Phaedo whoever he be, and wrangling Euclid, who inspired the Megarians with a mad passion for argument.

He wrote six dialogues entitled *Lamprias, Aeschines, Phoenix, Crito, Alcibiades,* and a *Discourse on Love*. To the school of Euclid belongs Eubulides of Miletus, the author of many dialectical arguments in a question and answer form, namely, *The Liar, The Disguised, Electra, The Veiled Figure, The Sorites, The Horned One,* and *The Bald Head*. One of the Comic poets says of him:

Eubulides the Eristic, who propounded his quibbles about horns and confused the orators with false and pretentious arguments is gone with all the brave dead useless display of a Demosthenes.

Demosthenes was probably his pupil and with his help corrected his pronunciation of the letter "R." Eubulides kept up a running controversy with Aristotle and said much to undermine his reputation.

Among others, the school of Eubulides included Alexinus of Elis, called Elenxinus because of his love of controversy. One famous controversy was that which he maintained with Zeno. Hermippus says that Alexinus left Elis and removed to Olympia, where he studied philosophy. His pupils inquired why he took up his abode here and were told that he planned to establish a school there, to be called the Olympian school. Their provisions ran out, however, and the place proved unhealthy, so they withdrew. Alexinus passed his remaining years alone with a single servant. As he was swimming in the Alpheus, a shark pierced him, and he died of his injury.

I have composed the following lines upon him:

It was not then a vain tale that once an unfortunate man, while diving, pierced his foot somehow with a nail; since that great man Alexinus, before he could cross the Alpheus, was pricked by a reed and met his death.

In addition to his reply to Zeno, he wrote other works, one against Ephorus the historian.

Euphantus of Olynthus also belonged to the school of Eubulides; he wrote a history of his own times. Also a poet, he composed several tragedies, which brought him considerable reputation at the festivals. He taught King Antigonus and dedicated a very popular work, *On Kingship*, to him. He died of old age.

Among the other pupils of Eubulides was Apollonius, called Cronus. He had a pupil Diodorus, the son of Ameinias of Iasus, who was also nicknamed Cronus. Callimachus in his *Epigrams* says of Cronus: "Momus himself wrote up on the walls 'Cronus is wise.' " Cronus was a dialectician too, and was credited with the discovery of the arguments known as the "Veiled Figure" and the "Horned One." When Cronus was staying with Ptolemy Soter, Stilpo put certain dialectical questions to him, but because he was unable to solve them on the spot, he was reproached by the king and, among other slights, given the nickname Cronus, in derision. He left the banquet. Later, he wrote an essay on the logical problem and ended his days in despondency. I have written lines about him, too:

> *Diodorus Cronus, what sad fate*
> *Buried you in despair,*
> *So that you hastened to the shades below,*
> *Perplexed by Stilpo's quibbles?*
> *You would deserve your name of Cronus better*
> *If C and R were gone.*

The successors of Euclid include Ichthyas, the son of Metallus, an excellent man, to whom Diogenes the Cynic addressed one of his dialogues; Clinomachus of Thurii, who was the first to write about axiom propositions, categormatics, and other such matters; and Stilpo of Megara, a renowned philosopher, of whom we have now to treat.

XVII
ANTISTHENES

ANTISTHENES, the son of Antisthenes, was an Athenian. Nevertheless, he was said not to be of pure Attic blood. When taunted on this point, he retorted: "The mother of the gods also is a Phrygian," because his mother was said to have been a Thracian. Consequently, when he had distinguished himself in the battle of Tanagra,[1] Socrates took the opportunity to remark that Antisthenes would not have proved so brave had both his parents been Athenians. Antisthenes personally showed his contempt for the airs which the Athenians assumed because they were native-born, by saying that this gave them no standing over snails or wingless locusts.

Antisthenes first became a pupil of Gorgias the rhetorician; this accounts for the rhetorical style of his dialogues, especially the *Truth* and the *Exhortations*. Hermippus says that Antisthenes planned to talk about the faults and virtues of Athenians, Thebans, and Lacedaemonians at the public gathering for the Isthmian games, but begged off when he saw many people from those cities convening.

Antisthenes later associated with Socrates and profited so much from the association that he used to encourage his own students to join him as pupils of Socrates. He lived in the Piraeus and every day would walk the five miles to Athens in order to listen to Socrates. From Socrates he learned endurance; he imitated Socrates's indifference to feeling and in this

[1] 426 B.C. cf. *Thucydides III, 91*.

way established the Cynic way of life. Antisthenes proved that pain is a good by the examples of the great Heracles and Cyrus – the one from the Greek world and the other from among the barbarians.

Antisthenes was the first to define "statement" (or assertion) as that which sets forth what a thing was or is. He frequently said, "I'd rather be mad than feel pleasure," and, "We ought to make love to women who will be properly grateful." When a boy from Pontus planned to attend his lectures and asked Antisthenes what he required, he answered, "Come with a new book, a new pen, and new tablets, if you have a mind to" (implying that he needed brains too).[2] When someone asked what kind of wife he should wed, he said, "If she's beautiful, you'll not have her to yourself; if she's ugly, you'll pay for it dearly." When told that Plato was abusing him, Antisthenes remarked, "It is a privilege of kings to do good and be ill spoken of."

When he was initiated into the Orphic mysteries, the priest said that those who were admitted into these rites would partake of many blessings in Hades. "Why then," he demanded, "don't you die?" Taunted because his parents were not both freeborn, he replied, "Nor were they both wrestlers, but yet I am a wrestler." Asked why he had so few disciples, Antisthenes replied, "Because I use a silver rod to drive them off." When asked why he reproved his pupils so harshly, he replied, "Physicians act the same toward their patients." One day, seeing an adulterer fleeing for his life, he exclaimed "Poor wretch, what danger you might have avoided for an obol." We learn from Hecato in his *Anecdotes* that Antisthenes used to say that it is better to fall in with crows than with flatterers; for the former devour you when you are dead, the latter while you are still alive.

Asked the highest moment of human happiness, Antisthenes replied, "To die·happy." When a friend complained that he had lost his notes, "You should have written them," he said, "on your mind, instead of on paper." He said that the envious

[2]*The pun turns about the word "new" and the phrase "a mind to."*

are consumed by their own passion, just as iron is eaten by rust. Those who aspire to be immortal, he said, must live piously and justly. States, said Antisthenes, are doomed when they are unable to distinguish good men from bad. Once, when applauded by some unsavory characters, he remarked, "I am horribly afraid I have done something amiss."

When brothers agree, no fortress is as strong as their common life, Antisthenes stated. The right outfit for a voyage, he said, is one which, in case of shipwreck, will go through the water with you. Once, criticized for keeping bad company, he replied, "Physicians attend their patients without catching their fever." "It is strange," he said, "that we weed out the tares from the corn and the unfit in war but do not exclude evil men from the service of the state." When asked what profit he had derived from philosophy, he answered, "The ability to converse with myself." Someone having called upon him to sing over the wine cups, he replied, "Then you must accompany me on the pipe." When Diogenes begged him for a coat, Antisthenes told him to fold his cloak around him twice. Asked what knowledge is the most necessary, he replied, "How to have nothing to unlearn." He advised men to endure slander better than they would bear being pelted with stones.

He used to taunt Plato with being conceited. When he saw a spirited charger in a procession, Antisthenes said, turning to Plato, "It seems to me that you would have made just such a proud, showy steed," because Plato was constantly praising horses. One day he visited Plato when the latter was ill, and seeing the basin into which Plato had vomited, Antisthenes remarked, "The bile I see, but not the pride." He advised the Athenians to vote that asses are horses, and when they declared this absurd, he replied, "Yet generals are found among you who have had no training but are only elected." "Many men praise you," someone said. "Why, what have I done wrong?" was his rejoinder. Once he turned the torn part of his cloak so that it came into view. Socrates, seeing it, said, "I can see your vanity through your cloak." Phanias, in his work on the Socratics, tells us that some one asked Antisthenes what he must do to be good and noble, and Antisthenes replied, "You must learn from those who know that the faults you have are to be avoided." When someone praised luxury, his reply was, "May the sons of your enemies live in luxury."

He asked a young man who was posing in a fantastic manner as an artist's model, "Tell me, if the bronze could speak, on what, think you, would it pride itself most?" "On its beauty," was the reply. "Then," said Antisthenes, "are you not ashamed of delighting in the very same quality as an inanimate object?" When a young man from Pontus promised to treat him with great consideration as soon as his boat with its freight of salt fish should arrive, he took him and an empty satchel to a flour dealer's, had it filled, and started to leave. When the woman asked for the money, "This young man will pay you," said he, "when his boatload of salt fish arrives."

Antisthenes is held responsible for the exile of Anytus and the execution of Meletus. He met some youths from Pontus whom the fame of Socrates had drawn to Athens and led them to Anytus, whom, ironically, he declared to be wiser than Socrates. Thereupon, it is said, those with him angrily drove Anytus out of the city. If he saw a woman anywhere bedecked with ornaments, he would hasten to her house and bid her husband bring out his horse and weapons; if the man possessed these, he would cease beriding his extravagance because, he said, a man could defend himself with these. If he had none, however, he would tell him to strip off his wife's finery.

These were Antisthenes's favorite themes. He would prove that virtue can be taught, that nobility belongs only to the virtuous. He held that virtue of itself is sufficient to ensure happiness, since it needed nothing except the strength of a Socrates. He held that virtue is a matter of deeds and not of words or learning. The wise man is self-sufficing, for all the goods of others are his. Ill repute is a good much as is pain. The wise man will be guided in his public acts not by the established laws but by the law of virtue; he will also marry in order to have children from union with the handsomest women. He will not disdain love, for only the wise man knows who are worthy to be loved.

Diocles records the following sayings of Antisthenes. To the wise men nothing is alien or impracticable. A good man deserves to be loved. Men of worth are friends. Make allies of men who are both brave and just. Virtue is a weapon that cannot be taken from one. It is better with a handful of good men to fight against all the bad than with hosts of bad men to fight against a handful of good men. Listen to your enemies, because they are the first to discover your mistakes. Esteem an honest man above a kinsman. Virtue is the same for women as for men. Good actions are fair and evil actions ugly. Count all wickedness foreign and alien. Wisdom is a most sure stronghold which never crumbles away or can be betrayed. Walls of defense must be constructed in our own unassailable reasons.

Antisthenes used to converse in the gymnasium of Cynosarges (White hound) at no great distance from the gates, and some think that the Cynic School derived its name from Cynosarges. Antisthenes himself also was nicknamed a hound. He was the first, Diocles tells us, to wrap his cloak about him twice and content himself with that single garment and to carry a staff and a wallet. Neanthes also says that he was the first to double his mantle. Sosicrates, however, in the third book of his *Successions of the Philosophers* says this was first done by Diodorus of Aspendus, who also let his beard grow and used a staff and a wallet.

Antisthenes is the only one of the Socratics praised by Theopompus, who says he had great skill and could by his agreeable discourse win over anyone he desired. This is clear from his writings and from Xenophon's *Banquet*. The strongest section of the Stoic School owed its origin to him. Hence Athenaeus the epigrammatist writes thus of them:

> Ye experts in Stoic story, ye who commit to sacred pages most excellent doctrines — that virtue alone is the good of the soul; for virtue alone saves man's life and cities. But that Muse that is one of the daughters of Memory approves the pampering of the flesh, which other men have chosen for their aim.

Antisthenes inspires the indifference of Diogenes, the continence of Crates, and the endurance of Zeno; he himself laid the foundations of their condition. Xenophon calls him the most agreeable of men in conversation and the most temperate in everything else.

Timon criticizes Antisthenes for writing so much and calls him a prolific trifler. Antisthenes died of an illness just as Diogenes, who had come in, asked him, "Do you need a friend?" Once, before his death, Diogenes, who was visiting Antisthenes, brought a dagger. Antisthenes cried out: "Who will release me from these pains?" Diogenes replied, "This," showing him the dagger. "I said," Antisthenes protested, "from my pains, not from life." It was thought that he showed some weakness in bearing his malady through love of life. These are the verses I wrote about him:

Such was your nature, Antisthenes, that in your lifetime you were a very bulldog to rend the heart with words, if not with teeth. Yet you died of consumption. Maybe someone will say, "What of that?" We must anyhow have some guide to the world below.

There have been three other men named Antisthenes: one a follower of Heraclitus, another a native of Ephesus, and the third of Rhodes, a historian.

Just as we have enumerated the pupils of Aristippus and of Phaedo, we will now add an account of the Cynics and Stoics who stem from Antisthenes.

XVIII
XENOCRATES

XENOCRATES, the son of Agathenor, was a native of Chalcedon. As a very young man he became a pupil of Plato. He also accompanied him on his journey to Sicily. He was slow and clumsy by nature. Comparing him to Aristotle, Plato said, "The one needed a spur, the other a bridle." And again, "See what an ass I am training and what a steed he has to compete with." Xenocrates was, nevertheless, in all other matters dignified and grave, a fact which made Plato say to him often, "Xenocrates, sacrifice to the Graces." He spent almost all his time in the Academy, and whenever he made his way to the city, all the noisy rabble and hired porters are said to have made way for him as he went along. Once the notorious Phryn tried to make his acquaintance. Pretending to be chased by some people, she took refuge in his house. He admitted her out of ordinary humanity and, since there was only one small couch in the room, permitted her to share it with him. After many solicitations, she left without success and told those who asked that Xenocrates was not a man but a statue. Another version of the story is that his pupils persuaded Lais to invade his couch. So great was his endurance that he submitted many times to amputation and cautery. His words were so absolutely trustworthy that although it was illegal for witnesses to give evidence without taking an oath, the Athenians allowed Xenocrates, and him alone, to do so. He was also extremely independent. When Alexander sent him a large sum of money, he took three thousand Attic drachmas and sent the rest back to Alexander, whose needs, he said, were greater than his own, because he had a greater number of people to support. He would not accept a present sent him by Antipater, as Myronianus attests in his *Parallels*. When he had been honored at the court of Dionysius with a golden crown as the prize for his prowess in drinking at the Feast of Pitchers, he went out and placed it on the statue of Hermes just as he had been accustomed to place garlands of flowers there. A story has it that when Xenocrates was sent with some others on an embassy to Philip, his colleagues, who had been bribed, accepted Philip's invitation to feasts and talked with him. Xenocrates did neither. For this reason Philip declined to see him. When the envoys returned to Athens, they complained that Xenocrates had gone with them but had rendered no service. The people were ready to fine him. But when he told them that now more than ever they ought to consider the interests of the state—"for," said he, "Philip knew that the others had accepted his bribes, but that he would never win me over"—the people paid him double honors. Later Philip said that of all who had come to his court Xenocrates was the only man whom he could not bribe. When he went as envoy to Antipater to plead for those Athenians taken prisoners in the Lamian war,[1] he was invited to dine with Antipater. He quoted the following lines to him:

> O Circe! what righteous man would have the heart to taste meat and drink ere he had redeemed his company and beheld them face to face?[2]

He thus so pleased Antipater with his ready wit that he at once released them. Once a sparrow pursued by a hawk flew into Xenocrates's tunic. He stroked it and let it go, saying that a suppliant must never be betrayed. He refused to reply to the banter of Bion. Tragedy, he says, does not condescend to the banter of comedy. A man who had never learned music, geometry, or astronomy still wished to attend his lectures; Xenocrates said, "Go your way, you offer philosophy nothing to

[1] 322 B.C.
[2] Cf. Odyssey, X, 383-385.

lay hold of." Others have it that he said, "You should not come to me to card a fleece."

When Dionysius told Plato that he would lose his head, Xenocrates, who was present, pointed to his own and added, "No man shall touch it till he cut off mine." When Antipater came to Athens and greeted him, he did not return the greeting until he had finished what he was saying. He was singularly free from pride; more than once a day he would retire himself, and he reserved, it is said, a whole hour to silence.

He left a very large number of treatises, poems, and addresses, of which I append a list:

These works comprise in all 224,239 lines.

Although he was this kind of man, when Xenocrates was unable to pay the tax levied on aliens living in Athens, the Athenians put him up for sale. Demetrius of Phalerum purchased him, thus making restitution twice; first, of his liberty to Xenocrates, second, of their tax to the Athenians. We learn this from the first book of the *Chapters on Historical Parallels* of Myronianus of Amastris. Xenocrates succeeded Speusippus and was head of the school for twenty-five years from the archonship of Lysimachides, beginning in the second year of the 110th Olympiad.[3] He died in his eighty-second year from the effects of a fall over some household item in the night.

Upon him I have expressed myself as follows:

Xenocrates, that type of perfect manliness, stumbled over a vessel of bronze and broke his head, and, with a loud cry, expired.

³*339-338* B.C.

XIX
ARISTIPPUS

ARISTIPPUS was a citizen of Cyrene and, as Aeschines informs us, came to Athens because of the fame of Socrates. A lecturer or sophist, as Phanian of Eresus, the Peripatetic, writes, he was the first among the followers of Socrates to charge fees and to send money to his master. Once, twenty minas which he had sent to Socrates was returned to him. Socrates declared his supernatural sign would not permit him to accept it; in fact, the offer annoyed him. Xenophon was not friendly with Aristippus; therefore he made Socrates direct his discourse denouncing pleasure against Aristippus. Theodorus in his work *On Sects* also criticized him, as does Plato in the dialogue *On the Soul*.

He was able to adapt himself to place, time, and person, and to play his part fittingly under all circumstances. He found greater favor than others with Dionysius, because he could turn any situation to good account. He took his pleasure in what was present and made no effort to secure the enjoyment of something which was not present. Hence Diogenes called him the king's pet cynic. Timon, too, sneered at him for luxury in these words: "Such was the delicate nature of Aristippus, who groped after error by touch."

He once bought a partridge for fifty drachmas; when someone questioned this, he asked, "Would you have been willing to pay an obol for it?" On receiving an affirmative answer, he replied, "Fifty drachmas are no more than an obol to me." When Dionysius asked him to choose among three courtesans, he took all three, saying, "Paris paid dearly for giving the preference to one out of three." When he had led them as far as the porch, however, he dismissed them. To such lengths did he carry choosing and disdaining. Hence the remark of Strato (or, some say, of Plato), "You alone are endowed with the gift to flaunt in robes or go in rags." He tolerated Dionysius's spitting on him, and when someone criticized this, he answered, "If fishermen let themselves be drenched with sea water to catch a fish, should I not endure to being spat upon to catch a 'blenny'?"

Diogenes, cleaning his vegetables, saw him passing and said to him jeeringly, "If you had become used to these as your diet, you would not have cultivated kings," to which Aristippus replied, "And if you knew how to live with men, you would not be washing vegetables." Asked what he had gained from philosophy, he replied, "The ability to feel at ease in any society." Reproached for his extravagance, he said, "If it were wrong to be extravagant, it would not be in vogue at the festivals of the gods." Asked what advantage philosophers have, he replied, "Should all laws be repealed, we would go on living just as we do now." When Dionysius inquired why philosophers go to rich men's houses while rich men do not visit philosophers anymore, his reply was, "The former know what they need while the latter do not." When Plato criticized him for his extravagance, Aristippus asked, "Do you think Dionysius is a good man?" When he received an affirmative reply, he said, "Still, he lives more extravagantly than I do. Obviously, nothing hinders a man from living extravagantly *and* well." To the question how the educated differ from the uneducated, he replied, "Exactly as horses that have been trained differ from those untrained." One day, as they entered the house of a courtesan, one of the young men in his company blushed. Aristippus remarked, "Going in is not dangerous, but being unable to come out."

Some one brought him a difficult problem with the request that he unravel it. "Why, you fool," said he, "should you want to untie it, since it causes trouble enough as it is?" "It is better," he said, "to be a beggar than to be uneducated: the one needs money, the others need to be made human." Once, when reviled, he tried to escape; his reviler followed him, asking, "Why are you running away?" "Because," said he, "just as you have the privilege of using abusive language, so my privilege is not to listen." When someone remarked that he always noted philosophers at rich men's doors, he said, "So, too, physicians are in attendance on those who are sick, but no one for that reason would rather be sick than a physician."

Once, on a voyage to Corinth, Aristippus was overtaken by a storm which left him in great distress. Someone said, "We plain men are not alarmed; are you philosophers become cowards?" He replied, "The lives at stake in either case are not to be compared." When a certain man took on airs because of his broad learning, he said, "Just as those who eat most and take the most exercise are not better in health than those who restrict themselves to what they require, so it is not wide but useful reading that promotes excellence." An advocate who pleaded and won a case for Aristippus put the question, "What good did Socrates do you?" "This much," was the reply, "that what you said about me in your speech was true."

Aristippus gave his daughter Arete very good advice, teaching her to despise excess. When asked how it would benefit his son to be educated, he replied, "At least in the theater he will not sit down like a 'bump on a log'." When someone brought him his son as a pupil, he asked a fee of five hundred drachmas. The father objected, "For that sum I can buy a slave." "Then do so," was the reply, "and you will have two." He said that he did not take money from his friends for his own use, but to teach them on what objects their money should be spent. Reproached for employing a rhetorician to conduct his case, he made reply, "Well, when I give a dinner, I hire a cook."

When Dionysius once forced Aristippus to expatiate upon a philosophical question, he said, "It would be ridiculous for you to learn from me what to say, and yet teach me when to say it." At this Dionysius was offended and made him recline at the end of the table. Aristippus said, "You must have wished to confer distinction on the last place." To someone who boasted of his diving skill, "Are you not ashamed," said he, "to brag of that which a dolphin can do?" Asked to differentiate between the wise man and the unwise, "Strip them both," said he, "and send them among strangers and you will find out." To one who boasted that he could drink a great deal without getting drunk, his rejoinder was, "So can a mule."

Once, Aristippus asked a man who had accused him of living with a courtesan, "What is the difference between renting a house in which many people have lived before and taking one in which nobody has ever lived?" The answer being "None," he continued, "Or again, between sailing in a ship in which ten thousand persons have sailed before and one in which nobody has ever sailed?" "No difference." "Then it makes no difference," said he, "whether the woman you live with has lived with many or with nobody." Accused of taking fees, though a pupil of Socrates, his reply was, "Of course I do, and Socrates, too, when certain people sent him corn and wine, used to take a little and return all the rest; thus he had the most prominent men in Athens for his stewards, whereas mine is my slave Eutychides." He enjoyed the favors of Lais, as Sotion states in the second book of his *Successions of the Philosophers*. To those who criticized him his defense was, "I possess Lais; she does not possess me. What is best is not abstinence from pleasures but mastery over them, without ever being overcome." To one who accused him of being extravagant in food, he replied, "Wouldn't you have bought this if you could have got it for three obols?" The answer was in the affirmative. "Very well, then," said Aristippus, "It is not I who am a lover of pleasure, but you who are a lover of money." One day when Simus, the steward of Dionysius, a Phrygian by birth and a rogue, was showing him costly houses with tessellated pavements, Aristippus coughed up phlegm and spat in the steward's face. When the steward protested, Aristippus said, "I could find no more suitable place."

When Charondas (others say Phaedo) asked, "Who is this who smells so strongly of ointments?" Aristippus replied, "It is I, hapless fellow, and the still more unlucky Persian king. Since no other animals suffer in this way, think whether it may not be the same with man. Confound the effeminates who make the use of good perfume unsuitable for us." When asked how Socrates had died, he answered, "As I myself would wish to die." Polyxenus the sophist once paid him a visit and, scandalized at the ladies present and other expensive entertainment, chided him. After a moment Aristippus asked him, "Can you join us today?" When the other accepted the invitation, Aristippus inquired, "Why, then, did you find fault? You seem to criticize the cost and not the entertainment." When a servant who was carrying money found the load too heavy, as Bion relates in his *Lectures,* Aristippus cried, "Pour away the greater part, and carry no more than you can manage." Once, on a voyage, he discovered that the vessel was manned by pirates; he took out his money and began to count it, and then, as if by chance, he let the money fall into the sea and naturally began to bewail his misfortune. Another version of this story attributes to him the further remark that it was better for the money to perish on account of Aristippus than for Aristippus to perish on account of the money. Dionysius once asked him what he was come for, and he said it was to impart what he had and obtain what he had not. Some, however, say he answered, "When I needed wisdom, I went to Socrates; now that I need money, I come to you." He complained that mankind, purchasing earthenware, tested it to see if it rang true, but had no norm by which to judge life. Others say Diogenes said this.

One day, in his cups, Dionysius ordered everyone to put on purple and dance. Plato refused, quoting the line: "I could not stoop to put on women's robes."[1] Aristippus, however, put on the dress and, as he was about to dance, was ready with the repartee:

> *Even amid the Bacchic revelry*
> *True modesty will not be put to shame.*[2]

Aristippus addressed Dionysius on behalf of a friend; failing to obtain what he asked for, he fell at Dionysius's feet. When

---

[1]Euripes, *Bacchae, 536.*
[2]Ibid., *317.*

someone jeered, he replied, "It is not I who am to blame, but Dionysius whose ears are in his feet." Once, in Asia, he was taken prisoner by Artaphernes, the satrap. "Can you be cheerful under these circumstances?" someone asked. "Yes, you fool," was the reply, "for when should I be more cheerful than now that I am about to converse with Artaphernes?" He likened those who went through the ordinary curriculum but stopped short at philosophy to the suitors of Penelope; for the suitors won Melantho, Polydora, and the rest of the handmaidens but failed to win the mistress. A similar remark is ascribed to Ariston, who said that when Odysseus went down into the underworld, he saw almost all the dead and made their acquaintance, but he never set eyes upon their queen.

Another time, when Aristippus was asked which subjects handsome boys ought to learn, his reply was, "Those which will be useful to them when they are grown up." To a critic who reproached him for leaving Socrates to go to Dionysius, his reply was, "Yes, but I came to Socrates for education and to Dionysius for recreation." When Aristippus had made some money by teaching, Socrates asked him, "Where did you get so much?" He answered, "Where you got so little."

When a courtesan claimed she was with child by him, he replied. "You are no more sure of this than if, after running through coarse rushes, you were to say you had been pricked by one in particular." Someone accused him of exposing his son as if he was not his own. He replied, "We know that spittle and vermin are of our own begetting; still, we cast them as far from us as possible, because they are useless." He received a sum of money from Dionysius at the same time that Plato carried away a book, and, when he was twitted with this, his reply was, "Well, I want money. Plato wants books." Someone asked him why he let himself be refuted by Dionysius. "For the same reason," said he "that others refute him."

Dionysus replied to a request from Aristippus for money, "But you told me that the wise man would never be in want." To which Aristippus replied, "Pay! Pay! And then let us discuss the question." When he was paid, "Now you see, do you not," said he, "that I was not found wanting?" When Dionysius quoted these lines to him:

Whoso betakes him to a prince's court
Becomes his slave, albeit of free birth,

he retorted: "If a free man he come, no slave is he." This is told by Diocles in his work *On the Lives of Philosophers;* other writers tell the anecdotes of Plato.

After a quarrel with Aeschenes, Aristippus said to him: "Shall we not make it up and leave off spouting words, or will you wait for someone to reconcile us over the wine bowl?" Aeschines replied, "Agreed." "Then remember," Aristippus went on, "that, though I am your senior, I made the first approaches." Thereupon Aeschines said, "Well done, by Hera, you are quite right. You are a much better man than I am. I began the quarrel but you make the first move to friendship." These are examples of his skill in repartee.

Four men known as Aristippus are: (1) our present subject, (2) the author of a book about Arcadia, (3) the grandchild by a daughter of the first Aristippus, who was known as his mother's pupil, (4) a philosopher of the New Academy.

Having sketched his life, let us now review the philosophers of the Cyrenaic school which sprang from him, although some call themselves followers of Hegesias, others followers of Anniceris, others again of Theodorus. We shall notice presently the pupils of Phaedo, the chief of whom were called the school of Eretria. This would seem to be the case. The disciples of Aristippus were his daughter Arete, Aethiops of Ptolemais, and Antipater of Cyrene. The pupil of Arete was Aristippus, who was called the mother-taught, and his pupil was Theodorus, known as the Atheist, subsequently as "god." Antipater's pupil was Epitimides of Cyrene, his was Paraebates, and he had as pupils Hegesias, who advocated suicide, and Anniceris, who ransomed Plato.

Those then who followed the teaching of Aristippus and were known as Cyrenaics held the following doctrines. They held that there are two states: pleasure and pain. The former is a smooth, the latter a rough, motion. Pleasure does not differ from pleasure nor is one pleasure more pleasant than another. The one state is attractive and the other repulsive to all living things. The bodily pleasure which is the end, according to

Panaetius in his work *On the Sects,* is not the quiet pleasure following the removal of pain, or the freedom from discomfort which Epicurus accepts and says is the end. They also hold that there is a difference between "end" and "happiness." Our end is particular pleasure, whereas happiness is the total of all particular pleasures, including both past and future.

Particular pleasure is desirable for its own sake, whereas happiness is desirable, not for its own sake, but for the sake of particular pleasures. The fact that from youth upward we are instinctively attracted to pleasure proves that pleasure is the end. Moreover, when we obtain it, we seek for nothing more, and there is nothing we shun so much as its opposite: pain. Pleasure is good even when it proceeds from the most unbecoming conduct, as Hippobotus says in his work *On the Sects.* Even when the action is irregular, the resulting pleasure is good and desirable for its own sake. The removal of pain, which Epicurus advances, does not seem to be pleasure at all, nor is the absence of pleasure pain. The followers of Aristippus hold that both pleasure and pain consist in motion, but absence of pleasure, like absence of pain, is not motion. The absence of pain, for example, is the condition of one who is asleep. Some people fail to choose pleasure because their minds are perverted. Not all mental pleasures and pains, however, are derived from bodily sources. We take unselfish satisfaction in the well-being of our country. This satisfaction is as real as our satisfaction in our own prosperity. They do not admit that pleasure is derived from the memory or expectation of good, as Epicurus taught. They hold that the movement which affects the mind wears down in course of time. Similarly, they hold that pleasure is not derived from sight or from hearing alone; for example, we listen with pleasure to imitation of mourning while the reality causes pain. They call the intermediate conditions absence of pleasure and absence of pain. They insist that bodily pleasures are far better than mental pleasures, and bodily pains far worse than mental pleasures. This is the reason that offenders are punished with bodily pains. They thought pain more repellent, pleasure more congenial. Therefore, they paid more attention to the body than to the mind. Although pleasure is in itself desirable, they believe that the things which bring about certain pleasures are often of painful nature – themselves, the very opposite of pleasure. Therefore, to accumulate the pleasures which produce happiness seems to them a most irksome business.

They do not subscribe to the opinion that every wise man lives pleasantly and every fool painfully, but regard it as only generally true. It is enough to enjoy each single pleasure as it presents itself. Prudence, they hold, is a good, desirable, not in itself, but in virtue of its consequences. We make friends from selfish motives, just as we cherish any part of the body so long as we have it. Some of the virtues, they feel, are to be found even in the foolish. Training of the body contributes to the achievement of virtue. The sage, they think, will not surrender to envy, love, or superstition, since these weaknesses are due to mere empty opinion; he will, nevertheless, experience pain and fear, for these are natural affections. Wealth, too, is productive of pleasure, though not desirable for its own sake.

Mental affections can be known, but not the objects from which they arise. The followers of Aristippus surrendered the study of nature because it seemed uncertain, preferring logical inquiries because of their usefulness. Meleager in the second book of his *On Philosophical Opinions* and Clitomachus in his first book *On the Sects* says that they think that dialectic and physics are both useless, for, once one has learned the theory of good and evil, one may speak with propriety, be free from superstition, and escape the fear of death. Nothing is just, honorable, or base by nature, but only by convention and custom. Nevertheless, the good man will be deterred from wrong-doing by the penalties imposed and the prejudices that it would stir up. Finally, there really exist some men who are wise. They think progress can be attained in philosophy, as well as in other matters. They hold that one man's pain may exceed another's and that the senses are not always true and trustworthy.

The school of Hegesias, as it is called, adopted the same ends, pleasure and pain. There is no such thing as gratitude, friendship, or beneficence, they believe, because we choose to do these things, not for themselves, but simply from motives of self-interest. Conduct other than that inspired by self-interest is not to be found. Happiness is impossible, for the body is infected with a great deal of suffering, while the soul shares the sufferings of the body and is vulnerable to disturbance. Fortune, moreover, often disappoints us. Happiness, therefore, cannot be realized. Life and death are desirable each in turn. But nothing is naturally pleasant or unpleasant. When some men are pleased and others pained by the same objects, this is due to the scarcity or surplus of such objects. Poverty and riches are not relevant to pleasure; for neither the rich nor the poor, as such, have any special access to pleasure. Slavery and freedom, nobility and low birth, honor and dishonor, all are alike indifferent in the calculus of pleasure. Life is a matter of advantage to the fool, of indifference to the wise. The wise man will be guided in all he does by his own interests, for no one else, he believes, is equally deserving. Though he secure the greatest profit from another, it would not equal what he himself contributes. The followers of Aristippus minimize the claims of the senses, because they do not give to accurate knowledge. Whatever appears rational should be done. Allowance should be made for errors, because no man errs voluntarily, but only under pressure of some suffering. We should not hate men; we should teach them what is better. The wise man surpasses others not in the choice of goods but in avoidance of evils; the purpose is to live without pain of body or mind. This they hold, is the advantage of those who do not distinguish among any of the objects which procure pleasure.

The school of Anniceris agreed with them in most respects but recognized that friendship, gratitude, and respect for parents do exist in real life, and that a good man may sometimes act out of patriotic motives. If the wise man suffers injury, he will still be happy though few pleasures come to him. A friend's happiness is not desirable in itself, for it is not enjoyed by his neighbor. Instruction by itself does not suffice to establish confidence in us or make us rise above the opinion of the multitude. Habits must be established in order to offset the bad dispositions which have grown up in us from the first. A friend should not be cherished merely for his usefulness (for, if that were to fail, we would no longer associate with him) but for the affection which inspires us even to endure suffering. Even though we make pleasure the end and suffer when deprived of it, we shall nevertheless cheerfully endure this deprivation because of our love for our friend.

The Theodoreans took their name from Theodorus, who has already been mentioned, and followed his doctrines. Theodorus completely rejected the current belief in the gods. I have encountered a book of his entitled *Of the Gods* which is not to be despised. Epicurus is said to have borrowed most of what he wrote on the subject from that book.

Theodorus was also a pupil of Anniceris and of Dionysius the dialectician, as Antisthenes mentions in his *Successions of the Philosophers*. He considered joy and sorrow the supreme good and evil, the one produced by wisdom, the other by folly. Wisdom and justice he called goods, and their opposites evils, while pleasure and pain are intermediate between good and evil. He rejected friendship because it does not exist between the unwise or between the wise. With the former, when the want is removed, the friendship disappears; the latter are self-sufficient and have no need of friends. It was reasonable, he thought, for the good man not to risk his life in the defense of his country, for he should never throw wisdom away to benefit the unwise.

The world was his country. Theft, adultery, and sacrilege might be allowed upon occasion, since none of these acts is by nature base, once you have removed the prejudice against them. Such prejudice is maintained in order to hold the foolish multitude together. The wise man indulges his passions openly without the least regard to circumstances. Theodorus used to employ such arguments as this: "Is a woman who is skilled in grammar useful insofar as she is skilled in grammar?" "Yes." "And is a boy or a youth skilled in grammar useful insofar as he is skilled in grammar?" "Yes." "Again, is a woman who is beautiful useful insofar as she is beautiful? And the use of beauty is to be enjoyed?" "Yes." When this was admitted, he would press the argument to the conclusion, namely, that he who uses anything for the purpose for which it is useful does no wrong. And by such interrogations he would carry his point.

Theodorus appears to have been called god in consequence of the following argument in which he engaged with Stilpo. "Are you, Theodorus, what you declare yourself to be?" To this he assented, and Stilpo continued, "And do you say you are god?" To this he agreed. "Then it follows that you are god." Theodorus accepted this, and Stilpo said with a smile, "But, you rogue, at this rate you would allow yourself to be a jackdaw and ten thousand other things."

Theodorus, sitting on one occasion beside Euryclides the hierophant, began, "Tell me, Euryclides, who violate the mysteries?" Euryclides replied, "Those who disclose them to the uninitiated." "Then you violate them," said Theodorus, "when you explain them to the uninitiated." He would not have escaped being brought before the Areopagus if Demetrius of Phalerum had not interceded. Amphicrates in his book *On Illustrious Men* says that Theodorus was condemned to drink the hemlock.

For a while Theodorus lived at the court of Ptolemy the son of Lagus and was once sent as his ambassador to Lysimachus. On this occasion his language was so bold that Lysimachus said, "Tell me, are you not the Theodorus who was banished from Athens?" To which he replied, "Your information is correct, for, when Athens could not bear me any more than Semele could Dionysus, she cast me out." And when Lysimachus added, "Take care you do not come here again." "I will not come," said he, "unless Ptolemy sends me." Mithras, the king's minister, standing by, said, "It seems that you ignore not only gods but kings as well." Theodorus replied, "How can you say that I ignore the gods when I consider you hateful to the gods?" On one occasion, in Corinth, he was walking abroad with a numerous train of pupils when Metrocles the Cynic, who was washing lettuce, remarked, "You, Sophist that you are, would not have needed all these pupils if you had washed vegetables." Thereupon Theodorus retorted, "And you, if you had known how to associate with men, would have had no use for these vegetables." A similar anecdote is told of Diogenes and Aristippus, as we have noted.

Such was the character of Theodorus and such his circumstances. He retired to Cyrene, where he lived with Magas and continued to be held in high esteem. The first time that he was expelled from Cyrene he is credited with a witty remark: "Many thanks, men of Cyrene," said he, "for driving me from Libya into Greece."

XX
ARISTOTLE

ARISTOTLE, son of Nicomachus and Phaestis, was a native of Stagira. Hermippus in his book *On Aristotle* relates that his father traced his ancestry to Nicomachus the son of Machaon and grandson of Asclepius. Aristotle resided with Amyntas, the king of Macedon, as court physician and counselor. Aristotle was Plato's most gifted disciple. He spoke with a lisp, as we learn from Timotheus the Athenian in his book *On Lives,* Also, his legs were slender (so they say), his eyes small, and he was conspicuous for his dress, his rings, and the way he wore his hair. Timaeus records that Aristotle had a son by Herpyllis, his concubine; this son also was called Nicomachus.

Aristotle withdrew from the Academy while Plato was still alive. Hence the remark of the latter: "Aristotle spurns me, as colts kick at the mother who bore them." Hermippus, in his *Lives,* mentions that Aristotle was away as Athenian envoy to the court of Philip when Xenocrates became head of the Academy; on his return, seeing that the school was under a new head, he chose a public walk in the Lyceum where he might walk up and down discussing philosophy with his pupils until it was time to rub themselves with oil. Hence the name "Peripatetic." Others, however, say that this name was given to him because, when Alexander was recovering from an illness and taking daily walks, Aristotle joined him and talked with him on various subjects.

Gradually, the circle about him became larger; he then sat down to lecture, saying: "It would be unfitting to be silent while Socrates speaks. He taught his pupils to discourse upon a given theme, in addition to exercising them in oratory." Later, however, he went to take up residence with Hermias the eunuch, tyrant of Atarneus. One account has it that he was on very affectionate terms with Hermias. Another has it that Hermias bound Aristotle to himself by ties of kinship, by giving him his daughter or niece in marriage; at least Demetrius of Magnesia says so in his work on *Poets and Writers of the Same Name*. The same author tells us that Hermias had been the slave of Eubulus, that he was Bithynian and had murdered his master. Aristippus in his first book, *On the Luxury of the Ancients,* says that Aristotle fell in love with a concubine of Hermias and married her with his consent; beside himself with joy, Aristotle sacrificed to this weak woman as the Athenians sacrificed to Demeter of Eleusis. Aristippus also says that Aristotle composed a song of praise in honor of Hermias, which is quoted below; that he stayed in Macedonia at Philip's court and was given his son Alexander as his pupil; that he asked Alexander to restore his native city, which had been destroyed by Philip, and that the request was granted him; and that he also compiled a code of laws for its inhabitants. On the example of Xenocrates, Aristotle established the rule that in his school a new president should be appointed every ten days. When it seemed to him that he had stayed long enough with Alexander, he went to Athens, after having first presented his kinsman Callisthenes of Olynthus to Alexander. When Callisthenes talked too freely before the king, thus disregarding Aristotle's advice, Aristotle is said to have chided him by quoting the line: "Short-lived, I ween, wilt thou be, my child, by what thou sayest." And so it happened, for Callisthenes, suspected of sharing the plot of Hermolaus against the life of Alexander, was confined in an iron cage and carried about until he became infested with vermin through lack of proper care. Finally, he was thrown to a lion and so died.

To return to Aristotle: he went to Athens and was head of his school for thirteen years. He then retired to Chalcis because he was indicted for impiety by Eurymedon the hierophant, or, as Favorinus has it is his *Miscellaneous History,* by Demophilius. The basis of the charge was a hymn he composed to Hermias, who was mentioned earlier, as well as the following inscription for his statue at Delphi:

This man in violation of the hallowed law of the immortals was unrighteously slain by the king of the bow-bearing Persians, who overcame him, not openly with a spear in murderous combat, but by treachery with the aid of one in whom he trusted.

Aristotle died at Chalcis, as Eumelus wrote in the fifth book of his *Histories,* by drinking aconite, at the age of seventy. The same writer says that Aristotle was thirty years old when he came to Plato, but here he is mistaken. Aristotle lived to be sixty-three, and he was seventeen when he became Plato's pupil.

The hymn in question runs as follows:

O virtue, toilsome for the generation of mortals to achieve, the fairest prize that life can win, for thy beauty, O virgin, it were a doom glorious in Hellas even to die and to endure fierce, untiring labors. Such courage dost thou implant in the mind, imperishable, better than gold, dearer than parents or soft-eyed sleep. For thy sake Heracles, son of Zeus, and the sons of Leda endured much in the tasks whereby they pursued thy might. And yearning after thee came Achilles and Ajax to the house of Hades, and for the sake of thy dear form the nursling of Atarneus too was bereft of the light of the sun. Therefore shall his deeds be sung, and the Muses, the daughters of Memory, shall make him immortal, exalting the majesty of Zeus, guardian of strangers, and the grace of lasting friendship.

There is, too, something I myself wrote upon the philosopher which I will quote:

Eurymedon, the priest of Deo's mysteries, was once about to indict Aristotle for impiety, but he, by a draught of poison, escaped prosecution. This then was an easy way of vanquishing unjust calumnies.

Favorinus in his *Miscellaneous History* says that Aristotle was the first to compose a forensic speech in his own defense written for this very suit, and he cites him as saying that at Athens, "Pear upon pear grows old and fig upon fig."[1]

According to Apollodorus in his *Chronology,* Aristotle was born in the first year of the 99th Olympiad.[2] He attached himself to Plato and, having become his pupil at the age of seventeen, remained with him twenty years. Aristotle went to Mitylene in the archonship of Eubulus in the fourth year of the 108th Olympiad.[3] When Plato died in the first year of that Olympiad, during the archonship of Theophilus, he went to Hermias and stayed with him three years. In the archonship of Pythodotus, in the second year of the 109th Olympiad,[4] he went to the court of Philip. Alexander then was fifteen years of age. Aristotle came to Athens in the second year of the 111th Olympiad,[5] and he lectured in the Lyceum for thirteen years. In the third year of the 114th Olympiad[6] Aristotle retired to Chalcis and died a natural death, at the age of about sixty-three, in the archonship of Philocles, in the same year in which Demosthenes died at Calauria. It is said that he earned the king's disfavor because he had introduced Callisthenes to him, and that Alexander, to annoy him, honored Anaximenes and sent presents to Xenocrates.

Theocritus of Chios, according to Ambryon in his book *On Theocritus,* ridiculed him in an epigram, which runs as follows:

To Hermias the eunuch, the slave withal of Eubulus, an empty monument was raised by empty-witted Aristotle, who by constraint of a lawless appetite chose to dwell at the mouth of the Borborus [muddy stream] rather than in the Academy.

[1]*Odyssey, VII 120.*
[2]*384-383* B.C.
[3]*345-344* B.C.
[4]*342-341* B.C.
[5]*335-334* B.C.
[6]*322-321* B.C.

Timon again attacked him in the line: "No, not even Aristotle's painful futility."[7]

Such then was the life of the philosopher. I have also come across his will, which runs thus:

All will be well, but, in case anything should happen, Aristotle has made these dispositions. Antipater is to be executor in all and sundry matters but, until Nicanor shall arrive, Aristomenes, Timarchus, Hipparchus, Dioteles, and (if he consent and if circumstances permit him) Theophrastus shall take charge both of Herpyllis and the children and of the property. When the girl is grown up, she shall be given in marriage to Nicanor, but if anything should happen to the girl (which heaven forbid and no such thing will happen) before her marriage, or when she is married but before there are children, Nicanor shall have full powers, both with regard to the child and with regard to everything else, to administer in a manner worthy both of himself and of us. Nicanor shall take charge of the girl and of the boy Nicomachus as he shall think fit in all that concerns them as if he were father and brother. If anything should befall to Nicanor (which heaven forbid!) either before he marries the girl, or when he has married her but before there are children, any arrangements that he may make shall be valid. If Theophrastus consents to live with her, he shall have the same rights as Nicanor. Otherwise, the executors in consultation with Antipater shall administer as regards the daughter and the boy as seems best to them. The executors and Nicanor, in memory of me and of the steady affection which Herpyllis has borne toward me, shall take care of her in every other respect and, if she desires to be married, shall see that she be given to someone worthy of her, and in addition to what she has already received they shall give her a talent of silver out of the estate and any three handmaids she may choose besides the maid she has at present and the manservant Pyrrhaeus, and if she chooses to remain at Chalcis, the lodge by the garden, if in Stagira, my father's house. The executors shall furnish whichever of these two houses she may choose with the furniture they think proper and with Herpyllis's approval. Nicanor shall take charge of the boy Myrmex and see that he is conducted to his own friends in a manner worthy of me with the property belonging to him which we received. Ambracis

[7] *Cf.* Iliad, XXIII, *70.*

shall be given her freedom and on my daughter's marriage shall receive five hundred drachmas and the maid whom she now has. Thale shall be given, in addition to the maid whom she has and who was bought, a thousand drachmas and a maid. Simon, in addition to the money paid him before for another servant, shall either have a servant purchased for him or receive a further sum of money. Tycho, Philo, Olympius, and his child shall have their freedom when my daughter is married. None of the servants who waited upon me shall be sold, but they shall continue to be employed, and when they arrive at the proper age, they shall have their freedom if they deserve it. My executors shall see to it that when the statues which Gryllion has been commissioned to execute are finished, namely, that of Nicanor, that of Proxenus, which it was my intention to have executed, and that of Nicanor's mother, they be set up. They shall also set up the bust of Arimnestus which has been executed, a memorial of him seeing that he died childless, and shall dedicate my mother's statue to Demeter at Nemea or whatever they think best. Wherever they bury me, there the bones of Pythias shall be laid, in accordance with her own instructions. And to commemorate Nicanor's safe return, as I vowed on his behalf, they shall set up in Stagira stone statues of life size to Zeus and Athena the Saviors.

Such is the tone of Aristotle's will. It is said that a very large number of dishes belonging to him were found, and that Lyco mentioned his bathing in a bath of warm oil and then selling the oil. Some relate that he placed a skin of warm oil on his stomach, and that, when he went to sleep, a bronze ball was placed in his hand with a vessel under it so that when the ball dropped from his hand into the vessel, he might be awakened by the sound.

A number of very felicitous aphorisms are attributed to him, which I quote. When asked, "What do people gain by lying?" his answer was, "Only this, that when they speak the truth they are not believed." Rebuked for giving alms to a man of evil life, he answered, "It was the man and not his character on whom I took pity." He used to say to friends and pupils, whenever or wherever he lectured, "As sight takes in light from the surrounding air, so does the soul from mathematics." He frequently said that the Athenians had indeed discovered wheat and laws, but that, though they used wheat, they had no use for laws.

"The roots of education," he said, "are bitter, but the fruit is sweet." When asked, "What is it that soon grows old?" he answered, "Gratitude." Asked to define hope, he replied, "A waking dream." Diogenes once offered him dried figs, and Aristotle perceived that he had prepared something sarcastic to say if he did not take them. He took them, consequently, and remarked that Diogenes had lost both his figs and his jest. On another occasion he accepted them when they were offered, lifted them up on high, as you do babies, and returned them, saying, "Great is Diogenes." He said that three things are necessary for education: natural endowment, study, and constant practice. Hearing that some one had calumniated him, he rejoined, "He may even scourge me so long as it is in my absence." He said that beauty is a greater recommendation than any letter of introduction. This saying is also attributed to Diogenes. Aristotle, they say, defined good looks as the gift of god, Socrates, as a short reign, Plato, as a superiority of nature, Theophrastus, as a silent deception, Theocritus, as an evil in an ivory frame, Carneades, as a monarchy that needs no bodyguard.

Asked how the educated differ from the uneducated, "As much," he said, "as the living from the dead." He called education an ornament in good times and a refuge in bad. Teachers who educated children deserved, he said, more honor than parents who merely gave them birth: the one gives only life, the other a good life. When a certain man boasted that he came from a great city, Aristotle replied, "That is not the point to be considered, the point is who is worthy of a great fatherland." To the question, "What is a friend?" his reply was, "A single soul dwelling in two bodies." Men, he said, were divided into those who were as thrifty as if they would live for ever, and those who were as extravagant as if they were going to die the next day. When someone asked why we spend much time with the beautiful, "That," he said, "is a question only a blind man could ask." Asked what profit he had ever drawn from philosophy, he replied, "This, that I do without being ordered what some are forced to do from fear of the law." Asked how students might make progress, he answered, "By pressing hard on those ahead and not waiting for those behind." To a chatterer who inundated him with talk and then asked, "Have I bored you to death with my chatter?" he replied, "Not at all, because I have not been listening." When someone chided him for having given a stipend to a dishonest man (the story is told in this form also), "I assisted not the man," he said, "but humanity." Asked how he should behave toward friends, he answered, "As we should wish them to behave to us." He defined justice as a virtue of soul which gives each what he deserves. Education he said is the best preparation for old age. Favorinus in the second book of his *Memorabilia* mentions as one of his favorite sayings, "He who has friends can have no friend." This is also to be found in the seventh book of the *Ethics*. These are the sayings attributed to him.

His writings are very numerous, and, in view of the man's excellence in every area, I think they ought to be listed:

Of Justice, four books
On Poets, three books
On Philosophy, three books
Of the Statesman, two books
On Rhetoric, or Grylus, one book
Nerinthus, one book
The Sophist, one book
Menexenus, one book
Concerning Love, one book
Symposium, one book
Of Wealth, one book
Exhortation to Philosophy, one book
Of the Soul, one book
Of Prayer, one book
On Noble Birth, one book
On Pleasure, one book
Alexander, or a Plea for Colonies, one book
On Kingship, one book
On Education, one book
Of the Good, three books
Extracts from Plato's *Laws,* three books

Extracts from the *Republic,* two books

Of Household Management, one book

Of Friendship, one book

On Being or Having Been Affected, one book

Of Sciences, one book

On Controversial Questions, two books

Solutions of Controversial Questions, four books

Sophistical Divisions, four books

On Contraries, one book

On Genera and Species, one book

On Essential Attributes, one book

On Arguments for Purposes of Refutation, three notebooks

Propositions Concerning Virtue, two books

Objections, one book

On the Various Meanings of Terms or Expressions Where a Determinant is added, one book

Of Passions or of Anger, one book

Of Ethics, five books

On Elements, three books

Of Science, one book

Of Logical Principle, one book

Logical Divisions, seventeen books

Concerning Division, one book

On Dialectical Questioning and Answering, two books

Of Motion, one book

Propositions, one book

Controversial Propositions, one book

Syllogisms, one book

Of Prior Analytics, eight books

Of Greater Posterior Analytics, two books

Of Problems, one book

Of Methodics, eight books

Of the Greater Good, one book

On the Idea, one book

Definitions prefixed to the Topics, seven books

Of Syllogisms, two books

Concerning Syllogism with Definitions, one book

Of the Desirable and the Contingent, one book

Preface to Commonplaces, one book

Of Topics Criticizing the Definitions, two books

Affections or Qualities, one book

Concerning Logical Division, one book

Concerning Mathematics, one book
Definitions, thirteen books
Of Refutations, two books
Of Pleasure, one book
Propositions, one book
On the Voluntary, one book
On the Beautiful, twenty-five books
Theses for Refutation, twenty-five books
Theses Concerning Love, four books
Theses Concerning Friendship, two books
Theses Concerning the Soul, one book
Politics, two books
Of a Course of Lectures on Politics like that
    of Theophrastus, eight books
Of Just Actions, two books
A Collection of Arts (that is, Handbooks), two books
Of the Art of Rhetoric, two books
Art, a Handbook, one book
Another Collection of Handbooks, two books
Concerning Method, one book
Compendium of the "Art" of Theodectes, one book
A Treatise on the Art of Poetry, two books
Rhetorical Enthymemes, one book
On Diction, two books
Of Taking Counsel, one book
A Collection or Compendium, two books
On Nature, three books
Concerning Nature, one book
On the Philosophy of Archytas, three books
On the Philosophy of Speusippus and Xenocrates, one book
Extracts from the *Timaeus* and from the Works of Archytas,
    one book
A Reply to the Writings of Melissus, one book
A Reply to the Writings of Alcmaeon, one book
A Reply to the Pythagoreans, one book
A Reply to the Writings of Gorgias, one book
A Reply to the Writings of Xenophanes, one book
A Reply to the Writings of Zeno, one book
On the Pythagoreans, one book
On Animals, nine books
On Dissections, eight books

A Selection of Dissections, one book
On Composite Animals, one book
On the Animals of Fable, one book
On Sterility, one book
On Plants, two books
Concerning Physiognomy, one book
Concerning Medicine, two books
On the Unit, one book
Prognostics of Storms, one book
Concerning Astronomy, one book
Concerning Optics, one book
On Motion, one book
On Music, one book
Concerning Memory, one book
Of Homeric Problems, six books
Poetics, one book
Of Physics According to the Lettering, thirty-eight books
Of Problems Which Have Been Examined, two books
Of Routine Instruction, two books
Mechanics, one book
Problems Taken from the Works of Democritus, two books
On the Magnet, one book
Analogies, one book
Miscellaneous Notes, twelve books
Descriptions of Genera, fourteen books
Claims Advanced, one book
Victors at Olympia, one book
Victors at the Pythian Games, one book
On Music, one book
Concerning Delphi, one book
Criticism of the List of Pythian Victors, one book
Dramatic Victories at the Dionysia, one book
Of Tragedies, one book
Dramatic Records, one book
Proverbs, one book
Laws of the Mess Table, one book
Of Laws, four books
Categories, one book
De Interpretatione, one book
Constitutions of 158 Cities, in General and in Particular,
    Democratic, Oligarchic, Aristocratic, Tyrannical

Letters of Philip
Letters of Selymbrians
Letters to Alexander, four books
Letters to Antipater, nine books
To Mentor, one book
To Ariston, one book
To Olympias, one book
To Hephaestion, one book
To Themistagoras, one book
To Philoxenus, one book
In Reply to Democritus, one book
Verses beginning "Holy One and Chiefest of Gods, Far-darting"
Elegiac verses beginning "Daughter of a Mother Blessed with Fair Offspring"

In all 445,270 lines.

This is the catalogue of the works written. The views he expressed in them are as follows. Philosophy has two parts, the practical and the theoretical. The practical part includes ethics and politics, and in the latter the doctrine of the household as well as that of the state is outlined. The theoretical part includes physics and logic. Logic, however, is not an independent science; it is developed as an instrument for the other sciences. Aristotle made it clear that he has a twofold aim, probability and truth. For each of these he employed two instruments: dialectic and rhetoric aim at probability; analytic and philosophy have truth as their end. He omits nothing which aids either discovery, judgment, or utility. As aids to discovery he left, in the *Topics* and *Methodics,* a number of propositions, in which the student would find an abundance of probable arguments for the solution of problems. As an aid to judgment he left the *Prior* and *Posterior Analytics.* By the *Prior Analytics* the premises are judged; by the *Posterior* the process of inference is tested. For practical use there are the precepts on controversy, and the works dealing with question and answer, with sophistical fallacies, syllogisms, and the like, are directed to the practical order. The test of truth, he holds, is sensation in the sphere of objects actually presented, while in the sphere of morals, which deals with the state, the household, and the laws, it is reason.

The sole ethical end, Aristotle held, is the exercise of virtue in a fully developed life. Happiness, he taught, is made up of three kinds of good: goods of the soul, to which he assigns the highest value; bodily goods, that is, health and strength, beauty and the like; and, thirdly, external goods, such as wealth, good birth, reputation, and so forth. He did not think that virtue alone is sufficient to guarantee happiness. Bodily goods and external goods are also necessary, for even the wise man would be miserable if he lived in the midst of pains, poverty, and similar circumstances. Vice, however, is sufficient in itself to secure misery, even though it possess an abundance of bodily and external goods. The virtues are interdependent of each other. A man might be prudent, or just, while at the same time profligate and unable to master his passions. The wise man is not immune to all passions, but he indulges them only in moderation.

Aristotle defined friendship as reciprocal goodwill, between equals. Under the term "friendship," as one species, he placed friendship among kinsmen, as another, that between lovers, as a third, that between host and guest. The end of love is not merely intercourse but philosophy. According to him, the wise man would fall in love and take part in politics; he would also marry and reside at a king's court. He distinguished three kinds of life — the contemplative, the practical, and the pleasure-loving — and gave preference to the contemplative. He held that the disciplines which make up ordinary education are useful for the achievement of virtue.

In the area of the science of nature Aristotle surpassed all other philosophers in the investigation of causes, so that he could explain even the most insignificant phenomena. Hence the extraordinary number of scientific notebooks he compiled. Like Plato, he held that God was incorporeal, that his providence extended to the heavenly bodies, that he was unmoved, and that earthly events are ruled by their affinity with the heavenly bodies. He held that in addition to the four elements there is a fifth, of which the heavenly bodies are made. Its motion is different from that of the other elements because it is circular. He also maintained that the soul is incorporeal, and he defined it as the first "entelechy," that is, actualization of a natural organic body potentially possessed of life. By the term actualization he means that which has an incorporeal form. This actualization, according to Aristotle, is twofold. Either it is potential, as that of Hermes in the wax, provided the wax be adapted to receive the proper moldings, or as that of the statue implicit in the bronze; or it is determinate, which is the case with the completed figure of Hermes or the finished statue. The soul is the realization "of a natural body," since bodies may be divided into two classes: artificial bodies made by the hands of craftsmen, such as a tower or a ship, and natural bodies which are the work of nature, such as plants, and the bodies of animals. And when he said "organic" he meant constructed as means to an end, as sight is adapted for seeing and the ear for hearing, capacities of a body "potentially possessed of life," that is, of possessing life in itself.

"Potential" has two senses, one answering to a determinate state and the other to its exercise in act. A man when awake has soul in the latter sense; a man asleep, in the former. Aristotle added the term "potential," then, in order to include the sleeper.

He held many other opinions on a list of subjects which would be too long to enumerate. His capacity for work and his inventiveness were amazing, as the catalogue of his writings given above proves; they come to nearly four hundred titles, counting only those whose authenticity is not questioned. Many other written works and pointed oral sayings are also attributed to him.

There were in all eight Aristotles: (1) our philosopher, (2) an Athenian statesman,[8] the author of graceful forensic speeches, (3) a scholar who commented on the *Iliad*, (4) a Sicilian rhetorician, who wrote a reply to the Panegyric of Isocrates, (5) a disciple of Aeschines the Socratic philosopher, surnamed Myth, (6) a native of Cyrene, who wrote upon the art of poetry, (7) a trainer of boys, mentioned by Aristoxenus in his life of Plato, (8) an obscure grammarian, whose handbook, *On Redundancy*, is still extant.

Aristotle of Stagira had many disciples; the most distinguished was Theophrastus, of whom we have next to speak.

---

[8]*Said to be the Aristotle who appears in Plato's dialogue* Parmenides.

XXI
THEO-
PHRASTUS

THEOPHRASTUS, a native of Eresus, was the son of Melantes, a fuller, as Athenodorus says in the eighth book of his *Walks*. He first heard his countryman Alcippus lecture in his native town and afterward he heard Plato, whom he left to follow Aristotle. When the latter retired to Chalcis, Theophrastus took over direction of the school himself in the 114th Olympiad.[1] One of his slaves, Pompylus by name, also was a philosopher, according to the first book of the *Historical Parallels* of Myronianus of Amastris. Theophrastus was a man of remarkable intelligence and industry and, as Pamphila says in the thirty-second book of her *Memorabilia*, was the teacher of Menander the Comic poet. He was very obliging and fond of discussion. Casander certainly granted him audience, and Ptolemy made overtures to him. So highly was he thought of at Athens that when Agnonides tried to indict him for impiety, the prosecutor himself narrowly escaped punishment. About two thousand pupils used to attend his lectures. In a letter to Phanias the Peripatetic, he speaks among other topics of a lecture as follows:

To get a public or even a select circle such as one desires is not easy. If an author reads his work, he must rewrite it. To shirk revision and ignore cirticism is a course which the present generation of pupils will no longer tolerate.

[1]*323* B.C.

And in this letter he also refers to someone as a "pedant."

Although his reputation was so great, Theophrastus, too, with all the other philosophers, had to leave the country for a short time. This was when Sophocles the son of Amphiclides proposed a law that on penalty of death no philosopher should preside over a school except by permission of the Senate and the people. The philosophers returned the next year, however, because Philo had prosecuted Sophocles for making an illegal proposal. The Athenians repealed the law, fined Sophocles five talents, and voted the recall of the philosophers, so Theophrastus also was able to return and live there as before. His original name was Tyrtamus; Aristotle renamed him Theophrastus because of his graceful style. Aristippus in the fourth book of his *On the Luxury of the Ancients* asserts that he was enamored of Aristotle's son Nicomachus, although he was his teacher. Aristotle is said to have applied to him and Callisthenes what Plato had said of Xenocrates and himself (as related earlier); namely, that the one needed a bridle and the other a goad, for Theophrastus was almost too clever in his interpretation of all his meanings, while the other was naturally backward. Theophrastus is said to have become the owner of a garden of his own after Aristotle's death through the good offices of his friend Demetrius of Phalerum.

There are aphorisms of his in circulation such as the following: "An unbridled horse ought to be trusted sooner than a badly ordered discourse." To someone who never opened his lips at a banquet, Theophrastus remarked: "Yours is a wise course for an ignoramus, but in an educated man it is sheer folly." He used to say that in one's budget the most expensive item is time.

Theophrastus died at the age of eighty-five, not long after he had relinquished his labors. My verses upon him are these:

> Not in vain was the word spoken to one of human kind, "Slacken the bow of wisdom and it breaks." Of a truth, so long as Theophrastus labored he was sound of limb, but when released from toil his limbs failed him and he died.

It is said that his disciples asked him if he had any last message for them, to which he replied:

> Nothing but this, that many of the pleasures which life boasts are but only apparent. When we are just beginning to live, behold we die. Nothing is so unprofitable as the love of glory. Farewell, and may you be happy. Either abandon my doctrine, which involves great effort, or excel as its worthy champions, for you will win great glory. Life holds more disappointment than advantage. But, as I can no longer discuss what we ought to do, do you go on with the inquiry into right conduct.

With these words, they say, he breathed his last. All the Athenians, out of respect for the man, accompanied his bier on foot. Favorinus says that as an old man he had to be carried about in a litter, and this he says on the authority of Hermippus, who had it from a remark of Arcesilaus of Pitane to Lacydes of Cyrene.

Theophrastus, too, has left a very large number of writings. I think it right to catalogue them because they abound in every kind of excellence. They are as follows:

Of Prior Analytics, three books
Of Posterior Analytics, seven books
On the Analysis of Syllogisms, one book
Epitome of Analytics, one book
Of Classified Topics, two books
Polemical Discussion on the Theory of Eristic Argument
Of the Senses, one book
A Reply to Anaxagoras, one book
On the Writings of Anaximenes, one book
On the Writings of Anaxagoras, one book
On the Writings of Archelaus, one book
Of Salt, Niter, and Alum, one book
Of Petrifactions, two books
On Indivisible Lines, one book
Of Lectures, two books
Of the Winds, one book
Characteristics of Virtues, one book
Of Kingship, one book

Of the Education of Kings, one book
Of Various Schemes of Life, three books
Of Old Age, one book
On the Astronomy of Democritus, one book
On Meteorology, one book
On Visual Images or Emanations, one book
On Flavors, Colors, and Flesh, one book
Of the Order of the World, one book
Of Mankind, one book
Compendium of the Writings of Diogenes, one book
Of Definitions, three books
Concerning Love, one book
Another Treatise on Love, one book
Of Happiness, one book
On Species or Forms, two books
On Epilepsy, one book
On Frenzy, one book
Concerning Empedocles, one book
Of Refutative Arguments, eighteen books
Polemical Objections, three books
Of the Voluntary, one book
Epitome of Plato's Republic, two books
On the Diversity of Sounds Uttered by Animals of the Same Species,
    one book
Of Sudden Appearances, one book
Of Animals Which Bite or Gore, one book
Of Animals Reputed To Be Spiteful, one book
Of the Animals Which Are Confined to Dry Land, one book
Of Those Which Change Their Colors, one book
Of Animals That Burrow, one book
Of Animals, seven books
Of Pleasures According to Aristotle, one book
Another Treatise on Pleasure, one book
Theses, twenty-four books
On Hot and Cold, one book
On Vertigo and Dizziness, one book
On Sweating Sickness, one book
On Affirmation and Negation, one book
Callisthenes, or On Bereavement, one book
On Fatigues, one book
On Motion, three books

On Precious Stones, one book
On Pestilences, one book
On Fainting, one book
Megarian Treatise, one book
Of Melancholy, one book
On Mines, two books
On Honey, one book
Compendium on the Doctrines of Metrodorus, one book
Of Meteorology, two books
On Intoxication, one book
Of Laws Distinguished by the Letters of the Alphabet, twenty-four
    books
Of an Epitome of Laws, ten books
Remarks upon Definitions, one book
On Smells, one book
On Wine and Oil
Introduction to Propositions, eighteen books
Of Legislators, three books
Of Politics, six books
A Political Treatise Dealing with Important Crises, four books
Of Social Customs, four books
Of the Best Constitution, one book
A Collection of Problems, five books
On Proverbs, one book
On Coagulation and Liquefaction, one book
On Fire, two books
On Winds, one book
Of Paralysis, one book
Of Suffocation, one book
Of Mental Derangement, one book
On the Passions, one book
On Symptoms, one book
Of Sophisms, two books
On the Solution of Syllogisms, one book
Of Topics, two books
Of Punishment, two books
On Hair, one book
Of Tyranny, one book
On Water, three books
On Sleep and Dreams, one book
Of Friendship, three books

Of Ambition, two books
On Nature, three books
On Physics, eighteen books
An Epitome of Physics, two books
Of Physics, eight books
A Reply to the Physical Philosophers, one book
Of Botanical Researches, ten books
Of Botanical Causes, eight books
On Juices, five books
Of False Pleasure, one book
One Dissertation on the Soul
On Unscientific Proofs, one book
On Simple Problems, one book
Harmonics, one book
Of Virtue, one book
Materials for Argument, or Contrarieties, one book
On Negation, one book
On Judgment, one book
Of the Ludicrous, one book
Afternoon Essays, two books
Divisions, two books
On Differences, one book
On Crimes, one book
On Calumny, one book
Of Praise, one book
Of Experience, one book
Of Letters , three books
On Animals Produced Spontaneously, one book
Of Secretion, one book
Panegyrics on the Gods, one book
On Festivals, one book
Of Good Fortune, one book
On Enthymemes, one book
Of Discoveries, two books
Lectures on Ethics, one book
Character Sketches, one book
On Tumult or Riot, one book
On Research, one book
On Judging of Syllogisms, one book
Of Flattery, one book
Of the Sea, one book

To Casander on Kingship, one book
Of Comedy, one book
(Of Meters, one book)
Of Diction, one book
A Compendium of Arguments, one book
Solutions, one book
On Music, three books
On Measures, one book
Megacles, one book
On Laws, one book
On Illegalities, one book
A Compendium of the Writings of Xenocrates, one book
Concerning Conversation, one book
On Taking an Oath, one book
Rhetorical Precepts, one book
Of Wealth, one book
On the Art of Poetry, one book
Problems in Politics, Ethics, Physics, and in the Art of Love, one
    book
Preludes, one book
A Collection of Problems, one book
On Physical Problems, one book
On Example, one book
On Introduction and Narrative, one book
Another Trace on the Art of Poetry, one book
Of the Wise, one book
On Consultation, one book
On Solecisms, one book
On the Art of Rhetoric, one book
The Special Commonplaces of the Treatises on Rhetoric, seventeen
    books
On Acting, one book
Lecture Notes of Aristotle or Theophrastus, six books
Of Physical Opinions, sixteen books
Epitome of Physical Opinions, one book
On Gratitude, one book
(Character Sketches, one book)
On Truth and Falsehood, one book
The History of Theological Inquiry, six books
Of the Gods, three books
Geometrical Researches, four books

Epitomes of Aristotle's work on Animals, six books
Of Refutative Arguments, two books
Theses, three books
Of Kingship, two books
Of Causes, one book
On Democritus, one book.
Of Becoming, one book
Of the Intelligence and Character of Animals, one book
On Motion, two books
On Vision, four books
Relating to Definitions, two books
On Data, one book
On Greater and Less, one book
On the Musicians, one book
Of the Happiness of the Gods, one book
A Reply to the Academics, one book
Exhortation to Philosophy, one book
How States Can Best Be Governed, one book
Lecture Notes, one book
On the Eruption in Sicily, one book
On Things Generally Admitted, one book
(On Problems in Physics, one book)
What Are the Methods of Attaining Knowledge, one book
On the Fallacy Known as the Liar, three books
Prolegomena to Topics, one book
Relating to Aeschylus, one book
Astronomical Research, six books
Arithmetical Researches on Growth, one book
Acicharus, one book
On Forensic Speeches, one book
(Of Calumny, one book)
Correspondence with Astycreon, Phanias, and Nicanor
Of Piety, one book
Evias, one book
On Times of Crisis, two books
On Relevant Arguments, one book
On the Education of Children, one book
Another Treatise with the Same Title, one book
Of Education or of the Virtues or of Temperance, one book
(An Exhortation of Philosophy, one book)
On Numbers, one book

Definitions Concerning the Diction of Syllogisms, one book
Of the Heavens, one book
Concerning Politics, two books
On Nature
On Fruits
On Animals

In all 232,808 lines. This concludes our consideration of his writings.

I have also come across Theophrastus's will, which reads as follows:

All will be well, but in case anything should happen, I make these dispositions. I give and bequeath all my property at home to Melantes and Pancreon, the sons of Leon. It is my wish that out of the trust funds at the disposal of Hipparchus the following appropriations should be made: First, they should be applied to finish the rebuilding of the museum with the statues of the goddesses, and to add any improvements which seem practicable to beautify them. Second, to replace in the temple the bust of Aristotle with the rest of the dedicated offerings which formerly were in the temple. Next, to rebuild the small enclosure adjoining the museum at least as handsomely as before, and to replace in the lower enclosure the tablets containing maps of the countries traversed by explorers. Further, to repair the altar so that it may be perfect and elegant. It is also my wish that the life-size statue of Nicomachus should be completed. The price agreed upon for the carving of the statue itself has been paid to Praxiteles, but the rest of the cost should be defrayed from the source mentioned above. The statue should be set up in whatever place seems desirable to the executors entrusted with carrying out my other wishes. Let all that concerns the temple and the offerings be arranged in this manner. The estate at Stagira belonging to me I give and bequeath to Callinus. The whole of my library I give to Neleus. The garden and the walk and the houses adjoining the garden, all and sundry, I give and bequeath to such of my friends hereinafter named as may wish to study literature and philosophy there in common, since it is not possible for all men to be always in residence, on condition that no one alienates the property or devotes it to his private use, but so that they hold it like a temple in joint possession and live, as is right and proper, on terms of familiarity and friendship. Let the community consist of Hipparchus, Neleus, Strato, Callinus, Demotimus, Demaratus, Callisthenes, Melantes, Pancreon, Nicippus. Aristotle, the son of Metrodorus and Pythias, also shall have the right to study and associate with them if he so desires. And the oldest of them shall pay every attention to him, in order to ensure for him the utmost proficiency in philosophy. Let me be buried in any spot in the garden which seems most suitable, without unnecessary outlay for my funeral or my monument. As previously agreed let the charge of attending, after my decease, to the temple and the monument and the garden and the walk be shared by Pompylus in person, living close by as he does and exercising the same supervision over all other matters as before, and by those who hold the property shall watch over his interests. Pompylus and Threpta have long been emancipated and have done me much service, and I think that two thousand drachmas certainly ought to belong to them from previous payments made to them by me, from their own earnings, and my present bequest to them to be paid by Hipparchus, as I stated many times in conversation with Melantes and Pancreon themselves, who agreed with me. I give and bequeath to them the maidservant Somatale. And of my slaves I at once emancipate Molon, Timon, and Parmeno; to Manes and Callias I give their freedom on condition that they stay four years in the garden and work there together and that their conduct is free from blame. Of my household furniture let so much as the executors think right be given to Pompylus and the rest be sold. I also give Carion to Demotimus, and Donax to Neleus. But Euboeus must be sold. Let Hipparchus pay to Callinus three thousand drachmas. And if I had not seen that Hipparchus had done great service to Melantes and Pancreon and formerly to me, and that now in his private affairs he has suffered disaster, I would have appointed him jointly with Melantes and Pancreon to carry out my wishes. Since I saw that it was not easy for them to share the management with him, and I thought it more advantageous for them to receive a fixed sum from Hipparchus, let Hipparchus pay Melantes and Pancreon one talent each and let Hipparchus provide funds for the executors to defray the expenses set down in the will, as each disbursement falls due. And when Hipparchus shall have carried out all these injunctions, he shall be released in full from his liabilities to me. Any advance that he has made in Chalcis in my name belongs to him alone. Let Hipparchus, Neleus, Strato, Callinus, Demotimus, Callisthenes, and Ctesarchus be executors to carry out the terms of the will. One copy of the will, sealed with the signet ring of Theophrastus, is deposited with Hegesias, the son of Hipparchus, the witnesses being Callippus of Pallene, Philomelus of Euonymaea, Lysandor of Hyba, and Philo of Alopece. Olympiodorus has another copy, the witnesses being the same. The third copy was received by Adeimantus, the bearer being Androsthenes Junior, and the witnesses are Arimnestus the son of Cleobulus, Lysistratus the son of Pheidon of Thasos, Strato the son of Arcesilaus of Lampsacus, Thesippus the son of Thesippus of Cerameis, and Dioscurides the son of Dionysius of Epicephisia.

So reads his will.

XXII

EPICURUS

341 - 270

Epicurus, son of Neocles and Chaerest-
rate, was a citizen of Athens of the deme Gargettus and, as
Metrodorus says in his book *On Noble Birth,* of the family of the
Philaidae. Heraclides[1] in his *Epitome of Sotion,* and other authorities as well, say Epicurus was brought up at Samos after the
Athenians had colonized that place and came to Athens when
he was eighteen years of age at the time when Xenocrates was
lecturing at the Academy and Aristotle in Chalcis. When Alexander of Macedon died and the Athenian settlers were ejected
from Samos by Perdiccas, Epicurus left Athens and joined his
father in Colophon. He remained there for a time and attracted some disciples, but he returned to Athens during the
archonship of Anaxicrates.[2]

Epicurus first pursued his studies with the other philosophers, but later he advanced his own views and established the
school that is named for him. He relates that his first contact
with philosophy came when he was fourteen years of age.
Apollodorus the Epicurean in the first book of his *Life of
Epicurus* says that Epicurus took up philosophy when dis-
gruntled because the schoolmasters could not explain the
meaning of "chaos" in Hesiod to him. Hermippus, however,
says that he began as a schoolmaster and was drawn to philoso-

[1]*Heraclides Lembos.*
[2]*307-306* B.C.

phy by the works of Democritus. This fact establishes the point of the allusion in the lines of Timon:

> Again there is the latest and most shameless of the physicists, the schoolmaster's son from Samos, himself the most uneducated of mortals.

According to Philodemus the Epicurean, in the tenth book of his extensive work, *On Philosophers,* Epicurus's three brothers, Neocles, Chaeredemus, and Aristobulus, joined in his studies, as his slave Mys did also, as Nuronianus in his *Historical Parallels* relates.

Diotimus the Stoic, an enemy of Epicurus, bitterly calumniates him, citing fifty scandalous letters that he claimed Epicurus had written. The writer who assigned to Epicurus the epistles that others ordinarily say are Chrysippus's also attacks him, as well as Nicolaus and Sotion, Posidonius the Stoic and his disciples in the twelfth book of his twenty-four-book work, *Dioclean Refutations,* follow them as does Dionysius of Halicarnassus. They claim he went with his mother from house to house, reading fortunes and helped his father in his school for a very small compensation. They also say that one of his brothers was a pimp and lived with Leontion the courtesan, and that he taught as his own the Democritian doctrines about atoms and those of Aristippus about pleasure. Timocrates and Herodotus, in a book *On the Training of Epicurus as a Cadet,* say that Epicurus was not really an Athenian citizen and others say he grossly flattered Mithras, the minister of Lysimachus, referring to him in his letters by Apollo's titles, "Healer" and "Lord." Others say Epicurus praised and flattered Idomeneus, Herodotus, and Timocrates because they had spread abroad his secret doctrines. In letters to Leontion, Epicurus addressed her: "O Lord Apollo, my dear little Leontion, with what thunderous applause we were moved while reading your letter." To Themista, the wife of Leonteus, he wrote: "If you do not come to see me I am prepared to spin three times on my own axis and be propelled to any place that you indicate." To the beautiful Pythocles he writes: "I will sit here and wait for your divine coming, my heart's desire." Theodorus says in the fourth book of his work, *Against Epicurus,* that in another letter to Themista he preaches to her. He is charged with corresponding with many courtesans, especially with Leontion, whom Metrodorus also loved. In his treatise *On the Ethical End* he writes in these terms: "I know not how to conceive the good, apart from the pleasures of taste, sexual pleasures, the pleasures of sound, and the pleasures of beautiful form." Again in his letter to Pythocles: "Loose all sail, my dear boy, and steer clear of all culture." Epictetus calls him a preacher of effeminacy and pours calumnies out on him.

Timocrates, the brother of Metrodorus, was a disciple of Epicurus at first but later left the school. In the book called *Amusement* he claims that Epicurus regurgitated twice a day from overindulging, and that he personally had great difficulty escaping from those notorious midnight philosophy sessions, as well as from the brotherhood, with all its secrets. Epicurus's acquaintance with philosophy, these calumniators claim, was slight, his acquaintance with life slighter still, and his bodily health deplorable. For many years he was unable to rise from his chair, and spent a whole mina daily on his table, as he himself confesses in his letter to Leontion and in another to the philosophers at Mitylene. Timocrates also alleges that Epicurus in his thirty-seven books *On Nature* frequently repeats himself and for the most part engages in polemic, especially against Nausiphanes. These are Timocrates's own words: "Pay no attention; for, he too, when struggling to bring forth an idea, was casually boastful, like the Sophists and many other servile creatures." In his letters, Epicurus says of Nausiphanes: "This infuriated him to the point that he abused me and called me a pedagogue." Epicurus used to call Nausiphanes a jellyfish, an illiterate, a fraud. He called Plato's school "the toadies of Dionysius," their master the "golden" Plato, and Aristotle a profligate who became a soldier and a drug-peddler after dissipating his inheritance. He called Protagoras a porter, the amanuensis of Democritus, and a village schoolmaster; Heraclitus, a muddler; Democritus, Derocritus (the idle-gossip); Antidorus, Sannidorus (servile gift-giver); the Cynics, foes of

Greece; the Dialecticians, robbers; and Pyrrho, an ignorant peasant.

These critics are clearly out of their minds. There are many witnesses who testify to our philosopher's goodwill to all men and to his native country, which honored him with statues in bronze. His friends were so numerous that they could be counted by cities and still fall short, and indeed all who knew him were made loyal by the siren-like attraction of his opinions—all, except Metrodorus of Stratonicea, who attached himself to Carneades, perhaps in reaction to his master's very goodness. The school itself is loyal, for it continues uninterruptedly under the direction of a numberless succession of scholarchs, while almost all others have died out. His piety toward his parents, his generosity to his brothers, his graciousness to his servants, as the terms of his will show, and his benevolence to all mankind, provide more proof. No words can tell his reverence toward the gods and his devotion to his country. He so deferred to others that he would not enter public life. He passed his entire life in Greece in spite of the disasters which befell it in that time; he left only once or twice to visit his friends in Ionia. Friends sought him out from all quarters and stayed with him in his garden. Apollodorus states this and also notes that Epicurus bought the garden for eighty minas. Diocles in the third book of his *Epitome* speaks of these people as living a very simple, frugal life together; they were content with half a pint of thin wine and were, for the most part, thorough-going water drinkers. He reports that Epicurus did not approve of their property being held in common, as the maxim of Pythagoras about the goods of friends required. He considered that such a practice implied distrust, and without trust no friendship can exist. In his letters he tells his correspondents that he was satisfied with plain bread and water, and again: "Send me a little pot of cheese, that, when I fancy, I may dine luxuriously." This was the man who held that pleasure was the end or purpose of life! Athenaeus praises him in the following epigram:

Ye toil, O men, for paltry things and incessantly begin strife and war for gain; but nature's wealth extends to a moderate bound, whereas vain judgments have a limitless range. This message Neocles's wise son heard from the Muses or from the sacred tripod at Delphi.

As we proceed, we will know this even better from his doctrines and sayings.

Epicurus's favorite among the early philosophers, Diocles reports, was Anaxagoras, though he disagreed with him on occasion, and Archelaus, who had taught Socrates. Diocles also reports that he exercised his friends by asking them to commit his treatises to memory.

Apollodorus in his *Chronology* says that Epicurus was a pupil of Nausiphanes and Praxiphanes, but Epicurus in a letter to Eurylochus denies this and claims that he was self-taught. Both Epicurus and Hermarchus deny that Leucippus the philosopher ever existed, though others, including Apollodorus the Epicurean, say that he had been the teacher of Democritus. Demetrius the Magnesian says that Epicurus also attended the lectures of Xenocrates.

The terms he used for things were ordinary terms, and Aristophanes the grammarian gives him credit for a very personal style. As a writer, Epicurus so prized clarity that, in his work *On Rhetoric,* he makes clearness the only requisite. And in his correspondence he replaces the usual greeting, "I wish you joy," with wishes for welfare and right living: "May you do well," and, "Live well."

Ariston in his *Life of Epicurus* says that Epicurus took his work entitled *The Canon* from the *Tripod* of Nausiphanes, adding that Epicurus had been a pupil of this man as well as of the Platonist Pamphilus in Samos. Ariston adds that Epicurus began the study of philosophy when he was twelve years old and founded his own school at the age of thirty-two.

Epicurus was born, according to Apollodorus in his *Chronology,* in the third year of the 109th Olympiad, in the archonship of Sosigenes, on the seventh day of the month Gamelion, in the seventh year after the death of Plato.[3] When he was thirty-two, he founded a school of philosophy, in Mitylene and Lam-

---

[3]*All this comes to 341* B.C. *Plato died in 347* B.C.

psacus, which he later, after some five years, moved to Athens. He died there in the second year of the 127th Olympiad,[4] in the archonship of Pytharatus, at the age of seventy-two. Hermarchus the son of Agemortus, a Mitylenaean, took over the school. Epicurus died of kidney stones after an illness that lasted two weeks, as Hermarchus says in his letters. Hermippus also says that he seated himself in a bronze bathtub of lukewarm water, requested unmixed wine, which he drank, and bidding his friends remember his teachings, passed away.

Here are some lines which I composed about him:

> *Farewell, my friends; the truths I*
> *taught hold fast:*
> *Thus Epicurus spake, and breathed his last.*
> *He sat in a warm bath and neat wine quaff'd,*
> *And straightway found chill death in that*
> *same draught.*

Such was the life of the sage and such his end.

Epicurus was a most prolific author and outdid all his predecessors in the quantity of his writings, which number three hundred and contain no quotations from other authors.

I will present the opinions contained in these works by citing three of his letters in which he had given a synopsis of his entire system. I will also quote his *Sovereign Maxims* and any other of his writings that seems worth citing, so that you may view his thought from all aspects and judge him accordingly.

The first letter is addressed to Herodotus and deals with physics; the second to Pythocles and deals with astronomy or meteorology; the third is addressed to Menoeceus and treats of human life. We may begin with the first after considering in general his division of philosophy.

Philosophy is divided into three parts: *Canonic, Physics, Ethics.* Canonic is the introduction to the system and is contained in a single work called *The Canon.* The physical part that embraces the entire theory of Nature is contained in the thirty-seven books *Of Nature* and, in summary form, in the letters. The ethical part deals with choice and rejection and is to be found in the books *On Human Life,* in the letters, and in the essay *Of the End.* The usual procedure is to associate canonic with physics; then canonic is described as the normative science that investigates the first principle, or the fundamental principles of philosophy, while physics concerns generation and corruption within nature. Ethics, finally, concerns the things that ought to be desired or avoided in human life and its supreme end or good.

Epicureans consider dialectic superfluous; in their investigations, physicists should be satisfied with ordinary language. In *The Canon,* Epicurus asserts that our sensations, preconceptions, and feelings are the standards of truth. The Epicureans generally accept perceptions of mental presentations as standards, too. Epicurus's own statements are to be found in the *Summary* addressed to Herodotus and in the *Sovereign Maxims.* Every sensation, he says, is alike without reason or memory, for it is not self-caused nor, if it be thought of as having an external cause, can it be conceived as adding to or subtracting from anything from that cause. Sensations are infallible; there is nothing which can refute them or prove them in error. One sensation cannot refute another similar sensation, for they are equally valid. Nor can one sensation refute another sensation that is not similar to it, but heterogeneous, for the objects that the two senses judge are not the same. Neither can reason refute them, for reason is wholly dependent on sensation; nor can one sense refute another, for we respond equally to all the senses. The reality of separate perceptions is warrant for the truth of our senses. Seeing and hearing are just as real as the sense of pain. Therefore, when we draw inferences about what lies beyond the senses, we must start from the plain "given of sense." All our ideas are derived from perceptions, either by direct contact, analogy, resemblance, or composition, or with some help from reasoning. The objects presented to the deranged and in dreams are true, because they produce effects—that is, movements in the mind—and the unreal never achieves such effects.

Epicureans mean by preconception an apprehension, correct opinion, notion, or universal idea stored in the mind, that is, a recollection of an external object often presented. For example, we say, "Such and such a thing is a man," because as soon as the word "man" is spoken, we think of his form by an act of preconception, in which the senses guide us. Therefore, the primary *denotatum* of every term is what is clear and distinct. No inquiry would ever be initiated did we not already know what it was we sought. For example, the object over there is a horse or a cow, let us say. Before such a judgment can be made, we must at some time or other have known by preconception the form of a horse or a cow. We could never have named anything if we had not previously learned its form by preconception. Preconceptions, therefore, are clear. The object of a judgment is derived from a notion previously grasped as clear; by reference to it we form the statement, for example, "How do we know that this is a man?"

Opinion is called conception or assumption; it may be true or false. It is true if it is later confirmed or if evidence does not contradict it. It is false if it is not confirmed later or is contradicted by the evidence. This is why they bring in the phrase, "What awaits confirmation."

There are two states of feeling, pleasure and pain. These arise in every animate being. The one, pleasure, benefits, the other, pain, is harmful to, the being in which it arises. Choice and rejection are determined, according to pleasure and pain. There are two kinds of inquiry, the one concerned with things, the other with words only.

Concerning the conduct of life, the things to be avoided and those to be sought, Epicurus's teachings are the following. We will preface his own words with a summary of his view and of that of his school on the character of the sage, or wise man.

Men are led to do injury to others by three passions: hatred, envy, and contempt. The wise man overcomes these passions by reason. The man established in wisdom never reverts to these motives, not even in appearance, so far as he can help it. Not that he will not feel passion; indeed he may be more sensitive than others. Not every bodily constitution nor every cultural origin permits a man to be wise. Though tortured on the rack, the wise man is still happy. Only the wise man feels gratitude toward friends, whether they be present or absent, and he shows it in speech and in action. When being tortured, he will cry out and groan. Where women are concerned, he will obey the requirements, as Diogenes says in his epitome of Epicurus's ethical doctrines of the law. He will not punish his servants; he will have compassion on them and recognize the merit of those of good character. The Epicureans do not think the sage should fall in love. Burial rites should not concern him, either. As Diogenes teaches in his twelfth book, Epicureans are suspicious of the view that love comes by divine inspiration. The wise man will not indulge in fine speeches. Sexual indulgence never has improved any man, and he should consider himself fortunate if he does not suffer harm as a result of it.

The sage will not marry and rear a family. Epicurus counsels against it in the *Problems* and in the *On Nature*. Under special circumstances of life, he may marry. Some wise men will also wander from the goal of wisdom, Epicurus says in the *Symposium*. The wise man will not slobber when in his cups. He will not be active in politics, according to the first books of *On Life*. He will not become a tyrant, turn Cynic (according to the second book of *On Life*). Finally, he will not beg. Even should he lose his sight, he will not withdraw from life, the same book tells us this. The wise man will feel sorrow, according to Diogenes in the fifth book of his *Epilecta*. He will take matters to court. He will leave written words, but he will not write panegyrics. He will take care of his property and be concerned for the future. He will love his country. He will be fortified against all vicissitudes of fortune and will never abandon a friend. He will have enough concern for his good repute, so that no one will be disdainful more toward him than toward others. He will take pleasure in common feasts of worship.

The wise will set up images to the gods. Personal wealth will not be a matter of great concern. He will converse well about music and poetry but will not himself write or compose. The wise man will make money, but only through his wisdom, if he be in straits. If necessary, he will even court a prince. He will exhibit gratitude for correction or counsel. He will establish a school, but not one that will attract an undiscriminating crowd. He will give public lectures, but only when invited. He will commit himself to substantive propositions and not remain a mere skeptic. He will be consistent with himself even when asleep. If need be, he will lay down his life for a friend.

The Epicurean school holds that sins are not all equal. It holds that health is in some cases a good, in others a matter of indifference; that courage is not a natural disposition but is learned by estimation of what is needed in different situations; and that in friendship we are drawn to those who meet our needs. One party must, however, make the first gesture (as a seed must be planted in the earth), but the friendship is maintained thereafter through mutual sharing of life's pleasures.

There are two kinds of happiness: the one is the highest possible, such as the gods enjoy, and this cannot be increased; the other is subject to increase and diminution.

Having noted these summary points we may now proceed to his letter.[5]

Epicurus to Menoeceus, greeting.
A man should not be slow in pursuing wisdom when he is young, nor grow weary of the quest when he is old. No age is too early nor any too late to seek the health of the soul. To say that the time for seeking wisdom is not yet, or that it has passed and fled is the same as to say that the time for happiness is not yet or that it is no more. Young and old alike, therefore, ought to seek wisdom: the young so that, while young, he may be like the old, free of fear of the things to come; the old so that, as age creeps over him, he may still be young at heart. We must practice the things that bring happiness; for, if we have happiness, we have everything else. And if we lack it, all our actions can have but the single end of attaining it.

Practice the things of which I have spoken to you ceaselessly and exercise yourself in them, considering them the fundamentals of right living. First, believe that God is a living being, blessed and immortal, as the common understanding of mankind holds God to be. Since you believe that he is such, say nothing of him that offends

[5]The third of the three mentioned above.

his immortality or does not concord with his blessedness; rather, believe of him everything that sustains both his blessedness and his immortality. For gods do exist and the evidence for them is manifest. They are not, however, such as the vulgar think them, for men are not constant in the ideas they have of the gods. The really impious man is not the one who rejects the gods that are worshiped by the vulgar, but the man who acquiesces to those gods. The beliefs of the many concerning the gods are not true preconceptions[6] but false assumptions. As a consequence, the greatest evils befall the wicked and the greatest blessings the good from the hand of the gods, because they are always partial to their own good characteristics, taking pleasure in men who are like themselves, but rejecting as alien whatever is not like them.

Form the habit of believing that death is nothing for us. Good and evil imply sensitivity while death is the deprivation of all sentience. To judge rightly, therefore—that death is nothing to us—heightens our pleasure in mortal existence, not by distending life over an immeasurable time, but by stilling the longing for immortality. Life holds no fears for one who has come to understand clearly that the cessation of life holds no terrors. That man is a fool who protests that he fears death, not because it will be painful when it comes, but because the prospect of it engenders pain. When a thing causes no pain by its presence, it can engender only groundless distress in the expectation of it. Death, therefore, the most fearsome of ills, is nothing to us; for, when we are, death is not, and when death comes, we are not. It is nothing, therefore, either to the living or to the dead, because it is not with the living and the dead are no longer. In the world, men at one time flee death as the greatest of all evils, while at another time they choose it as a respite from the ills of life. The wise man neither minimizes life nor fears its end. The thought of living is no burden to him, nor is the end of life considered an evil. Just as men who are dining do not select merely the larger portion, but rather the more pleasant, so the wise man tries to enjoy the time that is most pleasant and not that that is merely longest. The teacher who counsels the young to live well while advising the old to make a good end speaks without wisdom, not only because life is desirable, but because the same path of life teaches us to live well and to die well. Even worse is the man who says that it were better not to have been born, but that, once born, it is best to pass as swiftly as possible through the gates of Hades. If he

---

[6]*Preconceptions in the Epicurean sense explained above.*

really believes this, why does he not depart this life? If his conviction were really well established, this would not be difficult for him to do. If he says these words in jest, the words are foolishness, and those who hear do not believe him.

We must recall that the future is neither entirely in our hands nor entirely out of them. Therefore, we must not count on it as sure, nor despair of it as completely uncertain.

We must also consider that of our desires some are natural while others are foolish. Of those which are natural, moreover, some are necessary *and* natural, some only natural. Of those that are necessary, some are necessary if we are to be happy, some if the body is to be free of distress, some to life itself. One who understands all these things clearly will direct his choice and aversion to health of body and peace of mind, for these, in the end, are the sum and substance of the blessed life.

The end of all our actions is to free us from pain and fear. Once we have secured this, the storm of the soul is stilled. The living creature does not then need to go seeking something that it feels is lacking, nor to look for anything else to fulfill the good of the soul and of the body. Only when we feel pain at the absence of pleasure do we feel the necessity of seeking pleasure. That is why we call pleasure the beginning and the end of a blessed life. Pleasure is our first good, that most akin to our nature. It is the starting point of every choice and of every rejections, and we always return to it, since we make feeling the rule by which we judge the goodness of everything else.

Since pleasure is our first good, that closest to our nature, we do not take every pleasure indiscriminately. Frequently, we pass over many pleasures when they promise to bring a greater displeasure in their train. Frequently, we consider pains better than pleasures when endurance of such pains for a long time brings us, as a consequence, greater pleasure. While all pleasure is good because it is natural to us, not every pleasure is worth choosing; likewise, though all pain is evil, still not all pain is to be avoided. By measuring one against the other, and by considering the conveniences and inconveniences, these matters are all to be judged. At times we treat the good as an evil, and the evil as a good. Independence of external goods is considered a great good, not in the sense that we use little in every instance, but in the sense that we are contended with little if we do not have much, truly convinced that those who do not crave luxury enjoy it most and that what is according to nature is easily secured while what is worthless and useless is hard to win. Plain food gives as much pleasure as rich diet, once the pangs of hunger have been stilled; bread and water give the most intense pleasure when they touch hungry lips. Simple and inexpensive diet supplies all that is needful for health and enables a man to meet the inevitable demands of life without drawing back. Moreover, it enables us to get more enjoyment out of costly fare on occasion, and it frees us of concern as to what fortune may bring.

When we say that pleasure is the end and goal, we do not intend the profligate pleasures or sensual pleasures, as some people, by reason of ignorance, prejudice, or deliberate misrepresentation, claim we do. We mean by pleasure the absence of bodily pain and inquietude of soul. Pleasure is not an endless series of drunken carousels and gaiety: it is not sexual indulgence and enjoyment of fish and the other varieties of a gourmet table that makes life pleasureful. Rather it is sober thought and reflection, inquiry into the reasonable bases of every choice, eliminating those opinions that bring the greatest agitation to the soul. Prudence therefore is the point of departure and greatest good. Prudence is more precious than philosophy, for it is the soil of all other virtues. Prudence teaches that the life of pleasure cannot be attained save by prudence, honor, and justice; nor, on the other hand, can a life of prudence, honor, and justice lead to anything save a life of pleasure. All the virtues conspire to form the pleasant life, and a pleasant life cannot be separated from them.

Who, then, do you think, is superior to a man of this kind? His belief about the gods is pious and completely free from the fear of death. He has earnestly meditated the end established by nature, and perceives what goods can quickly and easily reach their limit and that the duration and the intensity of evils alike are of little measure. He scorns the notion of fate that pretends sovereignty over all events and sees rather that some things come about of necessity, others by chance, others through our own action. Necessity, he perceives, destroys responsibility, while chance or fortune is unstable. Our own actions, however, are free, and to them praise and blame accrue. Better, to accede to the myths about the gods than to submit to fate's yoke with which the philosophers of nature burden man. Those myths at least offer a hope that if we pay homage to the gods, we may escape, but the necessity of those philosophers of nature is deaf to all pleas. This man[7] does not think that chance is a god, as the world does, for the actions of a god exhibit no disorder; nor does he believe that chance is a cause, even an uncertain one, for he believes that no good that the dispensation of good and evil, which determines whether a life be blessed, is not one of chance, though the starting point of great good and great evil may be chance. He esteems that the ill fortune of the wise is better than the good fortune of the fool. An action based on sound judgment should not owe its fortunate outcome to chance.

Practice these precepts day and night both in private and in the company of him who shares your view; you will then never be troubled, whether waking or dreaming, but will live like a god among men. Man loses all traces of mortality when he lives among immortal blessings.

Elsewhere in the short epitome, Epicurus rejects divination in whatever form, saying "There is in fact no means of fore-telling the future. Even if there were, we ought not to consider what occurs on its basis as having anything to do with us."

These are Epicurus's views on life and conduct, and he has discoursed upon them at greater length elsewhere.

Epicurus's position on pleasure differs from that of the Cyre-naics. They include under the term, not the pleasure that consists in rest, but only that which consists in motion. Epicurus recognizes both: pleasure of mind as well as of the body, as he states in his work "On Choice and Rejection" in *On the Ethical End,* in the first book of his work *On Human Life,* and in the epistle to his philosopher friends in Mitylene. This is also true of Diogenes in the seventeenth book of his *Epilecta* and of Metrodorus in his *Timocrates.* The latter's words are: "Pleasure is understood to have two species, one consisting in rest the other in motion." The words of Epicurus in his work *On Choice* are: "Peace of mind and freedom from pain are pleasures that involve a state of rest; joy and delight consist in motion and activity."

A further point of difference with the Cyrenaics concerns their opinion that bodily pains are worse than mental pains; at

[7]*The prudent man.*

least, bodily pain is inflicted on evildoers. Epicurus holds, rather, that mental pains are worse; the flesh suffers the distresses only of the present while the mind suffers those of the past and future as well. Analogously, he holds that mental pleasures are greater than bodily pleasures. To prove that pleasure is the end, he recalls the fact that as soon as living things are born, they exhibit satisfaction with pleasure and aversion to pain, simply on the basis of nature, with no intervention of reason. Left to our own reactions, we shun pain; even Heracles, consumed by the poisoned robe, cries aloud,

> *And bites and yells, and rock to rock resounds,*
> *Headlands of Locris and Euboean cliffs.*[8]

Moreover, we cultivate the virtues because of the pleasure that attends them and not for their own sake, just as we take medicine for the sake of health. Diogenes in the twentieth book of his *Epilecta* says the same thing, and he also calls education recreation. Epicurus describes virtue as the indispensable condition of pleasure, that is, the one thing without which pleasure cannot be. Everything else, for example, food, is separable from pleasure, in the sense that pleasure can exist without it.

I may conclude my work and the account of this philosopher's life by citing his *Sovereign Maxims:*[9]

1. A blessed and eternal being knows no inquietude himself and brings no disturbance to anyone else; therefore, he knows movements neither of anger nor of partiality, for all such movement points to weakness.
2. Death is nothing. When the body has been resolved into its elements, it has no feeling, and what has no feeling is nothing to us.
3. The quantity of pleasure reaches its limit when all pain is removed. So long as pleasure is present, and is not interrupted, neither the body nor the mind nor both together experience pain.

---

[8]*Sophocles*, Tract, 787.

[9]*A collection of forty of the most important items in the Epicurean creed, drawn from many of Epicurus's voluminous and numerous writings. The collection is doubtless by one or a number of ardent disciples.*

4. Continuous pain does not endure long in the flesh. If extreme, pain persists a very short time, and even that degree of pain that borders closely on pleasure in the flesh does not last long. Illnesses that endure a long time are even compatible with greater bodily pleasure than pain.

5. A pleasant life is impossible without living wisely, well, and justly, and it is impossible to live wisely, justly, and well without, as a consequence, living pleasantly. If any one of these is lacking, when, for example, a man does not live wisely, though he lives well and justly, he cannot live a pleasant life.

6. Any means of obtaining security from other men is a good according to nature.

7. Some men have tried to make themselves secure from other men by becoming famous and illustrious. If their lives really became secure, they attained natural good; if, however, they were insecure, they have not attained the end that they originally sought under nature's own urging.

8. No pleasure is in itself evil, but the things that produce certain pleasures involve inconveniences much greater than the pleasures they procure.

9. If all pleasure could be accumulated—not only in time, but throughout the body, or, at least over the main elements of man's nature—there would be no difference between one pleasure and another. In fact, however, there is.

10. If the things in which sensualists find pleasure truly delivered them from the terrors of the mind—I mean fear of natural phenomena, of pain, of death—if these things instructed them to set bounds to their desires, we should find no reason to censure such people; for then clearly, they would abound in pleasure of all kinds and on every hand and would be free of pain, both of body and of mind—from all evil therefore.

11. If the phenomena of the air and the heavens never alarmed us, nor death awakened in us serious affright lest it hold some dread change for us, nor the unlimited excess of pain and desire tormented us, there would be no need to study nature.

12. Fear of things of greatest import to man cannot be put to flight unless man knows nature as a whole. Therefore, only the study of nature ensures the enjoyment of pure pleasures. Otherwise, he lives in dread of what the myths recount.

13. What would be the point in protecting ourselves against our fellowmen if we continued to be affrighted by what transpires above

our heads or beneath the earth or, in general, in the limitless universe?

14. When reasonable security against other men has been established, the power to repel and abundance of material good afford the basis for the genuine calm of a private life apart from the crowds.

15. The wealth of nature is at once of easy access and of limited supply, but fancy beguiles us with a vague wealth receding to a boundless distance.

16. Fortune seldom intrudes upon the wise man. His greatest and highest interests are directed by reason throughout the course of his life.

17. The just man enjoys the greatest peace of mind; the unjust is prey to all apprehension.

18. Bodily pleasure reaches its maximum once the pain of want has been relieved; thereafter, it can only be varied. The pleasure in the mind, by contrast, reaches its limit only when we contemplate things in themselves and the conjunctions that awaken greatest affright.

19. If the bounds of pleasure are measured by reason, length of time, short or long, affords equal satisfaction.

20. The body is receptive of pleasure, which is limited, as though it were unlimited, and unlimited pleasure requires limitless time. The mind, however, in thought perceives the end and limit of the body. Exorcising, therefore, the terrors of the future, it brings about a full and perfect life (in the present) and has no longer any need of limitless time. This does not mean, however, that it spurns pleasure; at the very moment of death, when fortune determines that it must leave this life, the mind still takes pleasure in the highest life.

21. The man who perceives the limits of life also perceives enough to ease the pain of want and make the whole of life full and complete. Therefore, he no longer feels the need of things that are to be secured only at the cost of strife and effort.

22. To determine the end (of life) we must accept all that is and submit to the clear testimony of our senses, to which all our opinions must conform. On any other condition, uncertainty and confusion will be supreme.

23. Opposing the senses, you will have no norm of reference, and no means of judging, not even of judging those statements that seem to you false.

24. If any single sensation is rejected unconditionally without con-

cern for the distinction between matter of opinion and that which is already present, either in sensation or in feelings or in any representational perception of the mind, all sensations will be plunged into confusion by your unfounded belief and every standard of truth will be repudiated. If, on the basis of opinion, you precipitously affirm as true what needs to be confirmed, failing to distinguish it from what does not need to be confirmed, you will surely fall into error and perpetuate complete ambiguity in all judgments of right and wrong.

25. Unless you refer all your actions on each and every occasion to the end prescribed by nature, and instead, in choosing, are deflected to some other end, your actions will not conform to your theories.

26. All desires are unnecessary if they induce no pain when permitted to go unsatisfied, if the longing they excite is readily dismissed, if the object of the desire is difficult to secure, or, finally, if its satisfaction promises to bring harm.

27. Friendship is the most important of all the means counseled by wisdom for securing happiness.

28. The belief that assures us that no object of our fear is eternal, or long endures, also assures us that even in the limited conditions of our existence nothing gives us so much security as friendship.

29. Some of the desires we have are natural and necessary; others are natural, but not necessary; others are neither natural nor necessary, but are due to illusory opinion.

30. Natural desires that bring no pain when not satisfied, though we seek their objects ardently, also spring from illusory opinion. When we do not free ourselves from them, this is due not to their being natural but to man's illusory opinion.

31. Natural justice expresses the need that one man not harm or be harmed by another.

32. Animals that are incapable of making agreements, or of inflicting or suffering pain on or from each other, know neither justice nor injustice. Tribes that either will not or would not form mutual agreements to the same purpose are in a similar situation.

33. Absolute justice has never existed; there have existed only reciprocal agreements, at different times and in different places, that provide against the infliction or the suffering of harm.

34. Injustice is not an evil in itself, but only because of its consequence, namely, the fear lest the injustice may be discovered by those whose office it is to punish offenses.

35. No man who, in secret, violates an injunction of the social agreement can be sure that he will not be discovered, though he

may have escaped detection innumerable times previously. To the very end of his life he cannot be sure he will not be discovered.

36. Justice as a general notion is the same for all; that is, it is that which is necessary in order to make social exchange possible. Its meaning in particular cases, under differing circumstances of time and places, varies.

37. Conventional law calls just whatever is expedient for social intercourse, whether or not it is identical for all. When a law, though duly passed, does not prove conformable to the demands of such intercourse, it is no longer considered just when the need recognized by the law changes, so that it corresponds only for the time being with an earlier notion—though for that time the law was just. Thus it is, if we look at facts and do not waste time on idle words.

38. When, despite no alteration in conditions, the conventional laws, judged by their consequences, prove not to conform to the concept of justice, those laws must be considered not to have been really just. When the laws prove no longer expedient, because conditions have changed, still they must be considered to have been just for the time during which they were expedient, and to have ceased being just when they ceased to be expedient.

39. The man who best understood how to overcome the fear of an external enemy formed a family of all the creatures he could bring together. Those he could not so gather, he still did not treat as aliens. When he found even this to be impossible, he avoided contact and kept them at a distance as best he could.

40. The men who could best protect themselves against those around them, supported by this sure warrant of safety, experienced the most acceptable life with each other. So complete was their enjoyment of this close society that though one of them died before his time, still those who survived did not mourn his death as though it were a sad event.

XXIII
ZENO

Zeno, son of Mnaseas of Demeas, was a native of Citium in Cyprus, a Greek city in which Phoenicians had settled. Timotheus of Athens in his book *On Lives* says that Zeno had a twisted neck. Apollonius of Tyre adds that he was slender, moderately tall, and dark-complexioned; for this reason, Chrysippus relates in the first book of his *Proverbs* that Zeno was called an Egyptian. He had heavy legs and was stout and sensitive. For this reason Persaeus in his *Convivial Reminiscences* claims that he refused many invitations to dine. Zeno liked to eat green figs and to lie in the sun.

As noted earlier, he was a pupil of Crates. Later, as Timocrates says in his *Dion,* he followed the lectures of Stilpo and Xenocrates for ten years, and of Polemos as well. Hecato and Apollonius of Tyre, in his first book on Zeno, relate that Zeno consulted the oracle to learn what he ought to do to achieve the best life, and that the god replied that he should take on the same aspect as the dead. He understood this to mean that he should study the ancient writers.

The following is the manner in which Zeno met Crates. On a voyage from Phoenicia to Piraeus with a cargo of dyestuff, he was shipwrecked. At that time he was thirty years old. He made his way to Athens and entered a bookshop. He was so enthralled by the second book of Xenophon's *Memorabilia* that he inquired where men such as Socrates might be found. At that moment Crates chanced opportunely to pass by, and the bookseller pointed to him and said, "Follow that man." From that day Zeno became Crates's pupil, exhibiting in other ways as well a strong talent for philosophy. He was, however, too modest by nature to take up the Cynic's attitude of disdain for the niceties. Crates considered this a defect and wanted to correct it, so he gave Zeno a potful of lentil soup to carry through the Ceramicus. When he saw that Zeno was ashamed and was trying to hide the pot, Crates broke it with a blow of his stick. As Zeno ran off with the lentil soup flowing down his legs, Crates cried out, "Why are you running away, my little Phoenician? Nothing terrible has happened to you."

For some time he was under Crates's tutelage, and during this period wrote his *Republic*. This called forth the jesting remark that he had written it on Cynosura, that is, the dog's tail. In addition to the *Republic* he wrote the following works:

Of Life According to Nature
Of Impulse, or Human Nature
Of Emotions
Of Duty
Of Law
Of Greek Education
Of Vision
Of the Whole World
Of Signs
Pythagorean Questions
Universals
Of Varieties of Style
Homeric Problems, in five books
Of the Reading of Poetry

There are also his:

A Handbook of Rhetoric
Solutions
Of Refutations, two books
Recollections of Crates
Ethics

Zeno parted from Crates and for twenty years studied with the other teachers mentioned above. For this reason, he is supposed to have said, "When I suffered shipwreck I made a prosperous voyage." Others, however, say he said this while studying under Crates. A different version of this story is that while already in Athens, he heard his ship was wrecked and said, "You have done well, Fortune, thus to drive me to philosophy in this way." It is also claimed that he sold his cargo in Athens before he devoted himself to philosophy.

It was Zeno's custom to discourse while pacing up and down in the painted arcade, which is called the arcade (stoa) of Pisianax, and which was named for the painting of Polygnotus. His purpose was to keep the area free of a crowd of loiterers. On this spot, in the time of the Thirty, fourteen hundred Athenian citizens had been put to death. People came to hear Zeno and for this reason were known as men of the stoa, or Stoics. The same name was given to his followers, who formerly had been known as Zenonians. Epicurus states this in his letters. Eratosthenes in his eighth book *On the Old Comedy* says that the name Stoic had earlier been given to the poets who passed their time there, and he adds that they had made the name of Stoic even more famous.

The Athenians esteemed Zeno very highly and evidenced this esteem by entrusting the keys of the city walls to him and by honoring him with a golden crown and a bronze statue. The citizens of his native town also extended this last mark of esteem to him and considered his statue an ornament to their city. The men of Citium living in Sidon also were proud to claim him as their own. Antigonus (Gonatas) also esteemed him, and every time that he came to Athens to hear Zeno lecture, Antigonus would invite him to his court. Zeno declined this offer but sent one of his friends, Persaeus, the son of Demetrius and a native of Citium, there. Thus Persaeus flourished in the 130th Olympiad[1] when Zeno was already an old man. Apollonius of Tyre in his work upon Zeno reports the letter of Antigonus in the following terms:

King Antigonus to Zeno the philosopher, greeting.
While in fortune and fame I think myself your superior, in reason

[1]*260-256* B.C.

and education as well as in the perfect happiness that you have attained I consider myself inferior. Therefore I have decided to invite you to visit me, certain that you will not refuse the invitation. By all means, then, make every effort to converse with me, with the clear understanding that you will be the instructor not of myself only but of all the Macedonians. It is obvious that whoever instructs the ruler of Macedonia and guides him in the paths of virtue will also be training his subjects to be good men. As is the ruler, such, for the most part, his subjects may be expected to become.

Zeno replied in the following words:

Zeno to King Antigonus, greeting.
I welcome your love of learning so long as you adhere to true education, which tends to improve, and not to its popular counterfeit, which only corrupts morals. Whoever has yearned for philosophy, spurning pleasure, so much vaunted but which makes the souls of some of the young effeminate, is clearly, and not by nature only, but by force of his will as well, inclined to nobility of character. If a noble nature is helped along by moderate exercise and receives instruction graciously, it readily acquires the perfection of virtue. However, bodily weakness due to old age limits me, for I am eighty years old. For this reason I am unable to join you. I am sending you, therefore, certain men, companions of my studies, whose mental powers are not inferior to my own, while their bodily strength is far greater. If you place yourself in their company, you will never fail to achieve the conditions necessary for perfect happiness.

Therefore he sent Persaeus and Philonides the Theban, and Epicurus, in a letter to his brother Aristobulus, mentions that both were living with Antigonus. I have thought it well to quote the decree that the Athenians passed about Zeno. It reads as follows:

In the archonship of Arrhenides, in the fifth prytany of the tribe Acamantis on the twenty-first day of Maemacterion, at the twenty-third plenary assembly of the prytany, one of the presidents, Hippo, the son of Cratistoteles, of the deme Xypetaeon, and his co-presidents put the question to the vote; Thraso, the son of Thraso of the deme Anacaea, moved:

"Whereas Zeno of Citium, son of Mnaseas, for many years has devoted himself to philosophy in the city and has been in all other respects as well a man of worth, exhorting the youth who come to him to be taught to virtue and temperance, directing them to what is best, offering, in his own conduct, a pattern to be imitated for everyone perfectly in accord with his teachings, it has seemed good to the people—and may it turn out well—to bestow praise upon Zeno of Citium, the son of Mnaseas, and to crown him with a golden crown according to the law, for his goodness and temperance, and to build him a tomb in the Ceramicus at public expense. To oversee the making of the crown and the building of the tomb, the people shall now elect six commissioners from all Athenians, and the Minister of State shall inscribe this decree on two stone pillars, and it shall be lawful for him to set up one in the Academy and the other in the Lyceum. The magistrate who presides over the administration shall indicate the expense incurred upon the pillars, that all may know that the Athenian people honor the good both in their life and after their death. Thraso of the deme Anacaea, Philocles of Piraeus, Phaedrus of Anaphylstus, Medon of Acharnae, Micythus of Sypalettus, and Dion of Paeania have been elected commissioners to oversee the preparation of the crown and the building."

It seems best to me to speak of all the Stoic doctrines here in the life of Zeno because he established the school. There are many books written by him in which he has written better than any other of the Stoics. His basic doctrines are the following. I touch on the major points, as I have in treating others.

The Stoics say that philosophic discourse falls into three parts: physical, ethical, and logical. Zeno of Citium first made this division in his *On Doctrine*, as did Chrysippus in the first book of his *On Doctrine* as well as in the first book of his *Physics*. Apollodorus and Syllus in the first part of their *Introductions to Stoic Doctrine,* Eudromus in his *Elementary Treatment of Ethics,* Diogenes the Babylonian, and Posidonius do the same.

Apollodorus calls these parts topics; Chrysippus and Eudromus call them forms; and others call them genera. The Stoics compare philosophy to an animal. Logic is like the bones and sinews; ethics like the fleshy parts; physics like the soul. Again, they compare it to an egg: logic is the shell, ethics the "white," and physics the yolk in the center. They also compare philosophy to a fertile field: logic is the enclosing wall, physics the soil or the trees, ethics the crop. Again they compare it to a city with strong walls that is ruled by reason. Some of the Stoics say that no individual part is independent of any other part, that all are interdependent. For this reason, the parts were not, ordinarily, taught separately, but mixed. Others begin with logic, take physics second, and ethics third. Zeno proceeds thus in his treatise *On Exposition,* as do Chrysippus, Archedemus, and Eudromus.

Diogenes of Ptolemais, on the other hand, begins with ethics, while Apollodorus places ethics second. Panaetius and Posidonius begin with physics, as Phanias, the pupil of Posidonius, relates in the first book of his *Commentaries on Posidonius.* Cleanthes distinguishes six, rather than three parts: dialectic, rhetoric, ethics, politics, physics, theology. Others, for example, Zeno of Tarsus, say that these are not parts of discourse but of philosophy as such. The logical part, some say, falls into the two sciences of rhetoric and dialectic. Others add a division that treats of definitions and another that treats of canons or criteria. Still others pass over the part that deals with definitions.

The part that treats of canons or criteria is a means of discovering truth. In it they discriminate our different kinds of perceptions. The part that treats of definitions is a means of recognizing truth, since facts are apprehended through common notions. The Stoics understand rhetoric as the science of speaking well on matters set forth in direct discourse and dialectic as that of treating subjects in due order by question and answer; for this reason they also offer the other definition as the science of statements that may be true, false, and neither true nor false.

Rhetoric falls into three divisions: deliberative, forensic, and panegyric. Rhetoric is divided into invention of arguments, expression of arguments in words, their ordering, and their delivery. Rhetorical speech is divided into introduction, narrative, replies to adversaries, and peroration.

Dialectic falls under two parts: meaning and language. The subjects fall under the following headings: representations and their consequences; stated propositions and the subjects and

predicates that make them up, whether axiomatic or cate-
gorematic; genera and species; arguments; moods; syllogisms
and fallacies due either to the subject matter or to the language
and including both false and true and negative arguments;
sorites and other similar forms, whether elliptical, apories, or
conclusive; and the fallacies known as the Veiled, or Horned,
No man, and The Mowers.

The second main division of dialectic noted above is that of
language; in this are included written language and the parts
of speech, the consideration of errors either in words or syntax,
poetical diction, verbal ambiguities, euphony and music. And
some writers include sections on terms, divisions, and style.

They believe that the study of syllogisms is very useful, for it
shows what can produce demonstration. This helps the forma-
tion of valid judgments, while the ordering and commitment to
memory of syllogisms impart scientific status to our notion of
things.

Any argument is a whole having premises and conclusions,
while an inference (syllogism) is an *inferential* argument composed of these elements. Demonstration is an argument inferring something less well known from something better known.

The phantasy is an impression on the soul; the name was
borrowed from the impression from a seal wax. Two kinds of
phantasies are distinguished, one that apprehends a real object,
the other not. The former, which they take as the test of
reality, is defined as that which comes from a real object, agrees
with that object, and has been impressed and stamped on the
mind in the manner of the seal; the latter, or non-appre-
hending, is defined as that which does not come from a real
object, or, if it does come, does not correspond to the reality,
failing either in clarity or distinctness.

They consider dialectic absolutely necessary and a virtue,
which includes other virtues. To be unprecipitous is to know
when to give and when to refuse assent to impressions. Caution
means a strong presumption against what appears, at the moment, probable. Irrefutability is a property that makes an argument so strong that one cannot be brought to take the opposite
side. Seriousness of mind is the habit of referring representa-

tions to right reason. Knowledge is defined either as infallible apprehension or as a habit or condition in the reception of presentations that cannot be shaken by argument. Unless he studies dialectic, the wise man cannot guard himself against failure in argument. By it, he is able to distinguish truth from falsehood, the merely plausible, and the ambiguous; lacking it, he cannot formulate questions and answers in due order.

Precipitousness in expression touches the course of events. Unless our perceptions are well ordered, we may fall into careless and indecorous conduct. Only by dialectical skill will the philosopher prove his acumen, alertness of mind, and general skill in argument. A person ought to be able to converse, to argue well, to put relevant questions, to respond intelligently to the questions put to him, and all these qualifications are proper to the skillful dialectician.

Such is, summarily stated, the substance of the Stoics' logical teaching. And in order to give it also in detail, let me now cite as much of it as comes within the scope of their introductory handbook. I will quote verbatim what Diocles the Magnesian says in his *Synopsis of Philosophers*. These are his words:

> The Stoics agree to put in the forefront the doctrine of presentation and sensation, inasmuch as the standard by which the truth of things is tested is generically a presentation. The theory of assent, and that of apprehension and thought, which precedes all the rest, cannot be stated apart from presentation. For presentation comes first; then thought, which is capable of expressing itself, puts into the form of a proposition that which the subject receives from a presentation.

Such, then, is the logic of the Stoics, by which they intend to establish the point that the wise man is the true dialectician. All things are discerned by means of logical analysis, whether it belongs in the area of physics or ethics. Without logic, as regards statement and reasoning, physics and ethics could not conduct their reasoning or make their proper statements; neither could they employ terms properly to determine how various human actions have been defined by law. Of the two kinds of inquiry included under virtue the first considers the nature of each particular thing, the second asks what it is named. Thus much for their logic.

The Stoics divide the ethical branch of philosophy in the following topics: (1) the topic of impulse; (2) the topic of which things are good and which evil; (3) the topic of the passions; (4) that of virtue; (5) that of the end; (6) that of primary value and of actions; (7) that of duties or the fitting; and (8) that of what induces to act or restraint from acting. This subdivision is followed by Chrysippus, Archedemus, Zeno of Tarsus, Apollodorus, Diogenes, Antipater, and Posidonius, and their disciples. Zeno of Citium and Cleanthes make the divisions less detailed, as is to be expected in an older generation. They do, however, subdivide logic and physics as well as ethics.

Self-preservation is the first drive in every living thing, the Stoics hold. Nature from the outset makes every living thing precious to itself. Thus Chrysippus writes in the first book of his work *On Ends*: "What is dearest to every animal is its own establishment in being and its own consciousness of that being." It would be strange should nature make the living thing alien to itself or should it leave the creature that it has made indifferent to its own state in being. The necessary conclusion, then, is that nature, in creating the animal, made it close and precious to itself. This relation to itself leads it to ward off all that is injurious to it and to be receptive to whatever serves its need or is like it.

The Stoics demonstrate that the assertion made by some people that the first drive of animals is directed to pleasure is false; for, they maintain, pleasure, when experienced, is not an end but a by-product, produced only after nature has sought out and discovered those things that minister to the animal's existence and well-being according to its kind. It is a consequence, to be compared to animals' being in good condition or to plants' being in full bloom.

They also say that originally nature did not distinguish between plants and animals, for it orders the life of plants (as it does that of animals), though in their case without drives and sensation, just as certain vegetative processes go on in us. Impulse is added in animals so that they can seek out the things that can sustain them. Then, the Stoics hold, nature establishes the law that animals must follow these drives. Reason, as a more perfect guide, is further granted to those beings we call rational; the rule of reason then becomes for them the norm of life according to nature, to order impulse by informing it with knowledge or science.

These reflections led Zeno to become the first to identify the end as "life in agreement with nature" (or living conformably to nature). This is the same as a virtuous life, for virtue is the goal toward which nature directs us. Cleanthes in his treatise *On Pleasure*, Posidonius, and Hecato in his work *On Ends* repeat this teaching. Living virtuously means living in accordance with individual experience of the actual course of nature, as Chrysippus says in the first book of his *On Ends*, because our individual natures are parts of the nature of the whole universe. This is why the end may be defined as life in accordance with our own human nature as well as that of the universe, a life in which we abstain from all actions that are forbidden by the common law of all things, that is, the right reason that is immanent to all things and is identical with Zeus, lord and ruler of all. Precisely, this defines the virtue of the happy man and the peaceful movement of life: the harmony of the spirit dwelling in the individual man in all his actions, with the will of him who orders the universe. Diogenes, therefore, says that the end is to act with good reason in the election of what is natural. Archedemus says the end is to perform all actions decorously.

Chrysippus understands by the nature with which our life ought to be in accord, first, universal nature and, then, in a more particular way, the nature of man. Cleanthes by contrast takes only the nature of the universe as the norm, not averting to the nature of the individual.

The latter also teaches that virtue is a state of harmony, worthy to be pursued for its own sake and not from hope, fear, or any external motive. Happiness, moreover, consists in virtue because virtue is that disposition of spirit that makes the whole life harmonious. The perversion of a rational being springs either from the pursuit of deceptive external ends or, occasionally, from the influence of those with whom it associates. Nature, in its basic movements, is never perverted.

In a first and most general sense, virtue is the perfection of anything in its kind, for example, a statue. Virtue may be nonintellectual, such as health, or intellectual, such as prudence. Hecato says, in his first book *On the Virtues*, that some virtues are scientific because they rest on theory, those, that is to say, that have a framework of theoretical principles. Prudence and justice are examples. Others are nonintellectual, such as health and strength: they are as extensive as the intellectual and parallel to them. Health is found to accompany and be coextensive with the intellectual virtue of temperance, just as strength results when an arch is well built. Such virtues are called nonintellectual because they do not demand the mind's assent. They are found to occur even in bad men, for instance, health or courage. The proof, says Posidonius in the first book of his treatise *On Ethics*, that virtue really exists is the fact that Socrates, Diogenes, and Antisthenes, and their followers made moral progress. The proof of the existence of vice as a basic fact is that it is the opposite of virtue. Chrysippus in the first book of his work *On the End* teaches that virtue can be taught. Posidonius in his *Protreptica* and Hecato concur. The fact that bad men become good proves that virtue can be taught.

Panaetius, however, divides virtue into two kinds, theoretical and practical. Others give a three-part division of it, into logical, physical, and ethical parts. The school of Posidonius recognizes four types. Cleanthes, Chrysippus, Antipater, and their followers recognize more than four. Apollophanes, however, recognizes only one, namely, practical wisdom.

Some virtues must be considered primary; others are subordinate to these. Wisdom, courage, justice, temperance are the primary virtues. Particular virtues are magnanimity, continence, endurance, presence of mind, good counsel. The Stoics define wisdom as the knowledge of things good and evil and of what is neither good nor evil; courage as knowledge of what we ought to choose, what we ought to beware of, and what is indifferent; justice . . .; magnanimity as the knowledge or habit of mind that makes one superior to anything that happens, whether good or evil; continence as an unshakable disposition toward that which concerns right reason, a habit that no pleasure can corrupt; endurance as a knowledge or habit that tells us what to hold on to, what not to hold on to, and what is indifferent; presence of mind as a habit that indicates what ought to be done in any particular situation or moment; good counsel as knowledge of what to do and how to do it, in consulting our own best interests.

In like manner, some vices are primary; others subordinate. For example, folly, cowardice, injustice, profligacy are accounted primary; incontinence, stupidity, ill-advisedness, subordinate. Vices, they teach, are forms of ignorance of those very things, the knowledge of which constitutes the complementary virtues.

In the most general sense, good is anything from which an advantage comes, what is identical with or not separable from benefit. It follows that virtue itself and whatever partakes in virtue is called good in these three senses, viz., as being (1) the source from which benefit results; or (2) that in respect of which benefit results, for example, the virtuous act; or (3) that by the agency of which benefit results, for example, the good man who partakes in virtue.

Another particular definition of good that they give is "the natural perfection of a rational being *qua* rational." Virtue corresponds to this, as do virtuous acts and good men because they participate in virtue. The same is true of joy, gladness, and the like, which accrue to virtue. Evils are either vices, such as folly, cowardice, injustice, or they partake of vice. Vicious acts and wicked persons are such by participation, as are the emotive states that accompany them: despair, moroseness, and the like.

Some goods are goods of the mind, others external, while some are neither. Goods of the mind include the virtues and virtuous acts. External goods include living in a well-governed land, having a good, and enjoying well-being. One's own personal happiness is one of those goods that is neither mental nor external. The same is true of non-virtuous actions: some are outward evils such as living in a poorly governed country or having a foolish friend and to see their unhappy condition. Other evils are neither mental nor external, for example, one's own unhappiness or viciousness.

Goods may be either ends or means to ends, or they may be
ends and means at once. A friend and the advantages derived
from him are means to good. Confidence, high-spiritedness,
liberty, delight, gladness, freedom from pain, and all virtuous
acts are ends.

The virtues, the Stoics say, are goods that are at once ends
and means. To the degree to which they cause happiness they
are means; to the degree that they make it complete, and so are
themselves part of it, they are ends. Likewise, some evils are
ends and some means, while others are both means and ends at
once. Your enemy and the harm he does you are means;
consternation, humiliation, slavery, gloom, despair, excess of
grief, and all vicious actions are ends. Vices are evils both as
ends and as means; since they make it complete, thus becoming
part of it, they are ends.

Some mental goods are habits, others dispositions, still others
neither the one nor the other. Virtues are dispositions; skills
and accomplishments reside in habit; exercise of one's faculties
simply as such are neither. There are also some mixed goods,
for example, to be happy in one's children or in one's old age.
Knowledge, however, is an unmixed good. Some goods such as
virtues are permanent, while others, such as joy and exercise,
are transitory.

All good is useful, unifying, profitable, expedient, serviceable, beautiful, beneficial, desirable, and either just or right. It
is useful because it occasions things that benefit us simply by
their occurrence. It is unifying because it brings about unity
where this is needed; it is profitable because it returns not only
what it costs but, in addition, a credit balance. It is expedient
because it makes it possible to enjoy benefits; it is serviceable
because the utility it renders merits recognition. It is beautiful
because the good is in proportion to the use made of it; it is
beneficial because by its very nature it endows us with other
goods. It is worthy of choice, for it is such that to choose it is
reasonable. It is just or right because it is in harmony with law
and tends to bring men together.

The Stoics call the perfect good beautiful because it has in
full all the elements that nature requires, and thus has perfect
proportion. They say that there are four species of the beau-

tiful, to wit: the just, the courageous, the orderly, and the wise. Under these forms are beautiful deeds accomplished. Correspondingly, there are four kinds of baseness or ugliness, to wit: the unjust, the cowardly, the disorderly, and the unwise. In the strict and proper sense, the beautiful is that good that makes its possessors deserving of praise; or, in another sense, it means an aptitude for one's proper function. In still another sense, the beautiful is that which endows something with new decorum as when we say that the wise man alone is good and beautiful.

The Stoics further add that only what is morally good is beautiful: thus Hecato in the third book of his treatise *On Goods* and Chrysippus in his work *On the Morally Beautiful*. This is the same as saying that all that is good is beautiful, and that the term "good" has force equal to the term "beautiful." "Since a thing is good, it is beautiful; now it is beautiful, therefore it is good." All goods are equal and all good is desirable in the highest degree and admits of no variation of intensity. All things may be divided into three groups: those that are good, those that are evil, and those that are neither, or morally indifferent.

Among those classed as good are prudence, justice, courage, temperance, and the rest; among those classified as evils are their opposites, namely, folly, injustice, and the rest. Classified as neutral or indifferent (that is, as neither good nor evil) are all those things that neither benefit nor harm a man. Such are life, health, pleasure, beauty, strength, wealth, fair fame, and noble birth, and their opposites, death, disease, pain, ugliness, weakness, poverty, ignominy, lowly birth, and the like. This is the doctrine of Hecato in the seventh book of his *On the End,* as well as of Apollodorus in his *Ethics,* and of Chrysippus. The Stoics say that such things as life, health, and pleasure are not in themselves goods; they are morally indifferent, though falling within the subdivision of "things preferred." As the property of heat is to warm, not to cool, so the property of good is to benefit, not to injure. Wealth and health, however, do no more benefit than injury; therefore, neither wealth nor health is good. They add that a thing cannot be called good, of which good or evil use can be made indifferently. Wealth and health can be used well or ill, indifferently; therefore they cannot be considered good. Posidonius, on the other hand, holds that these things should be classed as goods. Hecato in the ninth book of his treatise *On Goods* and Chrysippus in his work *On Pleasure* deny that pleasure is a good; some pleasures are indecorous and nothing indecorous can be considered good. To benefit means to initiate or to sustain in virtue; to harm is to initiate or sustain in accordance with vice.

The term "indifferent" has two meanings: first, it denotes those things that do not contribute either to happiness or to misery. Such are wealth, fame, health, strength, and the like. It is possible to be happy without having these, although, used in different ways, they tend to happiness or misery. In a second, quite different, sense those things are called indifferent that have no power to arouse either inclination or aversion; for example, the fact that the number of hairs on one's head is odd or even or whether you hold your finger straight or bent. This is not, however, the sense in which the things listed earlier were called indifferent; for they did possess such power. Some of them are preferred; others are rejected. But indifference in the second sense offers no basis either for choice or rejection.

Some indifferent things, the Stoics say, are "preferred," others "rejected." Those that have value, they say, are preferred, while those that have negative, instead of positive, value are rejected. They define value, first, as any contribution to harmonious living, such as belongs to every good; second, as some capacity or utility that contributes indirectly to life according to nature, which is to say, "any assistance made by wealth or health to living a natural life"; third, value is that which an expert estimator, one acquainted with the matter, assigns to it, for example, when the value of a quantity of wheat is said to be a certain quantity of barley with a mule added.

Things of the preferred class are those that have positive value, for example, among mental qualities, natural ability, skill, moral improvement, and the like; among bodily qualities, life, health, strength, good condition, soundness of organs, beauty, and so forth; and in the sphere of external things, wealth, fame, noble birth, and the like. To the class of rejected things belong, among mental qualities, lack of ability, want of skill, and the like; among bodily qualities, death, disease, weakness, being out of condition, mutilation, ugliness, and the like; in the sphere of external things, poverty, ignominy, lowly origin, and so forth. But again there are things belonging to neither class; such are neither chosen nor rejected.

Among preferred things some are preferred for their own sake, some for the sake of something else, and others both for their own sake and for the sake of something else. To the first of these classes belong natural ability, moral improvement, and the like; to the second, wealth, noble birth, and the like; to the last, strength, sound faculties, soundness of bodily organs. Things are preferred not for their own sake but for the sake of something else and those that are chosen not for their own sake but for the sake of something else are chosen because they secure many utilities. The same may be said of things which are rejected, in opposite terms.

The term "duty" is applied to things that, when done, may be justified by sound reasons, for example, harmony in the movement of life's process, that harmony that governs the growth of plants and animals. Even in plants and animals, they hold, decorous behavior may be perceived.

Decorous acts are all those that we do by the suasion of reason, and this is the case with honoring one's parents, brothers, and country and having amicable converse with friends. Those actions are indecorous that reason prohibits; such, for example, as neglect of parents, indifference to one's brothers, disagreement with friends, disregard for the interests of one's country, and so forth. Acts that do not belong under either of these classes are those to which or from which reason neither urges nor dissuades, such as picking up a twig, holding a stylus or a scraper, and the like.

Some duties are incumbent on us unconditionally, others only in certain circumstances. Unconditional duties are the following: to take proper care of health and one's organs of sense and things of that sort. Duties imposed by circumstances are such as maiming oneself and sacrifice of property. The same is true of actions that are violations of duty. Duties are also classified as those that are always obligatory and those that are only so on occasion. Thus it is always a duty to live virtuously; the exercise of dialectic by question and answer, or taking exercise by walking, is not so incumbent. There are also duties that fall between these classes, such as the obligation that boys have of obeying those who take care of them. The Stoics teach a division of the soul into eight parts: the five senses, speech, intellect—which is the mind itself—and the generative power. All are parts of the soul. Perversion flows from falsehood, which touches the mind as well. From perversion arise many passions or emotions, causes of imbalance, in the soul. Zeno sometimes defines passion or emotion as an irrational and unnatural movement of the soul, and sometimes as excessive impulse.

The main, or most universal, emotions, according to Hecato in the second book of his treatise *On the Passions* and Zeno in his treatise with the same title, include four great classes: grief, fear, desire or craving, pleasure. They teach that the emotions are judgments, as Chrysippus states in his treatise *On the Passions*. Avarice is a supposition that money is a good, and so are drunkenness, profligateness, and all other emotions.

Grief or pain, the Stoics say, is an irrational mental contraction. Its species are pity, envy, jealousy, rivalry, ennui, annoyance, distress, anguish, distraction. Pity is grief experienced before undeserved suffering; envy, grief at others' prosperity; jealousy, grief when another possesses what one desires for oneself; rivalry, pain when another possesses what one has oneself. Ennui is grief that weighs us down; annoyance, that which inhabits us and makes us feel a need for space; distress, pain that is induced by anxiety that endures and increases in intensity; anguish, painful grief; distraction, grief without reason, which grates on us and prevents our seeing the situation under all its aspects.

Fear is the expectation of evil. Fear includes the following emotions: terror, diffidence, withdrawal, shame, consternation, panic, mental agony. Terror is a fear that produces distraction; shame is fear of disgrace; diffidence is fear that one will have to act; consternation is fear due to confrontation by an unusual occurrence; panic is fear reinforced by sound; mental agony is the fear experienced, felt when the outcome of some matter remains in suspense.

Craving is an irrational appetite, and the following states fall under it: want, hatred, contentiousness, anger, lust, wrath, resentment. Want is a craving that is thwarted and prevented from reaching its object, while remaining in full tension toward it. Hatred is an enduring and intensifying craving that someone should suffer misfortune. Contentiousness is a craving or desire based on bias or partisanship. Anger is a craving or desire to punish someone who, you think, has done you an injury that you have not deserved. The passion of lust is a craving from which good men are liberated; for it is an attempt to win affection founded on the visible presence of beauty. Wrath is anger that has festered for a long time and therefore becomes filled, waiting with malice, waiting in ambush, as it were, as these lines illustrate:

> Even though for the one day he swallow his anger, yet does he still keep his displeasure thereafter in his heart, till he accomplish it.

Resentment is an early stage of anger.

Pleasure is an irrational excitation when one obtains something that seems worth choosing; under it are full ravishment, malevolent joy, delight, transport. Ravishment is pleasure that charms the ear. Malevolent joy is pleasure at another's ill fortune. Delight is the mind's tendency to softness; its name in Greek is related to the word "turning." Transport of delight meaning the dissolution of virtue.

Just as certain illnesses in the body, for instance, gout and arthritic disorders, are recognized, so are there ills of the soul, love of fame, love of pleasure, and the like. By an illness one means disease accompanied by weakness, while by disease (of the soul) is meant a fond daydreaming about something that seems desirable. Again just as there are tendencies in the body to develop or contract certain maladies, such as colds or dysentery, so there are in the soul tendencies such as enviousness, pitifulness, quarrelsomeness, and the like.

Three emotional states are recognized as good: joy, caution, and wishing. Joy, the counterpart of pleasure, is rational rejection; the wise man will never feel fear, but he will take caution. The Stoics say that wishing is the counterpart of desire (or craving), inasmuch as it is rational appetite. Just as the primary passions were seen to have others subordinate to them, so do the primary eupathies, (or good emotional states). Under wishing falls well-wishing or benevolence, friendliness, respect, affection; under caution, reverence and modesty; under joy, delight, mirth, cheerfulness.

The sage is passionless because he does not tend to fall into such infirmity as passion. In another sense, however, the term "apathy" is applied to the evil man, implying that he is callous and relentless. The sage is said also to be free from vanity; he is indifferent to good or evil report. This is not peculiar to him, however, for the rash man, who also must be accounted bad, is likewise free from vanity. Good men, the Stoics also say, are austere or harsh because they have no contact with pleasure themselves and little tolerance for those who do. The term "harsh," however, is applied to others as well, and in much the same sense—as a wine is said to be harsh when it is employed medicinally and not for drinking.

Good men are sincerely in earnest and watchful for their own betterment, following a way of life that banishes evil and brings out the good in things. They are also free from pretence; for they have stripped off all pretence or "makeup" whether in voice or in appearance. They are also free from business cares, refusing to do anything that is in conflict with duty. They will take wine, but not get drunk. They are also free from mental ills. This is not to deny that at times strange delusions, due to melancholy or delirium, will occur to the good man, ideas that are not determined by the principle of what is worthy of choice and therefore to nature. The sage will never feel grief, either, for grief is irrational contraction of the soul, as Apollodorus says in his *Ethics*.

The wise, it is also said, are godlike; for they have a divine something, whereas the bad man is godless. This word, "godless" or "ungodly," has two meanings: the one opposes it to the term "godly," the other denotes a man who denies the divine altogether. In the latter meaning, the term does not apply to bad men. The good also worship God; for they know the rites of the gods and piety is the knowledge of how the gods are to be served. The wise men sacrifice to the gods and keep themselves pure. They avoid all acts that offend the gods, and the gods esteem them well; for they are holy and just in what relates to the gods. The sages are the only priests; for they have made sacrifices, seen to the building of temples, purifications, and all the other matters appertaining to the gods, their chief object of knowledge.

The Stoics enjoin honoring one's parents and brothers in a manner second only to that used for honoring the gods. The affection of parents for their children is natural to the good, they believe, but not to the bad. One of their teachings is that sins are all equal, so Chrysippus writes in the fourth book of his *Ethical Questions,* as do Persaeus and Zeno. If one truth is not more true than another, neither can one falsehood be more false than another, nor one deceit more deceitful than another, nor, finally, one sin more sinful than another. He who is a hundred furlongs away from Canopus and he who is only one furlong away are equally not in Canopus, and so too he who commits the greater sin and he who commits the lesser are equally not in the path of right conduct. Heraclides of Tarsus, the disciple of Antipater of Tarsus, and Athenodorus, too, however, hold that sins are *not* equal.

The Stoics say that the sage man will take part in politics if there is no impediment. This is the teaching, for example, of Chrysippus in the first book of his work *On Various Types of Life.* By such participation, he will restrain vice and advance virtue. Also, the Stoics maintain, he will marry. Zeno, in his *Republic,* also says that the sage may marry and beget children. The wise man will never be content with mere opinions or assent to anything that is false. He will also adopt the role of Cynic, since Cynicism is a direct path to virtue, according to Apollodorus in his *Ethics.* Under great duress, he may even turn cannibal. The sage alone is free, the Stoics hold, while men subject to vice are slaves; for freedom is the power to act independently while slavery is loss or deprivation of that power. There is, however, a second form of slavery, which consists in subordination, and a third, which involves possession of the slave as well as his subordination. The condition corresponding to slavery is lordship. Lordship, in its own turn, is also an evil. The sages are not only free, they are kings as well. Kingship is rule that does not have to account to another, and only the wise can exercise such rule, so writes Chrysippus in his treatise in which he justifies Zeno's use of terms. Knowledge of good and evil is necessary in the ruler, but no evil man can possess such knowledge. Only the wise and good are fit for the role of magistrate, judge, or orator, for no evil man can qualify for these roles. The sages are infallible, not liable to error. They are without offense; for they do no harm to others or to themselves. They do not exercise pity, however, and are not indulgent to anyone; they never put aside the penalties that the laws impose for indulgence. Pity and even concern for equity are marks of a weak mind, which practices kindness instead of meeting due chastisement. They do not consider the punishments too severe. The sage man expresses wonder at seeming marvels, such as Charon's mephitic caverns, ebbings of the tide, hot springs, or volcanic eruptions. Nor yet, the Stoics go on to say, will the sage man live alone; for he is naturally disposed to society and action. He will gladly undergo conditioning to improve his capacity for bodily endurance.

The sage man will offer prayers, asking favors of the gods, thus Posidonius writes in the first book of his treatise *On Duties* and Hecato in his third book *On Paradoxes*. Friendship can exist only between the wise and good, because they are similar to one another. The Stoics mean by friendship a common use of all the necessities of life; in these matters we treat our friends as we would treat ourselves. A friend is worth having for his own sake, and it is good to have many friends. Among evil men, there can be no such thing as friendship, and the evil man, therefore, has no friends. The Stoics think that all men who are not wise must be mad. Since they do not act from wisdom, they must do so from madness.

The sage man does all things well, just as Ismenias plays all airs on the flute well. Everything belongs to the sage, for the law has conferred upon him a perfect right to all things. True enough, certain things can be said to belong to the bad, just as what has been acquired by fraud can be said, in a certain sense, to belong to the state and in another sense to those who are using it.

The virtues all involve each other, and a man who possesses one possesses all; for they have common principles, as Chrysippus says in the first book of his work *On Virtues*, Apollodorus in his *Physics According to the Early Schools*, and Hecato in the third book of his treatise *On Virtues*. If a man possesses virtue, he can immediately determine and do what he ought. Rules of conduct include rules for choosing, enduring, being steadfast, and distributing. If a man does some things by intelligent choice, some things with fortitude, some things by just distribution, and some steadfastly, he will be at once wise, courageous, just, and temperate. Each virtue deals with a particular matter. Courage, for instance, is concerned with what must be endured, practical wisdom with what must be done, what must be foregone, and what is indifferent. Similarly, each of the other virtues deals with its proper matter. Good counsel and understanding fall under wisdom. Good discipline and orderliness belong to temperance; equality and fair mindedness, to justice; constancy and vigor, to courage.

There is nothing intermediate between virtue and vice, according to the Stoics, while the Peripatetics say there is, to wit: the state of moral improvement. Just as a stick must be either straight or crooked, so a man must be either just or unjust, thus the Stoics. Likewise, there are no degrees of justice and injustice, and the same is true of the other virtues and their opposites. Chrysippus holds that virtue can be lost, but Cleanthes maintains that it cannot. The former says it may be lost as a consequence of drunkenness or melancholy; the latter says it cannot be lost by reason of the certainty of our mental comprehension. Virtue is worthy to be chosen for its own sake. We experience shame at evil conduct as if we understood that only the morally beautiful is really good. Virtue by itself suffices to ensure well-being, thus Zeno and Chrysippus in the first book of his treatise *On Virtues*, while Hecato in the second book of his treatise *On Goods* writes: "If magnanimity by itself can raise us above everything, and if magnanimity is only part of virtue, then virtue as a whole must be sufficient for well-being, leading us to disdain everything that seems troublesome." Panaetius and Posidonius by contrast deny that virtue is self-sufficing. On the contrary, health is necessary, and some means of livelihood and strength.

They also teach the perpetual exercise of virtue, as stated by Cleanthes and his followers. Virtue can never be lost, and the good man is always exercising his mind, which is perfect. Justice and right reason exist by nature and not by convention, thus Chrysippus in his work *On the Morally Beautiful*. The Stoics deny that the divergences of opinion among philosophers is any reason to give up the study of philosophy. If this were true, we would be constrained to give up life entirely, thus writes Posidonius in his *Exhortations*. Chrysippus holds that the ordinary Greek education is useful.

There can be no rights between man and the lower animals, because they are dissimilar, according to Chrysippus in the first book of his treatise *On Justice* and to Posidonius in the first book of his *On Duties*. The sage man will be attracted to young men who by their countenances show a natural disposition toward virtue. Zeno in his *Republic*, Chrysippus in book one of his work *On Modes of Life*, and Apollodorus in his *Ethics* all agree on these points.

Love is a movement toward friendship due to visible beauty, but its end is friendship not physical enjoyment. They say that Thrasonides had no commerce with his mistress, though she was in his power, because she despised him. This example proves that love depends upon respect, as Chrysippus says in his treatise *Of Love*, and is not an impulse from the gods. They define beauty as the flower and blush of virtue.

There are three kinds of life: the contemplative, the practical, and the rational. Of these, the last should be chosen because a rational creature exists, by nature, for contemplation and for action. The wise man will take his own life when reason dictates; for example, for the good of his country, for the sake of his friends, or if he suffers unbearable pain, mutilation, or incurable diesase.

The wise should possess wives in common, with free selection of partners, Zeno writes in his *Republic* and Chrysippus in his treatise *On Government* (Diogenes the Cynic and Plato hold this too). If such were the case, we would feel paternal affection for all the children alike, and the jealousies arising from adultery would not exist. The best form of government is a mixed form embracing democracy, kingship, and aristocracy, that is, the rule of the best.

Such are the ethical doctrines they profess. There are indeed many more each with its proper proof. What we have set down may, however, suffice for a concise and basic statement of them.

XXIV
CHRYSIPPUS

Chrysippus, the son of Apollonius, came either from Soli or from Tarsus, as Alexander states in his *Successions*. He was a pupil of Cleanthes. Earlier in life Chrysippus had practiced as a long-distance runner; later, however, he began to follow Zeno or, as Diocles and most others claim, Cleanthes. Even while Cleanthes was still alive, Chrysippus withdrew from his school and attained eminence as a philosopher in his own right. He possessed excellent talents and displayed the greatest acumen in every branch of philosophy. He came to differ on most points from Zeno as well as from Cleanthes; he often used to say to the latter that he wanted only to be told the doctrines. The proofs he would discover for himself. Nevertheless, whenever he had argued against Cleanthes, he would later feel remorse, so that he constantly exclaimed: "Blest in all else am I, save only where I touch Cleanthes: there I am ill-fortuned."

Chrysippus was so famous for his dialectical skill that people said that if the gods took to dialectic, they would adopt no other system than his. He had abundant matter but was not effective in his style. He surpassed everyone else in industry, as the list of his writings shows; there are more than 705 of them. He added to them by arguing repeatedly on the same subject, setting down anything that occurred to him, making many emendations and quoting numerous authorities. In one of his treatises Chrysippus copied out almost the whole of Euripides's *Medea,* so that when a man who had taken up the book was asked what he was reading, he replied, "The *Medea* of Chrysippus."

In his *Collection of Doctrines,* Apollodorus of Athens, wishing to show that the writings of Epicurus, written with force and originality, without the aid of quotations, were more numerous than the books of Chrysippus, says, "If one were to strip the books of Chrysippus of all extraneous quotations, his pages would be left bare." So much for Apollodorus. The old woman who attended Chrysippus used to say, on the word of Diocles, that he wrote five hundred lines a day. Hecato says that he took up the study of philosophy because his inheritance from his father had been confiscated by the king's treasury.

Chrysippus was unimpressive in his personal presence, as the statue in the Ceramicus proves; it is almost concealed by an equestrian statue nearby. This is the reason Carneades called him Chrypsippus, or "Horse-hidden." When somebody reproached him for not going with the crowd to listen to Ariston, Chrysippus answered, "If I had followed the multitude, I should not have studied philosophy." When a dialectician attacked Cleanthes, confronting him with sophistical fallacies, Chrysippus called out, "Stop distracting your elders from important matters; propose your conundrums to us younger men." On another occasion, a man who had a question to ask talked earnestly as long as they were in private, but when he saw a crowd was approaching, he began to be more contentious; so Chrysippus exclaimed,

> *Ah! brother mine, thine eye is growing wild:*
> *To madness fast thou'rt changing, sane to now.*

Chrysippus conducted himself quietly at drinking parties, even though he was unsteady on his legs, so that a slave woman used to say, "Lucky Chrysippus, only his legs get drunk." He had so high an opinion of himself that when someone inquired, "To whom shall I entrust my son?" he answered, "To me, for if I thought there was anyone better than myself, I should be studying with him myself." This is why the following lines are applied to him: "He alone has understanding; the others flit shadow-like around;"[1] and "If it had not been for Chrysippus, there had been no Porch."

At last, however — so Sotion says in his eighth book — he joined Arcesilaus and Lacydes and studied philosophy under them in the Academy. This explains why at one time Chrysippus argued against, and at another time in support of, ordinary experience, and why he used the method of the Academy in treating magnitudes and numbers.

On one occasion, as Hermippus relates, when Chrysippus had his school in the Odeum, his pupils invited him to a sacrificial feast. After he had taken a drink of sweet wine unmixed with water, he became faint. He died five days later, at the age of seventy-three years, in the 143rd Olympiad.[2] Apollodorus gives this date in his *Chronology*. I composed these slight lines on the subject:

> Chrysippus turned giddy after gulping down a draught of Bacchus; he spared not the Porch nor his country nor his own life, but fared straight to the house of Hades.

According to another account, his death was brought on by a violent fit of laughter. After an ass had eaten his figs, Chrysippus cried out to an old woman, "Give the ass a drink of pure wine to wash down the figs." At this remark he laughed so hard that he died.

He seems to have been a very arrogant man. At any rate, he dedicated none of his many writings to any kings. He was content with one old woman's judgment, says Demetrius in his work called *Men of the Same Name*. When Ptolemy wrote to Cleanthes requesting him either to come himself to his court or to send someone else, Sphaerus undertook the journey, while Chrysippus declined to go. On the other hand, Chrysippus sent for his sister's sons, Aristocreon and Philocrates, and educated them. Demetrius, whom we mentioned above, is also our authority for the statement that Chrysippus was the first who ventured to hold a lecture class in the open air in the Lyceum.

[1]Odyssey, *X, 495.*
[2]*208-204* B.C.

But to return to Chrysippus, he used to propound arguments such as the following: "He who divulges the mysteries to the uninitiated is guilty of impiety. Now, the hierophant certainly reveals the mysteries to the uninitiated, *ergo* he is guilty of impiety." Or again: "What is not in the city is not in the house either. Now, there is no well in the city, *ergo* there is none in the house either." Yet another: "There is a certain head, and that head you have not. Now, this being so, there is a head which you have not, therefore you are without a head." Again: "If anyone is in Megara, he is not in Athens. Now, there is a man in Megara, therefore there is not a man in Athens." Another: "If you say something, it passes through your lips." And further: "If you never lost something, you have it still, but you never lost horns, *ergo* you have horns." But others ascribe this last statement to Eubulides.

Some people criticize Chrysippus for having written much in a gross and indecent tone. In his work *On the Ancient Natural Philosophers,* line six hundred or thereabouts, he interprets the story of Hera and Zeus coarsely, with details with which no one would care to soil his lips. Indeed, his interpretation of the story is censured as being completely indecent. Chrysippus may be commenting on a physical doctrine, but the language used is more appropriate to street walkers than to deities. The work is not even cited by bibliographers, who wrote on the titles of books. Chrysippus's version is not found in Polemo, Hypsicrates, or even Antigonus; it is his own invention. In his *Republic* he permits marriage with mothers, daughters, and sons. He says the same in his work *On Things for Their Own Sake Not Desirable,* at the beginning. In the third book of his treatise *On Justice,* at about line one thousand, he permits eating of the flesh of the dead. In the second book of his *On the Means of Livelihood,* where he professes to be considering *a priori* how the wise man is to make his living, occur the words:

> And yet what reason is there that he should procure a living? For if it be to support life, life itself is after all an indifferent thing. If it be for pleasure, pleasure too is an indifferent thing. While if it is for virtue, virtue in itself is sufficient to constitute happiness. The

modes of getting a livelihood are also ludicrous as, for example, maintenance by a king, for he will have to be humored; or by friends, for friendship will then be able to be bought for money; or living by wisdom, for so wisdom will become mercenary.

As the reputation of his writings stands so high, I have decided to make a separate catalogue of them, arranged according to the class of subject treated. They are as follows:

I.   Logic
     Logical Theses
     The Philosopher's Inquiries
     Dialectical Definitions Addressed to Metrodorus,
          six books
     On the Terms Used in Dialectic, Addressed to Zeno,
          one book
     Art of Dialectic, Addressed to Aristagoras, one book
     Probable Hypothetical Judgments, Addressed to Dioscurides,
          four books

II. *Logic dealing with the subject matter, first series*
     Of Judgments, one book
     Of Judgments Which Are Not Simple, one book
     Of the Complex Judgment, Addressed to Athenades, two books
     Of Negative Judgment, Addressed to Aristagoras, three books
     Of Affirmative Judgments, Addressed to Athenodorus, one book
     Of Judgments Expressed by Means of Privation, Addressed to
          Thearus, one book
     Of Indefinite Judgments, Addressed to Dion, three books
     On the Variety of Indefinite Judgments, four books
     On Temporal Judgments, two books
     On Judgments in the Perfect Tense, two books

     second series
     Of a True Disjunctive Judgment, Addressed to Gorgippides,
          one book
     Of a True Hypothetical Judgment, Addressed to Gorgippides,
          four books
     Choosing from Alternatives, Addressed to Gorgippides, one
          book
     A Contribution to the Subject of Consequents, one book

On the Argument Which Employs Three Terms, Also Addressed to Gorgippides, one book

On Judgments of Possibility, Addressed to Clitus, four books

A Reply to the Work of Philo of Meanings, one book

On the Question: What are False Judgments, one book

third series

Of Imperatives, two books

Of Asking Questions, two books

Of Inquiry, four books

Epitome of Interrogation and Inquiry, one book

Epitome of Reply, one book

Of Investigation, two books

Of Answering Questions, four books

fourth series

Of Predicates, Addressed to Metrodorus, ten books

Of Nominatives and Oblique Cases, Addressed to Phylarchus, one book

Of Hypothetical Syllogisms, Addressed to Apollonides, one book

A Work, addressed to Pasylus, on Predicates, four books

fifth series

Of the Five Cases, one book

Of Enunciations Classified According to Subject Matter, one book

Of Modification of Significance, Addressed to Stesagoras, two books

Of Proper Nouns, two books

III. *Logic as concerned with words or phrases and the sentence, first series*

Of Singular and Plural Expressions, six books

On Single Words, addressed to Sosigenes and Alexander, five books

Of Anomalous Words or Phrases, addressed to Dion, four books

Of the Sorites Argument as applied to Uttered Words, three books

On Solecisms, one book

On Solecistic Sentences, addressed to Dionysius, one book

Sentences violating Ordinary Usage, one book

Diction, addressed to Dionysius, one book

second series

Of the Elements of Speech and on Words Spoken, five books

Of the Arrangement of Words Spoken, four books

Of the Arrangement and Elements of Sentences, Addressed to Philip, three books

Of the Elements of Speech, Addressed to Nicias, one book

Of the Relative Term, one book

third series

Against Those Who Reject Division, two books

On Ambiguous Forms of Speech, Addressed to Apollas, four books

On Figurative Ambiguities, one book

Of Ambiguity in the Moods of the Hypothetical Syllogism, two books

A Reply to the Work of Panthoides on Ambiguities, two books

Introduction to the Study of Ambiguities, five books

Epitome of the Work on Ambiguities, addressed to Epicrates, one book

Materials collected for the Introduction to the Study of Ambiguities, two books

IV. *Logic as concerned with syllogisms and moods, first series*

Handbook of Arguments and Moods, Addressed to Dioscurides, five books

Of Syllogisms, three books

Of the Construction of Moods, Addressed to Stesagoras, two books

Comparison of the Judgments Expressed in the Moods, one book

Of Reciprocal and Hypothetical Syllogisms, one book

To Agathon or Of the Problems That Remain, one book

On the Question: What Premises Are Capable of Demonstrating a Given Conclusion with the Aid of One or More Subsidiary Promises, one book

Of Inferences, Addressed to Aristagoras, one book

How the Same Syllogism May Be Drawn up in Several Moods, one book

Reply to the Objections Brought Against Drawing out the Same Argument Syllogistically and Without a Syllogism, two books

Reply to the Objections Against the Analyses of Syllogisms, three books

Reply to Philo's Work on Moods, Addressed to Timostratus, one book

Collected Logical Writings, Addressed to Timocrates and Philomathes: A Criticism of their Works on Moods and Syllogisms, one book

second series

On Conclusive Arguments, Addressed to Zeno, one book

On the Primary Undemonstrable Syllogisms, Addressed to Zeno, one book

On the Analysis of Syllogisms, one book

Of Redundant Arguments, Addressed to Pasylus, two books

Of the Rules for Syllogisms, one book

Of Introductory Moods, Addressed to Zeno, three books

Of Introductory or Elementary Syllogisms, Addressed to Zeno, one book

Of the Syllogisms, Under False Figures, five books

Syllogistic Arguments by Resolution in Undemonstrable Arguments, one book

Inquiries into the Moods, Addressed to Zeno and Philomathes, one book.(This appears to be spurious.)

On Explanatory Symbols, Addressed to Laodamas, one book

fifth series

Introduction to the Mentiens Argument, Addressed to Aristocreon, one book

Arguments of the Mentiens Type, To Serve as Introduction, one book

Of the Mentiens Argument, Addressed to Aristocreon, six books

sixth series

Reply to Those Who Hold That Propositions May Be at Once False and True, one book

To Those Who Solve the Mentiens by Dissecting It, Addressed to Aristocreon, two books

Proofs Showing That Indefinite Arguments Ought Not To Be Dissected, one book

Reply to Objections Urged Against Those Who Condemn the Dissection of Indefinite Arguments, Addressed to Pasylus, three books

Solution in the Style of the Ancients, Addressed to Dioscurides, one book

On the Solution of the Mentiens, Addressed to Aristocreon, three books

Solutions of the Hypothetical Arguments of Hedylus, Addressed to Aristocreon and Apollas, one book

seventh series

To Those Who Maintain That the Premises of the Mentiens Are False, one book

Of the Skeptic Who Denies, Addressed to Aristocreon, two books

Negative Arguments, To Serve as Logical Exercises, one book

Of the Argument for Small Increments, Addressed to Stesagoras, two books

Of the Arguments Affecting Ordinary Suppositions and on Those Who Are Inactive or Silent, Addressed to Onetor, two books

Of the Fallacy of "The Veiled Person," Addressed to Aristobulus, two books

On the Puzzle of "The Man Who Escapes Detection," Addressed to Athenades, one book

eighth series

Of the "Nobody" Puzzle, Addressed to Menecrates, eight books

Of the Arguments Derived from the Indeterminate and the Determined, Addressed to Pasylus, two books

Of the "Nobody" Argument, Addressed to Epicrates, one book

ninth series

Of Sophisms, Addressed to Heraclides and Pollis, two books

Of Dialectical Puzzles, Addressed to Dioscurides, five books

Reply to the Method of Arcesilaus, Dedicated to Sphaerus, one book

tenth series

Attack upon Common Sense, Addressed to Metrodorus, six books

Defense of Common Sense, Addressed to Gorgippides, seven books

V.   Under Logic
     Thirty-nine investigations outside the range of the four
     above-mentioned main divisions dealing with isolated logical
     investigations not included in separate wholes of the subjects
     enumerated. The total of the logical writings is 311.

VI. *Ethics dealing with the classification of ethical conceptions, first series*
     Outline of Ethical Theory, Addressed to Theoporos, one book
     Ethical Theses, one book
     Probable Premises for Ethical Doctrines, Addressed to Philo-
          mathes, three books
     Definitions of the Good or Virtuous, Addressed to Metrodorus,
          two books
     Definitions of the Bad or Vicious, Addressed to Metrodorus, two
          books
     Definitions of the Morally Intermediate, Addressed to Metro-
          dorus, two books
     Definitions of the Generic Notions (in Ethics), Addressed to
          Metrodorus, seven books
     Definitions Concerned with Other Branches of Science, Ad-
          dressed to Metrodorus, two books

     second series
     Of Similes, Addressed to Aristocles, three books
     Of Definitions, Addressed to Metrodorus, seven books

     third series
     Of the Objections Wrongly Urged Against the Definitions, Ad-
          dressed to Laodamas, seven books
     Probabilities in Support of the Definitions, Addressed to Dioscu-
          rides, two books
     Of Species and Genera, Addressed to Gorgippides, two books
     Of Classification, one book
     Of Contraries, Addressed to Dionysius, two books
     Probable Arguments Relative to the Classifications, Genera, and
          Species, and the Treatment of Contraries, one book

     fourth series
     Of Etymological Matters, Addressed to Diocles, seven books
     Points of Etymology, addressed to Diocles, four books

     fifth series
     Of Proverbs, Addressed to Zenodotus, two books

Of Poems, Addressed to Philomathes, one book
On the Right Way of Reading Poetry, two books
A Reply to Critics, Addressed to Diodorus, one book

VII. *Ethics dealing with the common view and the sciences and virtues thence arising, first series*
Against the Touching up of Paintings, Addressed to Timonax, one book
How It Is We Name Each Thing and Form a Conception of It, one book
Of Conceptions, Addressed to Laodamus, two books
Of Opinion or Assumption, Addressed to Pythonax, three books
Proofs That the Wise Man Will Not Hold Opinions, one book
Of Apprehension, Knowledge, and Ignorance, four books
Of Reason, two books
Of the Use of Reason, Addressed to Leptines

second series
That the Ancients Rightly Admitted Dialectic as well as Demonstration, Addressed to Zeno, two books
Of Dialectic, Addressed to Aristocreon, four books
Of the Objections Urged Against the Dialecticians, three books
Of Rhetoric, Addressed to Dioscurides, four books

third series
Of Formed State, or Habit, of Mind, Addressed to Cleon, three books
Of Art and the Inartistic, Addressed to Aristocreon, four books
Of the Difference between the Virtues, Addressed to Diodorus, four books
Of the Characters of the Several Virtues, one book
Of Virtues, Addressed to Pollis, two books

VIII. *Ethics, dealing with things good and evil, first series*
Of the Good or Morally Beautiful and Pleasure, Addressed to Aristocreon, ten books
Proofs That Pleasure Is Not the End-in-Chief of Action, four books
Proofs That Pleasure Is Not a Good, four books
Of the Arguments commonly used on Behalf of Pleasure

XXV
CARNEADES

CARNEADES, the son of Epicomus or (according to Alexander in his *Successions of the Philosophers*) Philocomus, was a native of Cyrene. He studied carefully the writings of the Stoics in general and those of Chrysippus in particular. By refuting the latter's successfully he gained such great fame that he would frequently say: "Where should I have been without Chrysippus?"

His capacity for work was without equal, but he was stronger in ethics than in physics. He permitted his hair and nails to grow long, so intense was his devotion to study. He was so outstanding in philosophy that even the rhetoricians would dismiss their classes and go to hear him lecture.

He had a very powerful voice, so that the keeper of the gymnasium sent to request him not to shout so loudly; he replied, "Then give me something with which to regulate my voice." The man hit upon a happy response, "Your audience is your regulator." His talent for criticizing opponents was astonishing, a fact which made him a controversialist to be feared. For these reasons he refused invitations to dine out. One of his pupils was Mentor the Bithynian; he tried to win over one of Carneades's concubines. On one occasion, consequently (according to Favorinus in his *Miscellaneous History*), when Mentor came to the lecture, Carneades, in the course of his remarks, spoke these lines by way of parody at Mentor's expense:

> Here comes an' old man of the sea, infallible, like to Mentor in person and in voice. Him I proclaim to have been banished from this school.[1]

[1]*Odyssey, IV, 384 II, 268, 401 (Carneades adapts these to his purpose).*

Thereupon Mentor stood up and replied: "Those on their part made proclamation, and these speedily assembled."[2]

He seems to have shown lack of courage in the face of death, often saying, "Nature, which shaped this whole, will also destroy it." When he learned that Antipater committed suicide by drinking a potion, he was greatly moved by the fortitude with which he met his end and exclaimed, "Give it then to me also." Those about him asked "What?" "A honeyed draught," said he. At the time he died the moon is said to have been eclipsed; one might also have said that the brightest orb in heaven after the sun thus expressed her sympathy.

According to Apollodorus in his *Chronology*, Carneades departed this life in the fourth year of the 162nd Olympiad,[3] at the age of eighty-five. Some letters of his to Ariarathes, king of Cappadocia, still remain. Everything else was compiled by his pupils; he himself left nothing in writing. I have written upon him in logaoedic meter as follows:

Why, Muse, oh why wouldst thou have me censure Carneades? For he is ignorant who knoweth not how he feared death. When wasting away with the worst of diseases, he would not find release. But when he heard that Antipater's life was quenched by drinking a potion, "Give me too," he cried, "a draught to drink." "What? pray what?" "Give me a draught of honeyed wine." He had often on his lips the words, "Nature which holds this frame together will surely dissolve it." None the less he too went down to the grave, and he might have got there sooner by cutting short his tale of woes.

It is said that his eyes went blind at night without his knowing it, and that he ordered the slave to light the lamp. The latter brought it and said, "Here it is." "Then," said Carneades, "read."

He had many other disciples, the most illustrious of whom was Clitomachus, of whom we shall speak next.

There was another Carneades, a formalistic elegiac poet.

[2] *Iliad, II, 52.*
[3] *129-128* B.C.